Professional Responsibility

Professional Responsibility: New Horizons of Praxis addresses the manifold and complex challenges inherent in professional responsibility. Since the beginning of the twentieth century, professions have been accorded a conjoined mandate – political and moral responsibility – to serve the interests of individuals and society. The quality of professional work, how professionals understand and live out their responsibilities in practice, is a matter of pervasive concern since, increasingly, they have such a prominent presence in most people's lives. Until the late 1960s, professionals' roles and responsibilities were rarely questioned, but such trust has since given way to collective scepticism concerning their commitment and willingness to live up to their moral and societal obligations. Abuse of power and privilege by some professionals has contributed to decline in trust by publics, the concept of 'good work' is increasingly challenged, and politicians and policymakers have sought to regulate and hold professions to account. It is timely, therefore, to investigate critically conflicting discourses and practices on what counts as professional responsibility, to question how professionals understand and are prepared for a life of professional responsibility, and what acting with integrity and authority looks like in practice.

One of the distinctive features of this book is the combination of normative and empirical dimensions that are used to dissect this question. The authors indicate from a diversity of disciplinary perspectives how professional responsibility includes particular thoughts and warranted actions yet remains multifaceted and inarticulate. The chapters articulate defining contours of professional responsibility by:

- focussing on normative dimensions of professional work and combining these successfully with attention to empirical aspects of professional practice in a variety of settings
- recognising the inevitable tensions between personal responsibility, and the largely depersonalised policies and strategies of quality control that exist when professional responsibility is situated within a policy environment.

This book moves beyond deconstruction and critique to a re-construction of new imagined horizons of professional responsibility from theoretical, conceptual and practical perspectives. It sets out to (re-)inscribe professional responsibility into discourses on professionalism through a re-configuration of its constituent elements in imaginative and creative ways and, crucially, by indicating the 'real world' import of re-charting the field.

Ciaran Sugrue is Professor of Education, University College, Dublin, Ireland.

Tone Dyrdal Solbrekke is Associate Professor at the Faculty of Education and Leader of the Master Program in Teacher Education, University of Oslo, Norway.

Professional Responsibility

New horizons of praxis

Edited by
Ciaran Sugrue and
Tone Dyrdal Solbrekke

Routledge
Taylor & Francis Group

LONDON AND NEW YORK

First published 2011
by Routledge
2 Park Square, Milton Park, Abingdon, Oxon OX14 4RN

Simultaneously published in the USA and Canada
by Routledge
711 Third Avenue, New York, NY 10017

Routledge is an imprint of the Taylor & Francis Group, an informa business

British Library Cataloguing in Publication Data
A catalogue record for this book is available from the British Library

Library of Congress Cataloging in Publication Data
   Professional responsibility: new horizons of praxis / [edited by]
   Ciaran Sugrue, Tone Solbrekke. – 1st ed.
      p. cm.
   1. Teachers–Professional ethics. 2. Professional ethics–Study and
   teaching. I. Sugrue, Ciaran. II. Solbrekke, Tone.
   LB1779.P77 2011
   371.100973–dc22   2011007660

ISBN: 978-0-415-61462-7 (hbk)
ISBN: 978-0-415-61463-4 (pbk)

Typeset in Galliard
by Cenveo Publisher Services

Printed and bound in Great Britain by the MPG Books Group

This book is dedicated to our professional colleagues and fellow professionals everywhere. We are particularly mindful of fellow professionals who struggle, with considerable risk to their personal and professional lives, to exercise their professional responsibilities and to vindicate the highest professional standards of integrity, expertise and service. We hope that you find words of solidarity, inspiration and encouragement in these pages.

Contents

Preface

Behind the vast majority of published books, even those of an academic bent, there is a 'story' as to how it came to be, if not a multiplicity of stories. It may be of assistance to the reader therefore, as Sky News does regularly – to provide the 'back story' that sheds light on this edited text on professional responsibility. With colleagues from Denmark, England, Ireland and Norway, we first collaborated a decade ago on a life history of school leaders project (see Sugrue, 2005).

Immediately after the fieldwork on the life history project was completed, one of us (Tone) became involved in the *Students as Journeymen Between Communities of Higher Education and Work*, which was funded as part of the fifth framework of the European Community. Known affectionately as 'the journeymen project', the professional formation of political science, psychology and law students within the university milieu was critically analysed and compared cross-nationally in institutions located in four countries. Data from the University of Oslo contribution to the study provided the raw material for a doctoral thesis the title of which was: *Understanding Conceptions of Professional Responsibility* (Solbrekke, 2007). Ongoing conversations have sought to connect the issue of professional responsibility and its potential as a generative concept not only in initial professional formation, but to professional lives and work more generally. In taking up this conversation opportunistically with colleagues in other disciplines and institutional contexts, we began to think of professional responsibility more in a cross-disciplinary manner but also with potential to bring apparently disparate disciplines together. As part of our collaboration on the topic of professional responsibility, more recently we contributed to *Professional Learning over the Lifespan: Innovation and Change* (A. Mc Kee and M. Eraut eds. Springer, forthcoming). The chapter we contributed to this edited collection (Learning from conceptions of professional responsibility and graduate experiences in becoming novice practitioners) furthered our thinking on professional responsibility.

We began to see professional responsibility as preferable to other prominent terms such as professionalism and professionalisation as it appeared to bring theory and practice into productive tension. More speculatively, we wondered if professional responsibility had the potential to bring some coherence and situated certainty to professional fields increasingly characterised by fragmentation.

With this in mind, we invited colleagues internationally who are located within different disciplines and with different research interest to contribute to this rainbow coalition from their perspectives as a means of generating a more generic conversation about professional responsibility in a cross-disciplinary manner. Such an approach, we thought, would be a distinct contribution to the literature while seeking simultaneously new directions. The ultimate litmus test for this endeavour however, is the extent to which you find the text to be a contribution to your thoughts and actions. With your assistance, then, its goal of creating new horizons of professionally responsible praxis will be advanced.

Acknowledgements

It is a most pleasant responsibility to acknowledge the many contributions made by several individuals to the completion of this text. We are most grateful to all our authors and co-authors whose work has fleshed out the manifold manifestations of professional responsibility. We are indebted to you all for completing work in a timely manner. We are also most grateful for the constructively critical comments provided on some of the draft chapters by our two discussants Gert Biesta and Eli Ottesen when they received a public airing during a double symposium at the ECER conference 2010. We are indebted to Routledge for accepting the manuscript, and in this regard Anna Clarkson has been a tower of integrity as she shepherded the work from concept to completion, assisted along the way by colleagues – James Hobbs and Vicky Parting. We record our gratitude to you individually and collectively; our Routledge 'family'. We want you and others to know that pleasant, cordial, efficient and professionally responsible service is appreciated and does not go unnoticed. We are most grateful also to Deepa Joshith and her production colleagues at Cenveo Publisher Services, Bengaluru, for their efficient and thorough management and final preparation of the manuscript. Not withstanding this sterling cooperation and support of all those mentioned, we acknowledge and take responsibility for those blemishes or inadequacies that may be legitimately laid at our door.

Collaboration on this 'project' has stimulated and intellectually enriched my own development. While all of the authors in the book have contributed to this, the work with Ciaran as co-editor has been particularly important. Deliberations about the project, its overall contributions and the struggle to reach legitimate compromises have all pushed me towards new horizons of understandings. For me, the challenges inherent in cross-linguistic and cross-cultural collaboration have created new insights in the field of professional responsibility. Where differences and misunderstandings occurred, these too have been catalysts for learning and for fulfilling a shared enterprise. For all of these reasons, I wish to record my gratitude to Ciaran for his sustained commitment and good humour, in themselves important contributions to the collaborative process.

Tone Dyrdal Solbrekke,
University of Oslo,
June 2011

Another important aspect of bringing this work to fruition has been collaboration between Tone and I as co-editors. From the outset, we were both enthusiastic about the project and saw the co-authoring of the first and final chapters as a challenge since we brought different expertise, culture and language to the task. However, it was also an equal partnership, premised on respect. I have learned much about our chosen topic while gaining important insights about the nature of collaboration. Although occasionally there were tensions and misunderstandings, commitment to the enterprise was never in doubt. For all of these reasons, I wish to record my gratitude to Tone, and to her husband Per for his tolerance, hospitality and generosity when I was a visitor in Oslo.

Ciaran Sugrue,
School of Education, University College Dublin,
June 2011

Notes on contributors

Ronald Barnett is Emeritus Professor of Higher Education, Institute of Education, London, UK, and Editor of the *London Review of Education*. His work has been focused primarily on the conceptual understanding of the university and higher education, a key question being: is it possible to sustain an educational idea of the university in the C21? His work as won several prizes throughout his career, including, for example, a DLit(Ed), conferred by the University of London for his scholarly work and 'Award for Outstanding Contribution to Higher Education, Research, Policy and Practice', first annual award of the European Association for Institutional Research (EAIR). His many publications include the following published by the Open University Press: *The Idea of Higher Education* (1990); *Improving Higher Education: Total Quality Care* (1992); *The Limits of Competence* (1994); *Higher Education: A Critical Business* (1997); *Realizing the University in an Age of Supercomplexity* (2000); *Beyond All Reason: Living with Ideology in the University* (2003); (with Kelly Coate) *Engaging the Curriculum* (2005); *A Will to Learn: Being a Student in an Age of Uncertainty* (2007). He is editor/co-author of eight other books and author of 200+ papers/chapters/reports. He has been an invited speaker in 30 countries (including China, Chile, Brazil, Japan, Mexico, New Zealand and Australia).

Tone Dyrdal Solbrekke is Associate Professor at the Faculty of Education and Leader of the Master Program in Teacher Education University of Oslo, Norway. She has been the editor of the *Norwegian Journal of Educational Research* for eight years. She worked as a teacher and principal for many years, and her academic career and research interests are wide ranging and include school development, leadership and professional identities, professional responsibility, qualification for professional life, and the relation between governance of, and practices in, higher education. She has published several articles in Norwegian and co-authored chapters in books on Scandinavian School Leadership, while more recent publications in English include: 'Professional responsibility as legitimate compromises- from communities of education to communities of work', *Studies in Higher Education* 33(4) (2008); 'Educating for professional responsibility – a normative dimension of higher education', *Utbildning &*

Demokrati [Education & Democracy] 17(2) (2008); 'Learning from conceptions of professional responsibility and graduate experiences in becoming novice practitioners' (co-authored with Ciaran Sugrue) (forthcoming in *Professional learning over the lifespan: Innovation and change* (ed.) Anne McKee and Michael Eraut) Springer); 'Bringing professional responsibility back' in *Studies in Higher Education forthcoming* 2011, (co-authored with Tomas Englund) and 'The avenue towards convergence in European higher education?' Special issue 'Bologna and the European Higher Education Area', *European Journal of Education* 45(4) (co-authored with Berit Karseth).

Tomas Englund is Professor of Education at the Department of Education, Örebro University, Örebro, Sweden. His research interests centre on curriculum theory and didactics, curriculum history, political socialization and citizenship education, professionalism and the philosophy of education. He directs the research group 'Education and Democracy' and is co-editor of the journal with the same name (in Swedish, *Utbildning & Demokrati*). He has recently been published in *Journal of Curriculum Studies, Journal of Education Policy, Scandinavian Journal of Educational Research, Journal of Human Rights, Education Inquiry, Educational Philosophy and Theory,* the *RoutledgeFalmer Reader in Philosophy of Education* and *Routledge International Studies in the Philosophy of Education.* Among recent publications in Swedish are *Utbildning som kommunikation. Deliberativa samtal som möjlighet* [Education as communication. Deliberative communication as a possibility] 2007 and *Vadå likvärdighet? Studier i utbildningspolitisk språkanvändning* [What about equivalence? Studies in the use of language in educational policy] 2008 both at Göteborg: Daidalos.

Peter Gronn is Professor of Education, University of Cambridge, UK, and a Fellow of Hughes Hall. At Cambridge he works in the area of leadership and school improvement. Previously he held professorial appointments at the University of Glasgow (2007–8) and Monash University (2003–7). Professor Gronn is a leading international scholar in the fields of general leadership, and educational and school leadership and is currently a member of a number of editorial boards of leading journals. He has had extensive research experience in government and non-government school systems in Australia and the UK, and is the author of numerous publications. In 2005–6, Professor Gronn was a consultant to the Australian Council for Educational Research (ACER) for the Teaching Australia project 'Standards for School Leadership' and in 2006–7 he also worked with ACER on the Country Background Report on school leadership in Australia which formed part of a 22-nation OECD comparative policy research project. Subsequently he has collaborated on projects with the National College for School Leadership (NCSL) and the Leadership Foundation for Higher Education (LFHE). He has co-authored two recent reports in Scotland on leadership coaching, and headteacher recruitment and retention. With Cambridge colleagues he is undertaking research into school autonomy in England.

Kristin Heggen is Professor for Health Sciences, Faculty of Medicine, University of Oslo, Norway. She has expertise in the humanities, social sciences and educational research. Her work is characterised by broadness in the clinical fields she has studied, including rehabilitation, care for elderly, supervision of care, acute psychiatry and acute hospital care. She is recognised for her expertise in qualitative methodologies, and she is an experienced user of unstructured observation in complex care settings, and interviews with participants as patients, care persons and health professionals. Her expertise is recognised through invitation to examine doctoral work in different disciplines and at several universities (nationally and internationally). She has been on the supervising team for seven doctoral students (one from Deakin University, Australia) who have completed their thesis, and is currently supervising six PhD-student. Heggen is regularly used as referee of international scientific journals and evaluator of proposals for the Norwegian Research Council. During the past 5 years she has published more than 25 papers in journals with peer-review, in addition to a number of book chapters. She has ongoing international collaboration with several well-known research groups at University of Melbourne (Australia), University of Ballarat (Australia), and The Carnegie Foundation for the Advancement of Teaching, (California/USA).

Berit Karseth is a Professor at the Institute for Educational Research at the University of Oslo, Norway. Her main research interests are curriculum policy and issues related to professionalism and knowledge development. Her most recent publications in English include "Qualifications Frameworks for the European Higher Education Area: A new instrumentalism or 'Much Ado about Nothing'?" *Learning and Teaching*, Vol. 1, No. 2, pp. 77–10; "Professional responsibility – an issue for higher education?" *Higher Education*, 52: 95–119 (co-authored with Tone D. Solbrekke), "Building professionalism in a knowledge society: Examining discourses of knowledge in four professional associations." *Journal of Education and Work*, Vol. 20, No. 4, pp. 335–35 (co-authored with Monika Nerland) and "Conceptualizing curriculum knowledge – within and beyond the national" *European Journal of Education*, Vol. 45, No. 1, (in press, co-authored with Kirsten Sivesind). She is currently a member of a national commission appointed to develop a new national curriculum for teacher education (primary and secondary education) in Norway.

Geert Kelchtermans is a Professor in Education and Director of the Centre for Educational Policy, Innovation and Teacher Education at the University of Leuven, Belgium. He studied educational sciences and philosophy and got a PhD in 1993 with a narrative-biographical study on the professional development of primary school teachers. His research interests are teacher development, leadership and innovation in schools, pedagogy of teacher education and qualitative research methodology. He has published widely in international journals such as *Teaching and Teacher Education, Teachers and Teaching: Theory and Practice, Journal of Curriculum Studies, Oxford Review of Education, Zeitschrift* *für Pädagogik, Pedagogische Studiën*, and has contributed several chapters to international edited book volumes. He also serves on the educational board of several international research journals.

Bruce Macfarlane is Associate Professor for Higher Education at the University of Hong Kong. He has held previous academic positions at four UK universities as a professor of education and a Head of Academic Development and worked as a visiting professor in Japan. The main focus of his research is applied and professional ethics in higher education. His publications include *Teaching with integrity: the ethics of higher education practice* (Routledge Falmer, 2004), *The Academic Citizen: the virtue of service in university life* (Routledge, 2007) and *Researching with integrity: the ethics of academic enquiry* (Routledge, 2009). He has also co-edited books about business and management education and higher education policy and management, including *Challenging Boundaries: managing the integration of post-secondary education* (Routledge, 2009). His latest research focuses on intellectual leadership. He is a former Vice Chair of the Society for Research into Higher Education and a Senior Fellow of the UK Higher Education Academy.

Maeve O'Brien is a Senior Lecturer in Human Development (Sociology) and Co-ordinator of a BA and MA in Human Development at St Patrick's College, Ireland. She has taught in schools and worked on educational initiatives to combat educational inequalities for over two decades. Her research interests focus on equality issues in education particularly in the areas of affective inequalities and wellbeing and how these cross cut with social class, gender and ethnicity. Recent publications include: O'Brien, M. (2009), 'Mothers' Capitals and their Impact on Love and Care Work' in Lynch, K., Baker, J. and Lyons, M (eds). *Affective Equality: Love, Care and Justice*, London: Palgrave; O'Brien, M. (2008) 'Gendered capital, emotional capital and mothers' care work in education,' *British Journal of Sociology of Education*, 29, 2; O'Brien, M. (2008), *Well-Being and Post Primary Schooling: A Review of the Literature and Research*, with the Human Development Team St Patrick's College, Dublin: NCCA.

Ciaran Sugrue is Professor of Education, University College Dublin. Previously he held the positions of – Reader in School Leadership and School Improvement, Faculty of Education, University of Cambridge, Director of Postgraduate Education at St. Patrick's College, Dublin City University and worked as a primary teacher, schools inspector, teacher educator and researcher in the Irish system. His research interests are wide ranging but primarily focused on School Leadership and Educational Change, as well as connecting these with continuing professional learning within the teaching profession, and on qualitative research methods. He was General Editor of Irish Educational Studies from 1998–2008, and is a member of the editorial boards of several international journals. With colleagues in Cambridge and the Faculty's Centre for Commonwealth Education he is engaged in research on Autonomy in English secondary schools and on

Pedagogy and Leadership in Tanzania. His most recent book is: *The Future of Educational Change: International Perspectives* (London: Routledge, 2008), while recent journal articles include: Sugrue, C. (2009). 'From Heroes and Heroines to Hermaphrodites: Emancipation or Emasculation of School Leaders and Leadership?' *School Leadership and Management*, 29(4), 361–372.

William M. Sullivan is a Senior Fellow at the Carnegie Foundation for the Advancement of Teaching, USA. He works on the Preparation for the Professions Programme. He also directs the Cross Professions Seminar, comparing education across professions, drawing out common themes and identifying distinct practices in professional education. The author of Work and Integrity: The Crisis and Promise of Professionalism in America and a co-author of Educating Lawyers: Preparation for the Profession of Law and Habits of the Heart: Individualism and Commitment in American Life, Sullivan has examined the link between formal training and practical reflection in effective education. Prior to his work at Carnegie, Sullivan was professor of philosophy at La Salle University. He earned a Ph.D. in philosophy at Fordham University. His books include: *Educating Engineers: Designing for the future of the field; A New Agenda for Higher Education: Shaping a Life of the Mind for Practice; Work and Integrity: The Crisis and Promise of Professionalism in America*, 2nd Edition.

Molly Sutphen is an Assistant Adjunct Professor in the Department of Social and Behavioral Sciences in the School of Nursing at the University of California San Francisco, USA. Formerly she was a Research Scholar at the Carnegie Foundation for the Advancement of Teaching and Co-Director of this Carnegie Foundation for the Advancement of Teaching National Nursing Education Study. Her research interests include the history of international health, faculty development, and ethics in nursing education. She received her doctorate from Yale University in the history of medicine and the life sciences. Her publications include: *Educating nurses: A call for radical transformation.* (Forthcoming) San Francisco: Jossey-Bass (co-authored with Patricia Benner, Victoria Leonard, and Lisa Day).

Sally Wellard is Professor of Nursing at School of Nursing, University of Ballarat, Australia. She has wide experience in research related to nursing practice with particular expertise in social sciences, chronic illness and educational research. Her current work includes the exploration of the social impact of disease on families, consumer participation in health care services, issues in aged care nursing and undergraduate clinical education. She is actively involved in the governance of community based health service, currently Chair of the Board of Management of Ballarat District Nursing and Healthcare. Wellard is recognised for her expertise in qualitative research methodologies, with particular interest in interviews with consumers, families, and health professionals. During the past 5 years she has published 22 papers in peer reviewed journals as well as two book chapters and 17 presentations at international and national conferences. Wellard has extensive experience in supervision and examination of doctoral work in nursing (nationally and internationally). Additionally, Wellard is frequently invited to review manuscripts for a number of international peer reviewed journals and is an assessor of grant proposals for a number of national and international competitive grant schemes.

Introduction

This book is about professional responsibility and the motivations for its under-taking are multiple. Those we consider most pertinent are indicated here. We recognise that, in many respects, the quality of life in contemporary societies is contingent on the quality of professionals' work, their knowledge and skills as well as their senses of moral and societal responsibility (Bauman 2005; Morgan 1994; Hoshmand 1998). It is generally accepted also that the fluid, uncertain and fast-paced nature of the lifeworlds of professionals pose considerable chal-lenges to acting in a professionally responsible manner. These challenges are complex, contextually unique and frequently give rise to competing and conflict-ing struggles regarding values and ethical stances – at the very heart of profes-sional practice (Noddings 1994, 2003; Schön 1983; Sockett 1993). Such value conflicts are rendered more real and fraught when confronted by an almost continuous stream of revelations that leave little to the imagination regarding the repeated failure of professionals – in banking, finance, organised religion and public life, where professionals have betrayed the trust placed in them by their publics by blatantly traducing their responsibilities, frequently exacerbated further by silence, secrecy, denial and subterfuge. When such betrayals are portrayed and perceived as ubiquitous, there is something of a crisis of confi-dence both within and between professional communities while eroded trust in the public mind is most difficult to restore. These circumstances provide compel-ling evidence that raising pertinent questions in light of contemporary realities regarding what professional responsibility entails is both timely and necessary.

Another significant contour on the contemporary terrain has been a prolifera-tion of professional roles: groups of workers who lay claim to the status of being 'professional'. As the middle classes expanded dramatically during the second half of the twentieth century, new careers with attendant roles and responsibili-ties are continuing to emerge. There is an emerging consensus that a greater proportion of the workforce need to be 'knowledge workers' rather than service or domestic workers. In order to be a knowledge worker, it is already necessary to serve a longer apprenticeship, to develop knowledge and expertise through acquiring a higher education, often to postgraduate level, while committing also to lifelong learning through workplace learning, to update one's knowledge continuously. As a means of regulating even the more established professions of law and medicine, for example, increasingly within national borders there are additional requirements to have one's licence to practise renewed. The nursing profession, by contrast, serves as a good example of a relatively recent arrival in the pantheon of professions. It has metamorphosed – from being largely an apprenticeship concerned with serving and caring for patients, to a graduate profession with limited rights to prescribe drugs, thus, arguably, invading a professional space until very recently occupied exclusively by members of the medical profession only. In such a diverse terrain, determining what professional responsibility entails becomes more onerous, challenging and subject to contestation from within and without.

Another facet of contemporary workplace conditions with consequences for how professional responsibility is understood and enacted is deregulation. Contemporary conditions differ profoundly from those of the industrial economy that prevailed when classical definitions of professions were being articulated. The labour market has been dramatically transformed (Castells 2000). It has become something of an established orthodoxy that professional lives are influenced immeasurably by secularisation, consumerism as well as intensified demands for flexibility and efficiency, effects frequently attributed to a new-liberal ideology (Barnett 2003; Beck & Beck-Gernsheim 2001; Sennett 1998). Personal identities are characterised by flux, with stability being more elusive while openness to change is a more definite requirement (Giddens 1991; Stronach et al. 2002). Such destabilising influences are exacerbated further by an increasing use of temporary work contracts, particularly among new entrants to the workforce. Such conditions may alter the very meaning of work and one's dedication to a profession and its moral and societal obligations (Sennett 1998). The cumulative impact of these forces of change strongly suggest that it is delusional to persist with a view that social structures, role models and values are 'given' or 'self-evident' (Bauman 2004, Stronach et al. 2002; Pahl 1995). Normative rules are no longer fixed and unquestioned. Rather, boundaries between what is moral and immoral are constantly disputed and collective rules monitoring individuals, to a large degree, have been replaced by self-monitoring (Giddens 1991). Contemporary working life is 'saturated with uncertainty' rather than having fixed reference points. Individual professionals are obliged to rely on their own ability to reflect critically and make immediate moral and responsible decisions (Bauman 2000; Munthe 2003). In the absence of certainties, there is an added urgency for ongoing deliberation on forces that insinuate themselves into professional decision making (Hoshmand 1998). Not surprisingly, there is increasing public clamour that social accountability and ethics are being compromised repeatedly by political power structures and economic arrangements.

Within and between these various evolutionary processes and mutations, there has been a proliferation of terminology too in an effort to capture and make sense of such rapid changes, shifting understandings, old loyalties and new alliances. Nevertheless, despite this rapidly altering professional landscape, it is appropriate to ask: are there commonalities regarding initiation into professional life and work, is it possible to create a shared language and to determine if some linguistic turns and attendant demands have an enhancing or detrimental impact, are energising and professionalising or de-motivational and de-professionalising, even if these dynamics play out very differently within national contexts due to different histories and trajectories. An understandable survival mechanism in such a linguistic and conceptual maelstrom is to switch off, tune out or find minimal means of conformity, compliance with imposed codes of conduct or ethics of practice, while other more thoughtful or considered views suggest that this is far too inadequate a response – unprofessional and irresponsible.

Such an altered, fractured and contested terrain, with attendant blurring of boundaries, is commonly accompanied by (potentially) destabilising conflicts and turf 'wars' characterised by resentment and disagreement regarding status, remuneration, roles and responsibilities that simmer just below the surface with frequent or irregular eruptions in workplaces and public arenas. When the impact of globalisation, competitiveness of market forces and their technological tentacles are inscribed into these contemporary cross-currents, professionals to varying degrees tend towards (inward-looking) preoccupation with enhancing their CVs to improve their prospects of employment and career advancement by focusing on expert knowledge, workplace experience, IT skills, etc. In such circumstances, privileging these elements of professional responsibility has tended to overshadow other older criteria, expectations and requirements such as character, morality, integrity, etc. These contemporary preoccupations, in many instances, result in collective amnesia regarding the historical legacies of professions, how their mandates have evolved, including the relationships between professionals, state and society. These realities are sufficient to convince us that a focus on professional responsibility has the potential to bring some situated certainty to a volatile field.

Therefore, the animating question of this text, addressed from a variety of perspectives within the individual chapters, is: 'In an increasingly insecure, unpredictable and de-regulated world, what does professional responsibility entail?' While the various chapters make distinct contributions, the collective intention is to move beyond deconstruction, complexity and critique, to new imagined horizons of professional responsibility from theoretical, conceptual and practical perspectives.

The text has 12 chapters divided into three parts. The first, 'Professional responsibility: a theoretical and practical matter', includes five chapters, all of which begin with theoretical considerations of professional responsibility while seeking simultaneously to identify and describe the implications for practice of such concerns, to give direction to the agency of professional actors. Part Two, 'Professional responsibility: from practice to theory', includes six chapters that are grounded more in empirical evidence while the distilling of evidence from a variety of sources becomes the basis of insights and understandings of professional responsibility in its various guises. The concluding part, 'Professional responsibility: Possible Futures?' has one chapter (Chapter 12) that self-consciously sets out to create an emergent discourse by giving voice to dormant, dominant and silenced aspects of professional landscapes. The reader is invited to become an active participant in the proliferation of reflective and critical conversations that are identified as necessary and ongoing if more holistic considerations of the complexities of professional life and work are to receive appropriate place and space alongside 'expert' or 'technical' perspectives in the (re-)creation of a more vibrant and vital sense of what is entailed in professional responsibility.

Chapter 1 'Professional responsibility: back to the future' sets the scene for the others by returning to the roots of professional responsibility. Since this is co-authored, we are working across cultural, linguistic, gendered and professional boundaries that sensitise us to the complexities of professional studies generally. Nevertheless, we isolate what we consider to be the dominant contours of professional responsibility as we survey selected aspects of the literature on professions, but with particular reference to the 'roots' of professions, their foundational mandates. This account has the additional intention of indicating why the term professional responsibility has potential to be a force for a more holistic approach to professions.

Chapter 2 'Towards an ecological professionalism' pushes the metaphor of ecological connectedness to its limits as it simultaneously argues for a more holistic approach to professional responsibility, beyond expertise and fragmentation. Within this framework, norms of sustainability both within and beyond a particular professional community are inescapable responsibilities that are integral to the life and work of professionals. As citizens and professionals, they have an individual and collective responsibility to care for the profession, to nurture and sustain it, and to extend such responsibilities also to planetary care, wellbeing and our ecological future – socially and professionally.

Chapter 3 'Professional responsibility and an ethic of care: teachers' care as moral praxis' takes as its point of departure a feminist critical perspective and, by drawing on a wide-ranging literature, builds a convincing case for care to be considered central to teachers' work, and, by implication, a dimension of other professions' responsibilities too. The case is made that it is necessary both to care for and to care about students, and if such aspirations are to be actualised, then the manner in which the work of teachers needs to be re-conceptualised to pay appropriate attention to an ethic of care becomes an urgent necessity, beyond performativity. The chapter concludes that re-inscribing care into teachers' scripts is a necessity and not an option if teachers' actions are to remain moral with emancipatory intent committed to a social justice agenda.

Chapter 4 'Professional responsibility under pressure?' begins from contemporary considerations of professional discretion, a degree of autonomy deemed necessary to make professional judgements and an increasing policy tendency to create a set of technologies that hold professionals to account, frequently on a narrow range of criteria, that are regarded by many commentators as anathema to professional responsibility. This chapter indicates clearly that the more technical language of new public management has privileged performative criteria to the detriment of a more broadly based understanding of what professional responsibility entails. By excavating the underlying logics of responsibility and accountability, the authors indicate their emergent perspective that responsibility is a more inclusive, challenging and demanding requirement than merely being held to account.

Chapter 5 'Teaching, integrity and the development of professional responsibility: why we need pedagogical phronesis' situates itself within contemporary higher education, its massification and its consequent emphasis on initiating new academic staff into the teaching role within the academy. It offers an insightful critique of what the author terms the psychologised curriculum leading to an impoverished pedagogy, and fragmentation of the academic role whereby teaching is both technicised in a means-end manner while being separated from research activities and other institutional responsibilities. Consequently, following Aristotle, the author posits phronesis as an important virtue with generative capacity to create a more potent disposition as well as practical wisdom that is qualitatively broader, deeper and richer than its technical relative (techne), with important consequences for how professional responsibility is construed.

As indicated above, Part two includes Chapters 6–11, and these are grounded more in empirical evidence, and from these evidentiary perspectives, the authors extrapolate and interpolate important insights into how professional responsibility is and ought to be conceived; they bridge the boundaries of theory and practice while beginning from the latter. The first of these empirical contributions, Chapter 6 'Risk, trust and leadership', is situated within dominant contemporary policies on accountability that create high-risk, low-trust environments in which school leaders are obliged to operate. In such circumstances, the chapter demonstrates, principals struggle against the odds to redress the balance between trust and risk, and this challenge becomes an important element of their responsibilities as leaders, setting the tone and climate as the basis for innovative endeavours, as well as being characteristic of leadership scripts.

Chapter 7 'Teaching professional responsibility: a clash of approaches in both legal and nursing education' through comparative data on the initial preparation of nurses and lawyers in US institutions undertaken at the Carnegie Foundation, indicates, illustrates and illuminates the manner in which a competency and skills orientation creates a culture of compliance and defensiveness rather than promoting more expansive, inquiry-oriented, ethical considerations of responsibilities with important implications for professional identity formation. Such an approach, the authors argue, includes attention to and understanding of relational responsibilities to themselves and professionals, their chosen profession, to the people they serve as well as to society, and the key role played by reflection in the creation of such identities and dispositions.

Chapter 8 'Professional responsibility: persistent commitment, perpetual vulnerability?' draws on a variety of empirical evidence from within the teaching profession to focus on the realities of teaching in a climate of accountability. In this regard, a key contribution to understanding professional responsibility inherent in the act of teaching is the vulnerability of the teacher as individual actor. Consequently, the argument advanced is that being professionally responsible necessitates also recognising vulnerability as an ontological and professional reality that should be celebrated rather than denied, and when this occurs, as is more likely in a performativity environment, teaching, as an activity and as a profession, is diminished.

Chapter 9 'Leadership: professionally responsible rule bending and breaking?' explores the extent to which rule bending and breaking is inherent in conceptions of leadership and its attendant actions, and the boundaries or latitude within which it is possible to defend such actions as being professionally responsible. Selected leadership text are interrogated in relation to the chapter's question, followed by a critical analysis of recent reports on UK politicians' expenses scandal and the abuse of children by Dublin priests. By focusing on instances of rule breaking that clearly violate norms of leadership, it is possible to identify what professionally responsible leadership might entail. However, on closer scrutiny of leadership vignettes provided by school principals, it becomes more difficult to decipher and to separate responsible rule breaking from behaviour that is 'beyond the pale', but it does become clearer that, without recourse to a moral compass, professionally responsible leadership is considerably more arbitrary and indeterminate, while such compass readings, as the empirical evidence indicates, is entirely fallible – a further challenge to professional responsibility, conceptually and practically.

Chapter 10 'Evidence-based practice, risk and reconstructions of responsibility in nursing' uses data from case studies of nursing practice in an Australian context to indicate how dominant policy discourses regarding evidence-based practice privileges and encourages particular routines of practice over others to the detriment of those patients such scientifically designed protocols are intended to serve. A key feature of the analysis is the identification of 'paper care', its time-consuming nature, its restrictive implications for practice and, ultimately, while ticking the appropriate boxes of accountability, the quality of care is diminished and restricted. Through a Foucauldian lens of governmentality, the analysis indicates that the iron logic of such practices imprison both the professional and the client and, if standards of care and quality of service are to be vindicated, it will be necessary for professionals to resist, technical rational rule, governed mindsets to loose professional responsibility from such restrictive chains.

Chapter 11 'Teacher education for professional responsibility – what should it look like?' undertakes a critical analysis of recent initial teacher education reforms in Norway through a triple theoretical lens each element of which, for different reasons, lays claim to being foundational in the professional formation of members of the teaching profession. This multifocal lens includes scientific knowledge and research, the moral basis of teaching and global situatedness – knowledge economy and competitiveness, and the positioning of contemporary professional schools within higher education. Not surprisingly, each foundational claim made though these three lenses seeks to privilege particular kinds of teaching, learning and research, frequently without adequate efforts to reconcile their underlying competing interests. The chapter contends that an adequate understanding of professional responsibility necessitates paying attention to the contributions of these competing perspectives, to understand their claims as a prerequisite to attempting a more holistic perspective on professional responsibility.

The third and final part contains one chapter, while part and chapter. Chapter 12 'Professional responsibility: new horizons of praxis' is more a beginning than an end. It imaginatively constructs a reflective conversation on professional responsibility, the intended purpose of which is to begin to weave a new tapestry of professional responsibility that echoes the concerns voiced in the foregoing chapters. However, it is also concerned to move beyond analysis and critique to crafting new horizons of professional responsibility, however tentatively, and invites the reader to become part of this conversation as a form of engagement and reflection, as well as a new beginning whereby new horizons are forged in conversation with colleagues in a variety of context. Recognising the ongoing necessity for such conversations and having the courage to take these initial steps we consider to be the most surefooted means of re-awakening the virtues of professional responsibility, building the necessary bridging capital for their enhancement and renewal through everyday professional conversations in workplace contexts and further afield.

References

Barnett, R. (2003) *Beyond All Reason. Living with Ideology in the University.* Buckingham: SRHE and Open University Press.

Bauman, Z. (2000) *Liquid Modernity.* Cambridge: Polity Press.

Bauman, Z. (2004) *Identity.* Cambridge: Polity Press.

Bauman, Z. (2005) The liquid modern challenges to education. In S. Robinson and C. Katulishi (eds) *Values in Higher Education.* pp. 36–50. Cardiff: Aureus Publishing Limited and The University of Leeds.

Beck, U. and Beck-Gernsheim, E. (2001) *Individualizaton. Institutionalized Individualism and its Social and Political Consequences.* London: Sage.

Castells, M. (2000) *The Institutions of the New Economy.* Summary of the address to the 'Delivering the Virtual Promise?' Conference, London, 19 June 2000. http://virtual-society.sbs.ox.ac.uk/text/events/castells.htm (accessed 17 December 2010).

Giddens, A. (1991) *Modernity and Self-Identity: Self and Society in the Late Modern Age.* Stanford: Stanford University Press.

Hoshmand, L.T. (1998) *Creativity and Moral Vision in Psychology. Narratives on Identity and Commitment in a Postmodern Age.* London: Sage Publications.

Morgan, D.F. (1994) The role of liberal arts in professional education. In C.M. Brody and J. Wallace (eds) *Ethical and Social Issues in Professional Education.* pp. 13–28. Albany: State University of New York Press.

Munthe, E. (2003) *Teachers' Professional Certainty. A survey study of Norwegian teachers' perceptions of professional certainty in relation to demographic, workplace, and classroom variables.* Doctoral dissertation. Oslo: Institute for Educational Research, University of Oslo.

Noddings, N. (1994) Foreword. In C.M. Brody and J. Wallace (eds) *Ethical and Social Issues in Professional Education.* Albany: State University of New York Press.

Noddings, N. (2003) *Caring: A Feminine Approach to Ethics and Moral Education.* Berkeley: University of California Press.

Pahl, R. (1995) *After Success-fin-de-ciecle, Anxiety and Identity*. Cambridge: Polity Press.

Schon, D. (1983) *The Reflective Practitioner*. New York: Sage Publications.

Sennett, R. (1998) *The Corrosion of Character. The Personal Consequences of Work in the New Capitalism*. New York: W.E. Norton & Company.

Sockett, H. (1993) *The Moral Base for Teacher Professionalism*. New York: Teachers College Press.

Stronach, I., Corbin, B., McNamara, O., Stark, S. and Warne, T. (2002) Towards an uncertain politics of professionalism: teachers and nurse identities in flux. *Journal of Educational Policy* 17(1), 109–38.

Part 1
Professional responsibility
A theoretical and practical matter

1 Professional responsibility – back to the future

Tone Dyrdal Solbrekke and
Ciaran Sugrue

Introduction

We have a preference for the term 'professional responsibility'. We think it has considerable traction and generative potential in an increasingly fluid, messy and complex world, in the spaces and places where professionals meet and work. Discussions about professions are frequently situated within the field of sociology, and often focus on professionalisation as well as the articulation of ideals to which professionals ought to aspire (Brante 1990; Evetts 2003; Macdonald 1995; Molander & Terum 2008). However, such idealisation tends to remain rather vague and obscured by considerations of status, remuneration and territory or spheres of influence and control By contrast, *professional responsibility* is a concept that is oriented more towards appropriate actions, and what it means to act in a professionally responsible manner. Professional responsibility, therefore, holds lofty ideals in tension with everyday professional workplace realities and how professionals navigate such turbulent situations or dissolve these Gordian knots.[1] Our preference for the term 'praxis' in the concluding chapter is premised on similar understandings, since it seeks to combine and connect in concrete ways – theoretical, ethical and practical considerations of responsibility and its attendant actions. Understood in this manner, professional responsibility no longer remains merely an imagined ideal, but something that is embodied by professionals as they attend to their work; being a professional is living a particular life.

While it is relatively easy to assert that professionals are persons obligated to undertake particular responsibilities, beyond such assertions, it can prove much more difficult to be more articulate about what these entail. The purpose of this chapter, therefore, is to identify significant conceptual landmarks on the professional terrain that contribute to understanding of its contours and dominant influences. It would be impossible to identify all the multiple forces and sources that influence conceptions of professional responsibility within the confines of this chapter (see Solbrekke, 2007, for further elaboration). Nevertheless, our intention is to identify those elements we consider to be required components whenever and wherever the tableau of professional responsibility is the focus of deliberation.

We excavate the original ideas of professions and re-interpret them in light of contemporary change forces. We identify the verities and power bases that lent substance to their anchoring influences on more traditional conceptualisations of what it means to be professional. As the title of the chapter suggests, we are going back to the future, to engage critically with foundational discourses, their roots and subsequent fortunes.

Despite as well as because of significant fracturing within the broadening contours of the vineyard in which professionals labour, we appropriate a common contemporary understanding of the term 'profession'. While wishing to avoid more traditional status hierarchies of old, new or semi-professions, we use the term professional to include those who have completed programmes of professional preparation in higher education (or equivalent) as an entry requirement to a profession.

The account we provide has four parts. It is not our intention to render an historical account, but we do identify important shifts in the conceptual terrain of professional responsibility over time and seek also to indicate the shaping influences that contributed to the emergence of new emphases that often silenced or marginalised dominant contours of the professional field at other times. The contribution is intended to provide a large canvas sufficient to accommodate the individual contributions contained in each of the other chapters. Second, the chapter constitutes the foundation on which the distinct contributions of the other chapters are woven into a deliberative conversation in the concluding chapter – a conversation that is intended to foster new horizons of professional responsibility.

Part One begins by identifying the 'roots' of professional responsibility as articulated by dominant voices of the early twentieth century. During this period, professions are positioned as mediators between the state and the citizen, while being accorded particular responsibilities by the state. By mid-century, however, alternative perspectives were beginning to raise questions regarding the authority of professions, resulting in greater diversity of accounts of professional responsibility. Arising from this mid-century diversification of perspectives, Part Two focuses on the impact of specialisation and expert knowledge as a significant shift in emphasis with implications for how professional responsibility was being understood. Additionally, intensification of marketisation and consumerism during this period contribute to the game-changing dynamics. Part Three revisits the earlier roots, identified in Part One, but through contemporary voices that in various ways and in different contexts have sought to rekindle extinguished or dormant dimensions of the field. Part Four re-configures these various contributions into a menu that we consider necessary for a more inclusive and holistic understanding of what professional responsibility entails. We conclude that twenty-first century complexities are here to stay, and professionals need to grapple with these realities through their initiation into professions and continue to reflect critically on them throughout a working life.

Excavating the roots of professional responsibility

Recourse to the Oxford Dictionaries (2010) provides several possibilities for understanding professional responsibility. The root of the word professional (profess) is associated with the concept of confession made by a person entering a religious order, and thus is connected with a sense of *calling*. Its Latin root 'profiteri' means *to declare publicly*. The Latin root of responsibility (respondere) means *to answer*, or *offer in return*. In combination therefore, from an etymological perspective, *professional responsibility* includes a sense of calling to provide service for the benefit of others, to take care of individuals as well as cater for the public welfare. Such understandings suggest being morally responsible for one's behaviour; to take on important duties while being willing to make independent decisions and being entrusted to do so. Responsibility, in this sense, resonates with the idea of teaching as a 'calling' (Hansen 2005). It connotes both the personal and moral dimensions of having a commitment to care that includes a combination of control, duties and decisions.[2]

Although etymological definitions are useful, they typically require additional elaboration. In seeking broader understanding of what professional responsibility entails, we ask: 'What particular features attach to the origins of professions and what particular responsibilities may be regarded as inherent in the very nature of professional work?'

Social trustee responsibility

The roots of professions and their embedded responsibilities may be traced to the beginning of the twentieth century and the work of Emile Durkheim, one of the early advocates of an emphasis on the professions as a positive force in social development (Johnson 1972). In his book *Professional Ethics and Civic Morals*, Durkheim elaborates the role of the professional as a *representative of a community* whose *responsibilities* include working for the emancipation of citizens in society (Durkheim 2001). He also defines professionals' responsibility as being central to the moral regulation of society (2001). All professional work therefore, he averred, must be founded in specific theoretical knowledge, skills and moral judgement beyond the level of lay people.

Similar assumptions are further elaborated in later sociological theories of professions, particularly in the work of Talcott Parsons (Parsons 1951, 1968). According to Parsons (1951: 434), professions are formally coupled to the public enterprise of being 'collectively oriented' rather than 'self-oriented'. This implies being able and willing to dedicate special and esoteric knowledge to the services of the members of society (Freidson 2001). Moreover, in this sense of professionalism, professionals value the meaning of professional work as being intimately bound up with the personal satisfaction derived from or inherent in doing 'qualitative' good work, while contributing also to their professional community and by serving the public. These are among

are further challenged by value conflicts that may arise from divergent roles the professional takes on during a career (Dreier 1999; Sinclair 1995). For example, shifting from a 'community of employees' to a new and peripheral role in a 'community of leaders' obliges the professional agent to negotiate and, at times, even change his or her practice of responsibility to fit new demands.

Another consequence of the hierarchical differentiation of professions that impacts understandings and practices of professional responsibility is an intensified specialisation of knowledge. Increasing specialist expertise tends also to rely on evidence-based knowledge, and a narrowing of who validates this knowledge (Grimen 2009). While specialist knowledge is useful in order to solve specified problems or to undertake distinct tasks, it may also create a kind of particularism and a possible sense of limited responsibility defined by local circumstances and the problem to be solved. Johnson (1972) captures this reality when he describes a situation in which the 'professional' does not look beyond the immediate consequences of his actions, and such possibilities are increasingly more likely. Increased specialisation in both education and work has tended to privilege expert or esoteric knowledge at the expense of moral and societal responsibilities. This shift in emphasis is the focus of the next part.

Professional responisbility: from 'social trustee' to 'expertise' and a utilitarian ethos

For the purpose of illustrating how some of the observed changes in societal structures have influenced professional responsibility in the latter part of the twentieth century, in this part we focus on empirical studies that indicate how professionals, in general, understand their professional role and responsibility. Significant analyses are Steven Brint's (Brint 1994, 2002; Brint and Levy 1999) extensive review of historical data on transformation of professions and broad empirical research on professionals, scholars and prospective professionals in the US. Central to the evidence provided is a fundamental movement among professionals from seeing themselves as 'social trustee professionals' to 'expert professionals' (Brint 1994: 203–5). A parallel shift in emphasis has been identified also in professional students' attitudes, orientations and engagement: what Brint characterises as *the rise of a utilitarian ethos* (Brint 2002: 245), a tendency to think of professional education merely as a means of obtaining credentials that will be valuable for each individual on the labour market. Consequently, as will be presented below, more recent formulations of professional responsibility scripts reflect little evidence to support the idea of professions as the source of a collective moral force in public life as promoted by Durkheim and Parsons.

A hollowing out of professional responsibility?

As indicated above, professionals increasingly define themselves by their marketable knowledge and skills. Their narratives are much more interwoven with the development of the economic forces regulating the labour market. In such circumstances, according to Brint (1994) powerful social and economic forces have brought the older idea of social trustee responsibilities – linking social purposes and knowledge-based authority – close to an end. Professionals rarely comment on the social importance of their work, as demonstrated by the statement from one life scientist who says: 'I see no reason to think that our work is more important to society than the work of an electrician or an auto mechanic' (10). While there is an appealing note of democratic egalitarianism in these words, they suggest also that being a professional requires no particular moral engagement – only expert knowledge.

Although there may be a residual heritage of 'social trustee professionalism' in state-regulated sectors and helping professions, 'expert professionalism' emerges as dominant even in the non-profit sector. It appears therefore that public welfare, high ethical standards in combination with claims to specialized authority has been replaced by an emphasis on the instrumental effectiveness of specialised, theoretically grounded knowledge with little concern for more traditional extended social responsibilities of ethical standards, or service in the public interest (pp. 27–37). Interviews with lawyers, doctors, engineers and scientists reveal that they tend to see professional responsibility primarily as a matter of being able to develop technical services in a complex world separated from moral and social concerns. The majority describe their work as involving broad and complex forms of knowledge, application of which requires sensitivity and discretion, but only a few mentioned their work in relation to its importance for society. There is evidence, therefore, that professionals in general have replaced the moral and societal dimension of responsibility with a private mindedness. This retreat from the public sphere is further exacerbated since many intellectuals have increasingly withdrawn from public life with the result that 'people who are responsible for educating sensibilities' no longer take 'principled positions on matters of public interest' (211). When celebrity culture and the darker art of 'spin' are added to this contemporary cocktail, a shared sense of professional responsibility is more difficult to identify, let alone promote and sustain.

However, Brint's thesis does not have direct universal application as indicated by results from recent studies in other countries such as, Norway with its strong social democratic orientation and commitments, where attitudes which move beyond mere self-interest and utilitarian concerns are more apparent (Jensen & Nygård 2000; Solbrekke 2007). Yet, values such as community service tend to diminish having entered the world of work in these contexts. Novice psychologists and lawyers in a work context typically have to negotiate their practice of professional responsibility to 'fit' with the culture, repertoire and enterprise of their new communities of work. During this process, even when they entered work life motivated to dedicate their knowledge for the benefit of clients *and* society, to a large extent, their focus changes. They appear to get caught up in local tasks and the societal dimension of their professional responsibility, in particular, is jeopardised (Solbrekke 2008).

Less surprising, yet worth recognising, the picture within business life is less promising with regard to moral and social responsibilities. A survey study on ethical dilemmas among managers in Norway concludes that they define their primary responsibility as being answerable to market culture. The 'manager role', based on a 'business moral', is perceived as the dominant responsibility, while the 'community member role' based on a 'community moral' becomes shadow rather than substance. Quite typically, many of these respondents stated that: 'ethics is important, but this is not the time to do something about it' (Olsen 2006: 248). Consequently, in practice, economic interests or demands of efficiency overshadow collective and public interests. In such circumstances, the moral dimension of professional responsibility is ignored or abandoned.

Despite a somewhat stronger focus on public service among professionals in the public rather than the business sphere, the general shift from public spiritedness to private mindedness among most contemporary professionals is evident. Other studies too indicate that professional life is shaped immeasurably by such influences as increased consumerism, flexibility, individualisation and efficiency which propel professionals into individualised practices in which social responsibility diminishes (Fishman et al. 2004; Sennett 1998).

There is a parallel story, however, that engenders more optimism regarding prospective professionals' attitudes and orientations. This cause for optimism documents a more holistic conception of professional responsibility that comprises technical, moral and civic dimensions. Drawing on previous experiences from research in diverse professional realms such as law, medicine, theatre, higher education and many more, Gardner, Csikszentmihalyi and Damon (2001) elaborated the meaning of 'good work' in an interview study of journalists and geneticists. Their study provides inspiring examples of professionals who are able to carry out work that is both excellent in quality and socially responsible. Nevertheless, their results also show that the conditions for living up to the ideals of a complex professional morality are perceived by many professionals as being poor. An increasing proportion of professionals find themselves 'squeezed' between competing interests of different stakeholders and the needs of clients. In order to respond to the demands of a specialised society characterised by powerful market forces, their moral principles very often are compromised in order to meet the requirements of efficiency and external goals. Such circumstances increase the risk that notions of professionally responsible performance become aligned more with 'excellence in quality' – of expertise and technique and less with being morally and socially responsible (Gardner, Csikszentmihalyi and Damon 2001: ix). Further challenges to more holistic understandings of professional responsibility emanate from the changing relationship between the neo-liberal state and its citizens where the state is perceived more as a 'provider and the taxpayer as consumer of public services' (Biesta 2010: 50–71).

New accountability regimes: their impact on professional responsibility

The more complex and shifting dynamics identified above have consequences for the relational role of professionals and their responsibilities. Additionally, in the new culture of consumerism, new systems of accountability have evolved to ensure more accountable services to the public with the help of measurement and legal standards. However, while this is intended to enhance the quality of professional practice, in terms of responsibility it appears to serve other purposes.[4] Within new forms of accountability and audit, professional responsibility tend to be perceived as a performance evaluated by indicators chosen for ease of measurement and control, rather than by the more complex standards of professions – a reductionist approach to professional responsibility.

Janice Gross Stein (2001) also highlights other problematic effects due to the manner in which good work is 'measured'. Though she is well disposed towards public accountability as a means of ensuring good-quality public services as well as building and maintaining public trust, she identifies also the increased risks of malpractice when the drive for efficiency has become an end rather than a means for good quality. She maintains that, in recent years, the drive for efficiency in terms of what is cost reducing has created a new vocabulary of accountability in which there is little or no room for asking the necessary questions: for what purpose and for whom the services are effective. Instead, the system of accountability tends to give paramount importance to standardised indicators which are effective and comparable at the expense of standards that are more time-consuming, but would create spaces and opportunities for evaluation of moral concerns and social trustee practice that embrace more inclusive conceptualisations of professional responsibility. Hargreaves (2003: 125–47) makes a very similar case in the field of education whereby high-stakes testing in US schools in particular reduces the professionalism of teachers to 'performance training sects'. However, he continues, teaching 'is not only a matter of technical skill and competence, but also involves personal, moral and political choices. It raises questions of values' (2003: 143); professional responsibility is not only a matter of expertise and technical competence.

Yet another fracturing influence on more holistic interpretations of professional responsibility is the flow of rapidly expanding information technology and distribution of knowledge. Lay people more often challenge the standards of professional work (Castells 2000). What is considered to be 'good work' is therefore, increasingly influenced by the interests and desires of 'customers', clients or patients, and questions of what is moral and immoral are disputed as postmodern relativism takes hold. The rise of such fracturing influences and the decline in potency of grand narratives has tended to privilege self-monitoring rather than being bound by collectively derived rules (Giddens 1991), a form of self-surveillance (Ball 2008).

In summary, professions have gradually moved away from professional responsibility as 'social trustee' to an increasing focus on specialisation and attendant emphasis on 'expert' knowledge. These developments, as well as the proliferation of professions, a questioning of authority and autonomy, have tended to create professional competition and new hierarchies. When market forces are added to this increasingly fractured terrain, a utilitarian ethos emerges with further negative consequences for larger social concerns and commitments. However, as some of the empirical evidence strongly suggests, the flame of the ethical and social trustee dimensions of professional responsibility continue to flicker. As researchers have become more aware of this fracturing of professional responsibilities, some have endeavoured to return to the roots of professional responsibility as a means of re-creating a more holistic and inclusive understanding of what professional responsibility involves. Such efforts are the focus of the next part.

Contemporary re-engagement with the roots of professional responsibility

There is a growing concern about how current workplace conditions thrust professionals towards a 'rational' and technical instrumental effectiveness of specialised work, at the expense of ethical standards, or service in the public interest. As a consequence, there is an emerging interest in how a more holistic understanding of professional responsibility may be addressed in a context of bottom-line thinking, market forces and global competition (Biesta 2010).

Although we readily recognise that returning to the stability, predictability and power relations that appeared to characterise professions during the earlier decades of the twentieth century is not an option, that a nostalgic return to a professional garden of Eden is fanciful, it would be foolhardy nevertheless to be dismissive of the ideas of Durkheim and Parsons on the normative dimension of solidarity and collectivity-orientation (Solbrekke 2007). Rather, the challenge is to re-interpret the concerns on which they focus attention but in ways that address professional responsibility in the context of twenty-first century realities. The particular prominence they accord to 'cognitive rationality' and 'affective neutrality' as the guarantee for advancing social welfare needs to be interrogated (Parsons 1951, 1968).[5] These ideas strongly influenced the postwar period, a period when the need to re-build societies permitted technical rationality to progress as the dominating reasoning in professional life as well as in professional education (Heiret 2003; Sullivan 2005). However, as Sullivan argues, it seems as though the proponents of this new order neglected to question whether this development was compatible with a long-term social mission of professions (Sullivan 2005: 147). Reviving the moral base for responsibility in terms of 'social trustee' values implies that we must critically examine and reconceptualise its meaning under current conditions of plurality and fluidity (Barnett 2003; Bauman 2000). Furthermore, contemporary economic fragility presents an important moment to revisit such considerations, as a means of bringing past, present and future into productive tension.

In 'an almost endless revision of taken-for-granted ways of doing things' as Giddens (1998: 28) puts it, the traditional frameworks, values and 'heroic' role models are in constant flux (Stronach et al. 2002). Thus, contemporary conditions both permit and require us to be active and independent professionals willing to make decisions despite the risk of making a wrong choice (Beck & Beck-Gernsheim 2001). Although constitutive rules of professional ethics are intended to provide guidance for professionals, actual decision making remains the individual's responsibility. Contemporary professionals are the inheritors of a professional responsibility legacy that obliges them to take responsibility for individual clients as well as the public interests.

Within this context, Ronald Barnett emphasises professionals' responsibility for 'speaking out' publicly, to engage in public inquires, debates or controversies, in which professionals have a legitimate voice (Barnett 1997: 33). Motivated by Habermassian 'critical reasoning' (Barnett 1990: 112–13), yet questioning the search for a set of universally 'valid' conditions (2003: 13), Barnett urges intellectuals as well as professionals to develop the capacity to be more open to multiple discourses and to engage with them. This implies that questioning dominant discourses within professional communities and public debates is essential for developing a conscious responsiveness to the wider society. In a postmodern, rapidly changing more fluid and less predictable environment, this questioning reflexivity becomes an urgent ongoing necessity rather than an occasional or episodic professional responsibility. Such reflexive attitude and courage to act, is also underlined by Edward Said (1994) who recognises the dynamics of power and emphasises that professional responsibility entails a special duty to address, when needed, the constituted and authorised powers of one's own society, whatever they might be.

These wider considerations of what professional responsibility entails come close to what William Sullivan (2005) identifies as 'civic professionalism'. Inspired by the pragmatic ideas of William James, George Herbert Mead and John Dewey, he links professional responsibility to moral reasoning in practice. Sullivan argues that professionals must, owing to their positions in social life, take the responsibility to handle ethical conflicts between societal interests and individual client's needs. As a professional it is impossible to escape the responsibility embedded in the multiple mandate – to foster respect for the individual *and* the public by offering quality services for *all* members in a society (Sullivan 2005).

Recapitulating these old ideals, returning to the roots does not make the life of professionals easier; quite the contrary. However, as the chapters in this book illuminate from a variety of perspectives, being a professional requires courage to articulate and enact practices that resonate with the values of their profession. It requires the ability to blend practical and analytical habits of mind, and ground decisions in professional discretion that resemble what Aristotle called *phronesis*; practical judgement that results from reflective reasoning – deliberation (Sullivan 2005). Practical judgement as essential to discretionary specialisation[6] may be characterised as encountering concrete situations with attentiveness and the ability to combine emotions and cognitive rationality as a means of arriving at good solutions – for the individual as well as the broader community. These contemporary currents in professional responsibility are a grounded means of reclaiming its future.

Professional responsibility: re-claiming the future

This chapter has described central features of professions and the responsibilities a professional is expected to shoulder. We have indicated also that such views are challenged in contemporary complex workplace contexts. Based on the foregoing analysis, we assert that in re-claiming the future of professional responsibility it is necessary to re-consider the ideals enshrined in the classical mandates of professions such as working for democracy and a collective orientation. However, to avoid possible accusations of being naive in expecting professionals to live up to such high standards, we readily recognise that professionals do not work in a vacuum unaffected by globalisation and political forces. Consequently, we focus on more recent approaches to the study of the 'world of professions' in order to take cognisance of contemporary realities – realities that in many instances have cultivated a collective amnesia regarding the roots of professional responsibility, sacrificed on the altar of a utilitarian ethos. Professional competition as well as market forces, and specialist expertise have enabled too many professionals to regard ethical and wider social commitments and responsibilities as primarily residing with others, partly determining that they have neither the time nor the autonomy to be responsible for them.

Professional norms and rules need to be reconceptualised so that they are consonant with the realities of professional as well as private lives (May 1996). Table 1.1 summarises the complex terrain of professional responsibility as a first step towards further explorations of its constituent elements and its possible reconstructions.

Given contemporary complexities, it is unlikely that this list is exhaustive and individual chapters are likely to extend it in a variety of ways. Nevertheless, it is within this 'jungle' of plural expectations and commitments that professionals are obliged to reach decisions that are based in knowledge as well as ethical discretion (Solbrekke 2007). This is no easy task, particularly if professional responsibility extends to the inclusion of decision making that embraces more than mere compliance with delineated professional ethics and norms (Colnerud 2006). Current societies characterised by the loss of power-assisted traditional stable and 'objective' ethical standards, pluralistic values and norms, increased uncertainty and competing interests, call for professionals who are attuned to individual clients' needs and open to multiple alternative solutions while not

Table 1.1 Reclaiming professional responsibility: necessary considerations

Professional responsibility includes combinations of appropriate attention to	
Client (individual/group needs)	Employer
Public/societal needs	Workplace conditions
Professional community/association	Personal career opportunities/advancement
Disciplinary/expert knowledge	Family and friends
	Personal/professional self (integrity)

being at odds with communal interests (Bauman 1995). Participation and personal involvement are welcomed, and differentiation is embraced rather than avoided (Benhabib 1992; May 1996). Rather than following conventional rules indifferently, morality requires a sensitive awareness entered into by commitment and participatory empathic concern (Bauman 1995: 56–7).

What are the implications of such complex considerations for the exercise of professional responsibility? Is there any sense in which 'legitimate compromise' may be reached between these competing interests? Chapter 12 will endeavour to lend some concrete reality to this question, while in the first instance, it is necessary to address the question: what would count as legitimate compromise?

The possibility of 'legitimate compromise'?

The moral philosopher Larry May insists that professional responsibility is discretionary (May 1996: 98), and the decisions we make as professionals are the dynamic consequences of the reciprocal interaction of personal and cultural factors in both their potentiating and constraining influences (Shotter 1984). Thus, applying a 'participationist communitarian'[7] (May 1996: 27), or group-orientated perspective to the development of individual practices of professional responsibility indicates that responsible decisions must be based on mutual adjustment and internal negotiations about the concept of 'good work' in solidarity with the purpose of the respective profession (May 1996: 27). Such an approach may encourage professionals to see themselves as part of a broader professional community – a community in which they may find support as well as provide them with a sense of belonging, of not being alone with an overwhelming responsibility. Such considerations represent a major challenge in a self-regulated world, where competitive individualism is pervasive in opposition to more collectivist perspectives.

However, becoming conscious of ourselves as participants in larger communities has the potential to strengthen the notion of social responsibility and to cultivate a mindset more attentive to collective relations. As outlined above, there is reason to believe that attentiveness to social responsibilities has diminished among professionals, while professionals are struggling with living up to the 'high standards' of professional work. Additionally, while priorities in work life often are made by politicians, the bureaucracy or a global firm at a distance from the professional's workplace, the individual professional is burdened with responsibility for the total quality of the work (Nerland & Jensen 2007). This is a responsibility that, in many cases, remains an obligation too heavy to bear. In such circumstances, the possibility of 'legitimate negotiated compromise' as May suggests, may help to cope, to avoid being overwhelmed by responsibilities while seeking to promote responsible behaviour.

May understands professional responsibility more in terms of 'exemplars and prototypes rather than rules' (May 1996: 96). Consequently, how to behave in a professionally responsible manner should evolve from collective negotiations and the results of 'mutual adjustment', 'moral negotiation' and 'compromises' that are based on dialogues and with a sensitivity to alternatives, presuppositions and ambiguities (May 1996: 97). However, for such compromises to retain their claim to legitimacy, it is necessary also to reserve a place and space for the individual to adapt the core values of his or her profession. This also involves critical reflections on how the normative obligations of the professional can be legitimately negotiated and lived out in a specific situation where professional competition and conflicting codes of conduct may be at odds rather than in synchrony with such deliberative obligations.

Whatever the workplace realities, it is necessary to acknowledge also, both from a practical and theoretical perspective, that not all compromises are legitimate. Some compromises may be a 'bridge too far' from the perspective of professional standards of 'good work' and thus become 'illegitimate' and an unacceptable exercise of professional responsibility. It hardly needs to be stated that there are obvious signs of immoral or irresponsible behaviour among current professionals.[8]

May's 'legitimate compromise' does not promote 'professional responsibility' as a relativistic concept without 'universal' obligations (May 1996: 130). Rather, professionals, owing to their unique professional expertise, are expected to be loyal to the obligation inherent in the professional claim – using knowledge to serve others – the individual client as well as the public. However, this does not imply unrealistic self-sacrifice on the professional's part. While professional self-sacrifice may be an unwarranted burden, taking professional responsibility seriously does entail grappling with the inevitable tensions between societal concerns and individual clients' interests as well as the ability to balance commitments in private life with diverse and multiple requirements of work life.

Before drawing this opening chapter to a conclusion, it would be remiss of us not to draw attention to the manner in which the language of professional responsibility has altered over time. If there is truth in the assertion that language does our thinking for us, then supplanting one language with another alters the discourse in perceptible and imperceptible ways. As the evidence here and in subsequent chapters attests, when the language of new public management becomes pervasive, accompanied by the surveillance implicit in various technologies of control (see Ball 2008) and the 'audits' or paper trails to which they give rise (Power 1999), they tend to engender compliance and conformity rather than more expansive and 'imaginative' understanding of professional responsibility (Power 2008).

Conclusions

While it is abundantly evident that the contemporary terrain of professional responsibility is complex and fragile, we have also tried to suggest that, by going back to the roots of professions, it is possible to undertake a process of anamnesis – of remembering marginalised, lost or silenced elements of professional discourses. It is clear from our selective excavations of the literature that ethical dimensions as well as wider social responsibilities have been caught in the cross-fires of increased specialisation, professional proliferation and attendant competition, and exacerbated by the influence of international market competition. When the language of new public management is added to this cocktail of competing interests, a 'narrowing of horizons' and a withdrawal from wider social commitments is not surprising (Gadamer 1989). However, rather than lament some lost golden age, it is necessary to embrace these contemporary realities, and from the 'bricolage' of these change forces, deploy the generative potential of professional responsibility as the glue that holds these competing perspectives in productive tension. It is through this lens that a potential 'fusion of horizons' will emerge in and beyond the distinct contributions of the individual chapters, thus contributing to new prospects for the future of professional responsibility.

Notes

1 The term 'Gordian Knot' is derived from a *legend* of *Phrygian Gordium*, which is associated with *Alexander the Great*. It is often used as a *metaphor* for an intractable problem solved by a bold stroke. In Shakespeare's *Henry V* (Act 1, Scene 1), the Archbishop of Canterbury states: 'Turn him to any cause of policy, The Gordian Knot of it he will unloose, Familiar as his garter'.
2 In the literature on professional responsibility the term 'accountability' is regularly used and some authors claim that accountability should be differentiated as one form of responsibility (Sinclair 1995). See Chapter 4 for a detailed account of this distinction and its significance for understandings of professional responsibility.
3 As will be illustrated in Chapter 4, responsibility requires autonomy to enact!
4 See Chapter 4 for further elaboration.
5 See Chapter 3 where the importance of care as inherent in professional responsibility is elaborated.
6 See Chapter 4 for a further elaboration.
7 In his version of communitarianism, May generally supports the ideas of Charles Taylor (1989) emphasising the importance of the frames of horizon in which human beings develop their identities and senses of morality and responsibility (May 1996: 13–14). His view is also understood to be close to Seyla Benhabib's (1992: 77–8) definition of 'participationist communitarianism', which endorses the value of multiple discourses and encourages non-exclusive principles of membership. It differs from an 'integrationist communitarianism', which stresses the importance of inculcation of, and a total loyalty to, a coherent value system. Application of 'participationist communitarianism' to professional responsibility implies that a legitimate demand of commitment to the moral order of a profession must be based on internal negotiations about the concept of 'good work' in solidarity with the purpose of the respective profession (May 1996: 27).
8 Chapter 9 exemplifies this.

References

Abbott, A. (1988) *The System of Professions: An Essay on the Division of Expert Labor.* Chicago: University of Chicago Press.

Ball, S. (2008) Performativity, privatisation, professionals and the state. In B. Cunningham (ed.) *Exploring Professionalism.* pp. 50–72. London: Institute of Education.

Barnett, R. (1990) *Higher Education: A Critical Business*. Buckingham: SRHE and Open University Press.

Barnett, R. (1997) *Higher Education: A Critical Business*. Buckingham: SRHE and Open University Press.

Barnett, R. (2003) *Beyond All Reason. Living with Ideology in the University*. Buckingham: SRHE and Open University Press.

Bauman, Z. (1995) Life in fragments: essays in postmodern morality. Oxford: Blackwell Publishers.

Bauman, Z. (2000) *Liquid Modernity*. Cambridge: Polity Press.

Beck, U. & Beck-Gernsheim, E. (2001) *Individualizaton. Institutionalized Individualism and its Social and Political Consequences*. London: Sage.

Benhabib, S. (1992) *Situating the Self. Gender, Community and Postmodernism in Contemporary Ethics*. Cambridge: Polity Press.

Biesta, G. (2010) *Good Education in an age of Measurement Ethics, Politics, Democracy*. Boulder & London: Paradigm Publishers.

Brante, T. (1990) Professional types as a strategy of analysis. In M. Burrage, and R. Thorstendahl (eds) *Professions in Theory and History. Rethinking the Study of the Professions*. pp. 75–93. London: Sage Publications.

Brint, S. (1994) *In an Age of Experts*. Princeton: Princeton University Press.

Brint, S. & Levy, C. (1999) Profession and civic engagement: trends in rhetoric and practice 1875–1995. In T. Skocpol and M. Fiorina (eds) *Civic Engagement in American Democracy*. pp. 163–210. Washington, DC: Brookings Institution Press.

Brint, S. (2002) The rise of the 'practical arts'. In S. Brint, (ed.) *The Future of The City of Intellect*. pp. 231–259. Stanford: Stanford University Press.

Castells, M. (2000) *The Institutions of the New Economy*. Summary of the address to the 'Delivering the Virtual Promise?' Conference, London, 19 June 2000. http://virtualsociety.sbs.ox.ac.uk/text/events/castells.htm (Accessed 10 May 2005)

Colnerud, G. (2006) Teachers ethics as a research problem: syntheses achieved and new issues. *Teachers and Teaching: Theory and Practice* 12(3), 365–85.

Dreier, O. (1999) Personal trajectories of participation across contexts of social practice. *Outlines, Critical Social Studies* (1), 5–32.

Durkheim, E. (2001) *Professional Ethics and Civic Morals*. London: Routledge.

Evetts, J. (2003) Reinterpreting professionalism: as discourse of social control and occupational change. In L. Svensson and J. Evetts (eds) *Conceptual and Comparative Studies of Continental and Anglo-American Professions*. Research report no. 129. from the Department of Sociology. Göteborg: Gothenburg University.

Fauske, H. (2008) Profesjonsforskningens faser og stridsspørsmål [The phases of research on professions and controversial questions]. In A. Molander and L.I. Terum (eds) *Profesjonsstudier* [The Studies of Professions]. pp. 31–53. Oslo: Universitets forlaget.

Fishman, W., Solomon, B., Greenspan, D. & Gardner, H. (2004) *Making Good: How Young People Cope with Moral Dilemmas at Work*. Cambridge, MA: Harvard University Press.

Freidson, E. (1988) *Profession of Medicine. A Study of the Sociology of Applied Knowledge*. Chicago: University of Chicago Press.

Freidson, E. (2001) *Professionalism: The Third Logic*. Cambridge: Polity Press.

Gadamer, H.G. (1989) *Truth and Method* (Translated by J. Weinsheimer and G. Marshall), 2nd edn. London: Sheed & Ward.

Gardner, H., Csikszentmihalyi, M. & Damon, W. (2001) *Good Work – When Excellence and Ethics Meet.* New York: Basic Books.

Giddens, A. (1991) *Modernity and Self-Identity.* Cambridge: Polity Press.

Giddens, A. (1998) *Risk Society: the Context of British Politics,* in Jane Franklin (Ed.) The Politics of Risk Society. (Cambridge, Polity Press) 23–34.

Grimen, H. (2009) Debatten om evidensbasering – noen utfordringer [The debate on evidence base (ing) – some challenges]. In H. Grimen and L.I. Terum (eds) *Evidence-based Professional Practice.* pp. 191–222. Oslo: Abstract Publisher.

Gross Stein, J. (2001) *The Cult of Efficiency.* Toronto: Anansi Press.

Hansen, D. (2005) *The Call to Teach.* New York: Teachers College Press.

Hargreaves, A. (2003) *Teaching in the Knowledge Society.* Buckingham: Open University Press.

Heiret, J. (2003) Profesjoner og profesjonsbegreper i norsk historieforskning [Professions and concepts of professions in Norwegian historical research]. *Historisk tidsskrift.* (3), 201–28.

Jensen, K. & Nygård, R. (2000) *Studentidentitet og Samfunnsmoral. Søkelys på høyere gradsstudenters norm- og verdisettingsmønster* [Student identity and societal moral issues. On graduate students' norms and value structures]. Innsatsområdet Etikk, Skriftserie. 4 Oslo: University of Oslo.

Johnson, T.J. (1972) *Professions and Power.* London: Macmillian Press Ltd.

Macdonald, K.M. (1995) *The Sociology of Professions.* London: Sage Publications.

May, L. (1996) *The Socially Responsive Self. Social Theory and Professional Ethics.* Chicago: University of Chicago Press.

Molander, A. & Terum, L.I. (eds) (2008) *Profesjonsstudier* [The Studies of Professions]. Oslo: Universitetsforlaget.

Nerland, M. & Jensen, K. (2007) Insourcing the management of knowledge and occupational control: an analysis of computer engineers in Norway. *International Journal of Lifelong Education* 26(3), 263–78.

Olsen, J.B. (2006) *Om doble normer i næringslivet – etikken i tidsklemma* [Double standards in the business industry – ethics in tight squeeze]. Doctoral thesis, Göteborg: University of Gothenburg, Företagsekonomiska Institutet, Handelshögskolan.

Parsons, T. (1951) *The Social System.* New York: The Free Press.

Parsons, T. (1968) Professions. *International Encyclopedia of the Social Sciences,* vol 12. pp. 536–47. New York: The Free Press and Macmillian.

Power, M. (1999) *The Audity Society Rituals of Verification.* Oxford: Oxford University Press.

Power, S. (2008) The imaginative professional. In B. Cunningham (ed.), *Exploring Professionalism.* pp. 144–60. London: Institute of Education.

Said, E. (1994) *Representations of the Intellectual: the Reith Lectures.* New York: Pantheon Books.

Sennett, R (1998) *The Corrosion of Character. The Personal Consequences of Work in the New Capitalism.* New York: W.E Norton & Company.

Shotter, J. (1984) *Social Accountability and Selfhood.* Oxford: Basil Blackwell.

Sinclair, A. (1995) The chameleon of accountability: forms and discourses. *Accounting Organisations and Society* 20(2/3), 219–37.

Solbrekke, T.D. (2007) *Understanding conceptions of professional responsibility.* Ph.D. dissertation, University of Oslo.

Solbrekke, T.D. (2008) Professional responsibility as legitimate compromises – from communities of education to communities of work. *Studies in Higher Education* 3(4), 485–500.

Solbrekke, T.D. & Heggen, K.M. (2009) Sykepleieansvar – fra profesjonelt moralsk ansvar til teknisk regnskapsplikt? [A nurse's responsibility – from professional moral responsibility to technical accountability?] *Arbejdsliv* 11(3), 49–61.

Sullivan, W. (2005) *Work and Integrity. The Crisis and Promise of Professionalism in America*. New York: Harper Business.

Svensson, L. (2008) Professions and accountability. Challenges to professional control and collegiality. Paper presented at the *5th Interim Conference of the International Sociological Association: Sociology of Professional Groups*. Challenges to professionalism. Limits and benefits of the professional model. Centre for the Study of Professions, 12–13 September, Oslo University College, Oslo, Norway.

Taylor, C. (1989) *Sources of the Self: The Making of Modern Identity,* Cambridge: Cambridge University Press.

Turner, B.S. (2001) Preface to 2nd edition of *Professional Ethics and Civic Morals* (E. Durkheim). London: Routledge Sociology Classics.

2 Towards an ecological professionalism

Ronald Barnett

Introduction

The modern professional is embedded in overlapping networks, some of his or her own choosing and some inadvertently.[1] The networks are intra-professional (with one's own profession) and inter-professional (increasingly with other professions); they are with clients and with the state; and they are with discourses and understandings. Many of these networks have degrees of formality attaching to them but others involve largely informal and ephemeral interactions.

There is nothing new in this, it may be felt. What is new is the scope and challenge of this phenomenon of the networked professional. The scope is marked out by such further concepts as lifewide learning, supercomplexity and the emerging conceptual age. In turn, value questions arise: how does the new professional secure his or her own legitimacy? Is it through an adherence to universal or particular values? How, if at all, might the concept of responsibility come into play here? Might the idea of the ecological professional offer a way forward?

I want to explore these issues in this chapter. I shall do so by advancing and developing the concept of 'the ecological professional' itself and, in the process, I shall also identify and try to tease out a number of related concepts – such as the 'being' of the professional (as in 'professional being'), 'liquid professionalism', 'authentic professionalism', professional 'networks', 'registers' of professionalism, professional 'responsibility' and professional 'authenticity', professional 'dispositions' and 'qualities', 'supercomplexity' and professional 'sustainability'. This chapter is, therefore, as it might be said, an essay in the philosophy of professionalism. I shall draw on 'modern' European philosophy, in particular, 'The Three Ecologies' by Félix Guattari (2005) but also on Heidegger (1998). Nietzsche will also hover in the background.

Implicitly, this chapter explores the question: how might the ideas of 'the professional' and 'professionalism' be understood in the contemporary world? I shall try, however, to go further than offering a kind of conceptual geography of the territory by also exploring, on the basis of the conceptual ground covered, the *possibilities* that attach to being a professional in the modern age.

Professionalism, I shall argue, is beset by considerable challenges but yet there remain positive possibilities in the very idea.

The professional in space and time

The modern professional is caught in space and time complexes. The professional has her being in multiple spaces and multiple timeframes; and these spaces and timeframes themselves interconnect in complex ways. Professional being looks forwards and backwards as well as at the demands of the moment. It looks outwards to external spaces and inwards to interior spaces. Part of today's professionalism lies in the handling of the juxtaposition of the interior and the exterior callings.

The spaces themselves characteristically have their own rhythms and pacings; and these can collide. The timeframe for the doctor–patient encounter has differing logics. On the one hand, the doctor works within a timeframe logic set by the local and national performance indicators and the resourcing envelope of the doctor's practice. On the other hand, the patient has a different timeframe modality, drawn from his or her personal needs and even anxieties. In this doctor–patient encounter, the different timeframe logics collide; and this is due partly to their being reflective of differing clinical spaces, on the one hand a space of professional care and understanding (and even empathy) in which the patient has his or her being; and on the other hand, a bureaucratic-technical space in which the clinical practice has its being.

But the doctor has her being in widening space–time complexes. She may be a member of international medical 'communities of practice', or of local and more informal such networks; she will be subject to local and national and even international norms of medical practice; she will be receiving several journals, each with its own rhythm of publication, reporting on studies perhaps taking several years of research; and she will be bombarded daily with data and news and information (of new drugs, new routines and new clinical practices and audit procedures). Here and now, distant and in the past and into the future; overlapping and colliding: the modern professional somehow manages these time–space complexes and her place amid them.

There is a phenomenology at work here that has barely begun to be understood. When it is said that the modern professional has the challenge of managing her time, that simple phrasing stands duty for complexes of time–space *being*. What is it to live amid multiple spaces, each with its mix of discourses, voices, ideologies and understandings? What is it to live in the future – the 'extended present' (Nowotny 1996) – as well as the present? What is it to live amid multiple timeframes, at once short and fast, and long and slow, in which the professional has both to live in the moment and to live in the future (as long-term projects are contemplated)?

This professional's identity is distributed in time and space. Perhaps a bureaucratic identity in one place (a number on a professional register or a nodal point in resource management); perhaps a clinical identity; a quasi-pedagogical identity; and horizontally – perhaps extending across other countries – and into the future. The term 'matrix' hardly begins to do justice to this complex identity structure. Increasingly, too, there is no hiding place in this welter of identities: the modern professional is on show, her actions transparent to the wider world and subject to account from diverse directions and manifold stakeholders. The modern professional's identity is increasingly not of her own making, being less under her control but subject to the perceptions of others and the various resource, accountability and communicative structures in which she has her professional being.

While straddling these time–space complexes, the modern professional endeavours to construct her own subjectivity. How does she see the world? What is her perspective on it? Does she have, is there available to her, a stable horizon of values? Or, rather, does she inhabit several ethical territories simultaneously, to which she is subject? Is it possible for the modern professional to have a personal and unitary hold on the world? Does the idea of *authentic professionalism* make sense anymore in such a fluid world?

Surely, these challenges to modern professionalism are only going to increase. The modern professional lives amid a set of infinities, not of her making; of expanding accountability demands, resource challenges, global horizons of standards and developing techniques, shifting knowledge and changing client relationships. There is no end to these changes; rather, they accumulate and expand, entering new regions of uncertainty. In this infinity of openness and contestability, the modern professional moves uncertainly and even hesitantly. Any overt confidence can only be a pretence of security, for the reflexive professional knows that she skates on thin ice. Her only hope is to keep skating so as to stay ahead of the cracking ice behind her.

The networking professional

Willy-nilly, the modern professional is a networked professional. The idea of 'network' here, though, takes on its own complexity. Three distinctions should be observed. First, network here is both *verb* and *noun*. The professional 'networks' (verb): she engages with groups and communities, with a spread of interests. But she also is herself a node amid networks (noun) (cf. Castells 1996: 470). The modern professional, indeed, may be construed as just that: a meeting point of a number of networks. At the conjunction of a particular set of communities, agencies and groups, each with its own force and influence, sits a particular professional. This structural conception of professional life, as a set of interlocking networks, has a certain poignancy, for the idea of professional contains precisely the idea of allegiance to wider constituencies beyond the individual. The individual acquires a professional self only insofar as she interconnects with and acknowledges responsibilities to wider communities. There can be no *alone-professional*.

A second distinction is that between professional as *agent* and as *subject*. As an agent, the professional works at extending her networks. The doctor may reach out to certain pharmaceutical companies, to other professionals in certain specialties (perhaps even across the world), to particular kinds of client in extending the client base and to other groups (in the political and bureaucratic domains) which might help in developing the practice's infrastructure. In all of this, the professional is intentionally networking: she networks strategically. The practice's website will be continually updated, in projecting certain kinds of image and resonance so as to reflect the networks that are deliberately being fostered and even extended. Intentionally or otherwise, she is a *networked professional*. She is caught in networks, being both positioned and influenced by them. The idea of the network, therefore, is a nice cameo of the relationship between structure and agency. In the network, the professional is both structured and agentic all at once.

The third distinction in relation to the networked professional is that of *systems* and *discourses*, a kind of hard–soft distinction. On the one hand, as noted, the professional has her professional being among systems of client interaction, resource provision, bureaucratic accountability mechanisms and physical infrastructures. But, on the other hand, the professional moves within softer networks, of discourses, conversations and ethical horizons. These *discursive networks* are networks of ideas, concepts and beliefs.

These two features of the networked professional – systems and discourses – are inter-related and overlap, but they are also discrete and even contending. The professional, in the single clinical encounter, interacts with the client or patient as a centre of reflective consciousness (a 'human being' to whom 'care' is extended) but in the same moment, conducts that encounter against the background of an ever-constraining resource 'envelope'. The patient is perceived both as a human being and as a consumer of expensive resources (not least the time of the professional herself). But this is to say that the clinical encounter is conducted within intermingling swirls of ideas and considerations, which may compete with each other. The fluid currents of ideas may be reluctant to mix together.

These dimensions of networks are themselves inter-related. The networked professional has her being among soft and hard discursive networks, which may themselves be intended or unintended. A matrix of networks could be plotted here quite easily, its two axes being those of soft–hard networks and intended–unintended networks. But the temptation to produce such a network grid should be resisted for, even if its vertical and horizontal lines were to take a dotted form to reflect their porosity, still such a grid would imply a too definite sense of orderly structure. Rather, this *liquid professionalism*, as we may term it, is characterised precisely by multiple fluid currents, both intermingling and colliding with each other (cf. Bauman 2000).

To understand the modern professional as an inescapably networked professional – in real and virtual networks, in obligatory and self-directed networks, in networks of communities and of discourses – prompts searching questions. In whose interests is or might this networking take place? What kind of responsibility, if any, is upheld in this networking? To what ends is it taking place?

An ecological calling

The concept of ecology may be helpful in taking these reflections forward. Ecology is a 'thick concept' (Williams 2006). It refers us to facts about the world, notably its interconnectedness, its internal interdependencies and humanity's part in sustaining (or injuring) those interdependencies. However, it also connotes ethical dimensions, notably a sense that humanity has a responsibility in sustaining the ecological systems in which it finds itself. There is here an idea of stewardship, that humanity has been bequeathed the powers and resources that may help to sustain the ecology of the world and so has a duty to do just that, over generations ahead. The idea of 'deep ecology' goes even further, serving to remind humanity that the world is not out there, even as an object to be saved from extinction by humanity's efforts, but that humanity is deeply implicated in ecological systems.

Originally developed in relation to the natural physical environment, 'ecology' has been taken up in many domains. Guattari (2005) depicts 'three ecologies', namely those of the environment, social relations and the psyche of the human subject. The large issues of living together on this planet call for 'an ethico-political articulation' between these three ecological registers, which Guattari terms 'ecosophy'. Guattari, I sense, is aware that the term 'ecological', even extended so as to embrace these three registers, scarcely exhausts its potential conceptual reach. After all, he begins the relevant chapter with this aphorism from Gregory Bateson: 'There is an ecology of bad ideas, just as there is an ecology of weeds'.

And, indeed, the idea of ecology has been taken up in many domains, including that of ideas itself, so that there is a growing literature on 'knowledge ecology'.

For our purposes, in the domain of professionalism and professional life, the idea of ecology comes into play in no less than five domains, namely all of the four domains so far identified plus one other. In the context of what it is to be a professional, we can pick out five ecological registers.

1   The ecology of the professional self: is there or can there be a unity to the professional self or is it necessarily fragmented? To what degree and in what ways are its components held together or held apart?
2   The ecology of the client relationship: what are the bonds of the relationship? To what extent might concepts such as duty, allegiance, trust and care have a bearing on contemporary professionalism?
3   The knowledge ecology of professionalism: what forms of knowledge come into view in the framing of professionalism? Does the term 'knowledge' even bear weight here, or should we not at least speak of contrasting knowledges? What is their ecology? Are some knowledges dominant? (Are practical knowledges supplanting more discursive knowledges?) Are some being suppressed? Are yet others struggling to be born?

4   The ecology of the professional environment: what are the interconnections
between the professional, the client and the wider physical, technological
and societal environment? How might those interconnections be
understood (or even 'modelled')? Are, for example, mathematical models of
those complex interactions helpful (akin to those being developed in model-
ling cities) or are they misleading?

Each of these four registers has already been implied in our discussion but
there is surely a fifth register that has to come within this ecological horizon,
namely, the following.

5   The discursive ecology of professionalism: what are the registers of ideas
and concepts that might come into play in conceptualising contemporary
professionalism? And from which domains might they be drawn: From
management and organisational studies, ethics, economics, philosophy
or even theology or anthropology? And what might their interconnections and their tensions be?

It might be objected that the use of the idea of the ecological to embrace all
of these five domains of professional life is to over-stretch the concept. Or it may
be objected that to affix the idea of the ecological to these five domains is to
link them together artificially. The five domains deserve and require separate
consideration, so it might be said; advantage is to be had neither by linking
them together nor by placing them in the company of the idea of the ecological.
I accept this line of thought but only in part: that the five domains deserve
separate treatment is right but there is still advantage in placing them together
under the idea of the ecological. For, to return to an earlier point, the idea of
the ecological is a thick concept; and its thickness is particularly helpful here.

For our purposes, the essence of the idea of the ecological lies in its dual
connotations of interconnectedness *and* an ethical orientation towards that
interconnectedness. It is both fact and value intertwined. The ecological professional has a sense of the ecological registers within which she has her professional
being and their interconnectedness *and* has an orientation of care towards those
registers. The professional is aware of the *interconnectedness* of the registers of
her professional being – they do not present as discrete spaces but, to the
contrary, are acutely felt as indivisible, as, in the course of a single day, she juggles
a wide array of professional challenges and responsibilities *and* possibilities that
she sees for herself. In turn, the *ethical dimension* of her professional presses
itself. The professional is reflective about her professional self and its integrity
across its registers; about the changing structure of her client relationships; about
the developing knowledge structures within which her professional practices are
situated; about the wider environment surrounding her professionalism;
and about the ideas and concepts that contour the ideational territory of that
professionalism. However, she goes beyond merely being cognisant of those five
registers and does what she can to sustain and even promote the integrity and

wellbeing of those registers. The ecological professional has not just a care for her professionalism but works out that professionalism in a serious way in the crucial five domains of her professional life.

This is truly an ecological calling. Professionalism itself imbues an allegiance to the exterior; the exterior (clients, knowledges, practices, etc.) are not outside the professional's professionalism but are a part of it. The exterior in all its manifestations not so much presses on the professional but is held within her. It is a set of callings, inwardly felt. There is here a spirit of professionalism, at once energising the professional to hear and to respond to callings and to imagine how they might be improved. The ecological professional has a care (Heidegger 1998: 225ff) towards the five ecological domains of her professional being and so is moved to work towards their development. The ecological professional is called to action in those five ecological registers.

An ecological responsibility

The idea of the ecological, then, when placed in the context of professional life, becomes a particular complex set of ideas. It works in at least five registers, it connotes levels of professional being (as in 'deep ecology'; Moog 2009), it allows for varying forms of intensity and engagement, it has potential scope and it invites multiple perspectives; and all of these domains – *registers, levels, intensity, scope* and *perspectives* – inter-relate in complex and even inchoate ways. It is hardly surprising, therefore, against this set of considerations, that it is difficult to give a full or even an adequate account of the idea of professionalism in the contemporary age.

Professional being is not given; it has to be constructed. In itself, the assertion is trite. But the forms of construction are not given either. It is surely clear that professional being can be constructed in a bewildering variety of ways, given the many domains of its potential formation.

Here, though, in the presence of the idea of an ecological professionalism, certain facets press themselves. The idea of the ecological, to reiterate, is both fact and value intertwined. The ecological professional is one who is not just sensitive to the complexity of the environment – personal, social, technological, physical – in which professional life has its place but who is also concerned to promote the sustainability and even the wellbeing of that multilayered environment. All professional life to be worthy of the name has been conducted against a horizon of the ethical: it is there, if at all, that it gains its authenticity (cf. Taylor 1991). But the idea of an ecological professionalism presses this reflection further. For the ecological professional is minded to work so as to improve the wellbeing of her environment, in all its networked complexity. But how might the idea of improvement be understood? Can it be conceptualised?

Here, the concept of responsibility gains its entrance; and it may be distinguished from authenticity. Authenticity is a matter of being true to oneself, an idea that may be further understood in two ways (cf. Cooper 2002). One may be true to oneself through being unencumbered by unduly constraining forces and situations: here, one has the freedom to become oneself as one really wants and even needs to be. Alternatively, one may be true to oneself through venturing forward fearlessly, relying only on oneself and one's own resources and capacities. This is a more Nietzschian conception of authenticity, of actually striking out boldly no matter what the circumstances. On either conception, authenticity is that state of affairs in which one heeds one's own inner callings. It looks to the interior of being. Authenticity is a crucial concept for our purposes for, in being fully professional, the professional has to be herself to a significant extent.

Pit, then, responsibility alongside authenticity. If authenticity is a matter of heeding one's inner callings (or at least being accorded the space to do so), responsibility is the opposite idea, for it betokens a regard for the exterior world, and almost a disregard for self. Responsibility calls precisely for responsiveness to the claims of the world. Again, in parallel with authenticity, two versions of responsibility may be distinguished. On the one hand, there is the situation in which it is commonly recognised that to a particular profession attaches certain kinds of responsibility. This is a form of *epistemic responsibility*, a spelling out of the conditions of professionalism for a particular setting. On the other hand, there is the situation in which a professional not just acknowledges such a set of responsibilities (and even acts on them) but feels them as part of her own professional identity. They constitute her professional being. This is a form of *ontological responsibility*. It is the form of responsibility that comes to constitute what Heidegger called 'care' or 'concern', or what used also to be termed 'vocation', that state of self-*less* being in which individuals are called out to and yield to an inner calling. Such a calling has been especially associated with the so-called caring professions, in the church, in nursing or in teaching.

Both forms of responsibility are important *and* they are inter-related. Ontological responsibility – the felt responsibility – has to be anchored in a frank and realistic acknowledgement of the professional's particular responsibilities, and so given weight through her epistemic responsibility. Equally, her epistemic responsibility is sheer intellectualism unless, in turn, it is given substance in the professional's own interior being, such that her responsibilities impart a spirit that impels her forward into the professional fray, with all its complexities and challenges. For this, there has to be an ontological responsibility at work; her professional being has to be layered with not just a sense of responsibility but with responsibility itself. Her professional identity is structured in part by her exterior callings: her 'duty'.

This professional identity, structured with responsibilities, is prompted in turn towards assuming an ecological orientation. The ecological professional is, it will be recalled, precisely a professional who recognises the multidimensionality of her professionalism and has a care towards the several domains of her professional being – personal, inter-personal, environmental and so on. The ecological professional is already, by definition therefore, a responsible professional; as stated, she recognises the domains of her professionalism and her responsibilities in sustaining and in advancing the wellbeing of her several networks (intended and unintended).

In both its epistemic and ontological aspects, this analysis of the concept of responsibility points up the severity of what it is to be an ecological professional. For the ecological professional now is a professional who is sensitive to her professionalism having its place amid several dimensions *and* who is on a journey to explore her (epistemic) responsibilities in each domain and also to take on those responsibilities as part of her ontological continuous becoming as a professional. This is a never-ending and demanding set of challenges.

The ecological professional, accordingly, is always forging her own professionalism. She is conscious of the (five) domains of her professional being, which she is always exploring, and to each one she has, as indicated, an abiding care or concern. After all, 'Dasein's Being reveals itself as *care*' (Heidegger 1998: 227). More, since the domains of her professionalism are themselves inter-related in dynamic and ever-changing forms, her responsibilities as an ecological professional are always shifting, like patterns in the sand. The ecological professional is always on the move, as the horizons of her ethical responsibilities themselves continue to move.

A professional ecosophy

In sketching his idea of the ecological environment in which humanity is embedded (with its different ecologies), Guattari spoke of 'a new ecosophy, at once applied and theoretical, ethico-political and aesthetic …' (Guattari 2005: 67). Surely, we have seen this 'new ecosophy' in this liquid professionalism that constitutes the emerging ecological professionalism. The idea of professionalism underwent a revolution, amid the arrival of the so-called 'new public management', from an autonomous professionalism founded on a command of a knowledge field interpreted in the interests of a client, to an accountable professionalism bounded by technical constraints and performance indicators. In that shift of professional technicisation and bureaucratisation, responsibility itself shifted from a twin responsibility to profession and client to external stakeholders and management systems. Now, understood as ecological professionalism, the professional has a *worldly* responsibility towards the wellbeing of the ecological registers in which her professional being is located.

We see this in the very name of an international charity: 'Médicins sans Frontieres'. We see it in graphic form when professionals of many kinds respond immediately to world crises – tsunamis, earthquakes, famines, floods – or to chronic world problems (such as physical malformations or diseases) and travel to distant lands to deploy their professional skills and care in helping to alleviate suffering and pain. We see it too on the battlefield when doctors and others treat the injured of opposing armed forces. These professionals identify – qua professionals – with peoples across the world. This professionalism is truly a worldly professionalism. Perhaps it was always there to some extent, but now – with modern communications and transport systems, this professionalism is doubly heightened: the professional's awareness is heightened and the possibilities for response are also heightened.

This worldly professionalism has yet other properties. Returning to Guattari, the earlier quotation is instructive, especially when placed in the context of the five ecological registers that we have delineated. An ecological professionalism is itself 'at once applied and theoretical, ethico-political and aesthetic ...'. The ecological professional, we may say, is a practising epistemologist *and* a practising ontologist: she believes that there is a world around her and it has definite forms and structures, even if their character is far from clear. She acts in and on the world, and struggles to go on learning about the world in which she has her professional being.

But she has a care for, a concern for, the world: her professionalism has an 'ethico-political' character. She has a concern for all of the networks, the registers that mark out her professional life. She is mindful of her being within each of them, and tries in the first place to ensure that nothing she does or says brings harm in any of them.

Her actions and thoughts also have an aesthetic character. It is not too fanciful to say that the ecological professional is a professional poet – of a kind. For she imagines a world of beauty into being, so far as she can. In having a concern for the multiple environments within which she has her professional being, she makes her interventions with care, and with refinement, so as to advance the registers within which she works. Her concern has a natural aesthetic quality, which expresses itself in the micro aspects of her engagements with her world. It would approach a contradiction to say that the ecological professional had a concern for the world but yet was insensitive to the aesthetic character of her interactions with it.

This ecological professional has both dispositions *and* qualities, and these should be distinguished. In order to *be* an ecological professional, to engage with the world and to struggle relentlessly to play a part in its improvement, certain *dispositions* are called for. These include a will continuously to learn, a will to discern the world in all its complexity (its five registers), a will to engage, a will to be receptive to the world and a will to be creative in the world. These dispositions propel a professional into the world and with some care towards it.

To such dispositions (required of every ecological professional) is brought to bear numerous *qualities*, and here ecological professionals will differ as they interpret their callings as ecological professionals. Such qualities may include courage, resilience, aesthetic sensitivity, imagination, humour and modesty. To repeat, the enumerated dispositions are *necessary* ingredients of an ecological professional, though they are not sufficient. Qualities, in contrast, are much more extendable and subject to individual take-up. The enumerated qualities are simply *examples* of qualities evinced by ecological professionals; there will be other qualities and ecological professionals will vary in their exemplification of those qualities. It is in their holding on to the necessary *dispositions* that individuals become ecological professionals; it is in their exhibiting certain kinds of *qualities* that such individuals bring their own interpretations as to what it can be to be an ecological professional.

The ecological professional, therefore (and to pick up Guattari's term) is a professional ecosophist. It may be that she would not easily be able to articulate her challenges and her aspirations as an ecological professional (though she may come close to doing so) but yet her professional being is held reflexively in this multidimensional way, in its playing out of the individual's dispositions and qualities in the regions of the ecological registers with their multiple timeframes and spaces. No wonder that contemporary professional life is demanding. The ecological professional feels the call of the registers of her life, and responds, drawing on all her resources (cognitive, experiential, emotional, financial, empathy and her time management skills as she moves across multiple timeframes). Choices have to be made and ethical judgements reached and actions taken, as she extends herself across her ecological registers. This professional life is inexorable in the burdens it loads on to the individual. Care exerts its ontological toll, as the emotional and existential demands, infinite in their scope, *necessarily* outstrip the resources of the professional.

Supercomplexity

'Supercomplexity' is a shorthand for many of the challenges facing the ecological professional. Whereas complexity here connotes the character and interwovenness of the manifold systems in which professional life is embedded, supercomplexity refers to the openendedness of the conceptual or narrative challenges facing the professional as she works through and at her practices.

To some extent, what is at issue here is the hard–soft distinction that we encountered earlier; the hardness of systems as against the fuzziness of concepts and ideas through which the professional gains some kind of self-understanding and self-interpretation. On the one hand, systems are relatively tractable: they can be subjected to analysis and prediction and control. On the other hand, ideas and concepts are relatively intractable, yielding only dispute and never-ending interpretation. The question: 'To what systems of evaluation and accountability is the professional subject?' yields a confined set of responses such that there could be agreement and a consensus: the professional can comprehend the systems in which she is placed even if she does not support them. The question: 'What is to count as professionalism?' not only evinces a lack of consensus but downright conflict. Here, the professional can justifiably suffer from uncertainty and even some angst, as she perceives quite different interpretations of her professionalism which conflict with each other. Questions as to systems could yield agreement; questions as to concepts and ideas never could yield agreement.

It is in relation to such utter openendedness that the idea of 'supercomplexity' gains its purchase. But the idea takes on even more force in the context of the ecological professional. For, as we have seen, the ecological professional has her being among complexes of ecological registers (plural), complexes of time and space *and* of different ethical horizons. Her professional being moves on various planes – the local and the global, the performative and the therapeutic, the personal and the impersonal – and she is minded, willed even, to play her part, however modest, in promoting wellbeing in the domains in which she lives out her professionalism. Her professional being is all the time, and ineradically so, challenged to make *choices*.

This has been a long-standing and even an abiding feature of professional life; the autonomy afforded to the professional bequeathing a regime of choices. But for the ecological professional, her life is saturated with choices; it is a thoroughly choice-laden life. And the choices are not just matters of decisions – over systems and system-located actions – but they are very much matters of ethical choices and choices over the very registers in which to work. To what extent might a busy professional doctor concern herself with the health needs of people in developing countries and in what ways? To what extent might a doctor lobby for a change in health policy? Just how should the clinical relationship be construed (in a global and a digitised age, in which patients have recourse to all manner of resources and advice)? The ecological professional hears different voices expressed in different languages – of virtues, performance indicators, rights, needs, resources – and responds to these voices through her own inner conversation. Living in a supercomplex world, the ecological professional is necessarily multilingual.

Conclusions

An ecological professionalism is within reach. It is a kind of feasible utopia. It is already apparent in some professionals' lives. Some, if not many, are already living out the callings of ecological professionalism. They sense themselves as embedded in multiple timeframes and spaces, the local and the global, the shortterm and the longer term. And while they are bound to live amid performative discourses – of efficiency, and cost-effectiveness and performance goals and indicators – they seek also to place those discourses against ethical horizons. This is a liquid professionalism that calls the professional self-reflexively continually to make choices, choices that in turn bring instrumental strategies and actions to self-summoned ethical tribunals. In all this, the professional considers and acts so as to assist the wellbeing of the manifold registers that structure her professionalism.

This ecological professionalism can threaten to overwhelm individuals who heed its callings. All the time, this ecological professional senses a gap, even a gulf, between her perceived possibilities of a better world and the limitations of her actions. Such limitations are both practical and ethical. The ecological professional is aware always of other possibilities for her actions and utterances; she is acutely aware that she could have spoken and acted otherwise, and not just in confined situations but that her time and resources could have been deployed to further other registers (the interests of the client, collective practices among the profession, her own professional learning, the wider society and even the wider world). But the ecological professional is also aware that other ethical concerns could have been brought to bear on her actions and utterances. This is a heavy load to bear; even an intolerable one.

There is a nice irony here: that a concern for the sustainability of the registers within which the ecological professional has her being may lead to particular challenges for her own sustainability. Living out a care for the world, and a will to help in its development, levy a heavy personal burden. Two necessary and interconnected – if not sufficient – conditions of self-sustainability are those of self-belief and a wider collective affirmation in the individual professional, an affirmation that may come variously from the client base, the profession itself and even from domains – the political, the mass media, the technological – in the wider society. Both of these conditions – the self-belief and the wider collective affirmation – are fragile; which is to say that an ecological professionalism is itself fragile. But, like the bringing off of a memorable performance of a musical concert, an ecological professionalism, for all its fragility, is possible. Like the musical performance, too, it also needs continual reflection, practice, effort, creativity, imagination and renewed performance. Its possibilities need continually to be realised. An ecological professionalism is never satisfied with yesterday's utterances and actions, or even today's, but always looks ahead, considerate of its 'being-possible'. It lives always in its possible futures.

Note

1 The construction 'his/her' here is intended to indicate that the discussion in this chapter refers to all professionals. Subsequently, to avoid being cumbersome, I mostly restrict the construction simply to 'her'. In every case, it should be understood as being inclusive of 'his'.

References

Bauman, Z. (2000) *Liquid Modernity*. Cambridge: Polity Press.

Castells, M. (1996) *The Rise of the Network Society*. Oxford: Blackwell.

Cooper, D. (2002) *The Measure of Things: Humanism, Humility, and Mystery*. Oxford: Clarendon Press.

Guattari, F. (2005 [1989]) *The Three Ecologies*. London: Continuum.

Heidegger, M. (1998 [1962]) *Being and Time*. Oxford: Blackwell.

Moog, S. (2009) Ecological politics for the twenty-first century: where does 'nature' fit in? In S. Moog and R. Stones (eds) *Nature, Social Relations and Human Needs*. Basingstoke: Palgrave Macmillan.

Nowotny, H. (1996) *Time: The Modern and the Postmodern Experience*. Cambridge: Polity Press.

Taylor, C. (1991) *The Ethics of Authenticity*. Cambridge: Harvard University Press.

Williams, B. (2006 [1985]) *Ethics and the Limits of Philosophy*. Abingdon: Routledge.

3 Professional responsibility and an ethic of care

Teachers' care as moral praxis[1]

Maeve O' Brien

Introduction

It is increasingly the case in the twenty-first century that education in the West is shaped by international policy discourses that emphasise performativity and measurable outcomes for schools, teachers and students (Ball 2003; Sugrue 2004), at the expense of less tangible, but at least equally significant, issues concerning human wellbeing, care and happiness (Cohen 2006; Noddings 1992, 2003; O'Brien 2008). If the aims of education are merely to supply human capital in the form of skilled, technical, rational capital for the market, then this neglect of human flourishing or concern for the wellbeing of society and its citizenship is not an issue for educators. It would seem, however, that among teachers themselves (Farrelly 2009; Hargreaves 2000; Nias 1996), and within the philosophical, educational and social scientific discourses, care, wellbeing and the 'good of society'[2] are seen to be inter-related in important ways (Baker et al. 2004; Cohen 2006; Lynch, Lyons & Cantillon 2007; Noddings 2003). Scholarship and research on schooling and wellbeing have indicated that care and relationality and the affective context or dimensions of school life are funda-mental to students' positive affect and perceptions of their school experiences (Engels et al. 2004; Opendakker & Van Dame 2000; Smerdon 2002; UNICEF 2007), despite the increasing intensification of a regulative performativity that condones detachment, entrepreneurship, self-sufficiency and rationality. It is interesting that, while schools may not seem to be explicitly focused on happiness, care or wellbeing, research suggests that 'happy' people live longer, have better health and are more engaged in life (Seligman 2002). This raises an obvious normative question as to whether schools, and therefore teachers, should be concerned with the overall wellbeing and care of their students and how this is interpreted, while balancing this against the demands they face for performativ-ity and student learning. It also raises an empirical question as to how we under-stand the parameters of the professional responsibility of teachers relative to their own understandings of themselves as caring, emotional and rational subjects.

In this chapter, I make the case from a feminist critical interdisciplinary perspective that teachers' care work and the time and energies they devote to caring for and about students should be recognised as a central and significant aspect of their professional practice and their ethical responsibility as educators. I argue that caring and specifically the professional care of teachers is and thus should be recognised as a moral praxis.

First, I explore some major interdisciplinary perspectives on care, care work and its necessity for human flourishing at the levels of the individual and society. The second part of the chapter then explores how care scholarship and research relates to teachers' work and care, their practice and their professional identity. In this discussion I emphasise some of the dilemmas and costs of teachers' care as routine work, while at the same time highlighting its significance for wellbeing to school communities and the broader society. In the concluding part, I indicate how emergent concerns from the analysis relate to the issue of professional responsibility and teachers' daily work.

Discourses and perspectives on care and wellbeing

Care, emotions and wellbeing

In Western philosophy, wellbeing or human flourishing had its roots in the idea of the 'good life' coming to us from the ancients, and Aristotle in particular. 'Eudaimonia' is the concept that captures the view of the life 'well-lived' through virtuous practice, thus contributing to the good of the society and thus to one's own personal wellbeing. This perspective on *rational* moral praxis, has infused the work of more recent contemporary thinkers including educationalists. Liberal education has inherited this Aristotelian legacy in that the educated person in this tradition is understood as one who lives a virtuous rational life and, in the process of good living, achieves wellbeing (Mulcahy 2008). Living well (i.e. virtuously) as an individual is related to the notion of caring about others and for the society in which one lives. It is believed that adherence to virtue at the level of the individual produces a 'just' society at the level of the collective (see Sen 2009). Rationality, the taming and education of the emotions for virtuous living, for wellbeing, forms the basis of justice ethics and modern rational society.

From the later decades of the twentieth century onwards, the influence of feminist discourses have been felt across many disciplines and have challenged overly rational views of the human subject and thus understandings of human flourishing. Neo-Aristotelians such as Martha Nussbaum (1995) have written extensively on the significance of our emotions to care and moral action. Feminist theorists and researchers have likewise suggested that it is our emotional capacities that enable us to care and to love, and that these are capacities that are fundamental to our own wellbeing and that of others. Collins (1990: 28) suggests that at the level of societal wellbeing, emotions and affectual relationships are the glue of moral solidarity and the energy of mobilisation. Carol Gilligan's (1982) work has been seminal in the area of human emotions and moral development particularly, and has counteracted Kohlberg's gendered assertions about women's restricted moral development. Her work indicates how, for many women, orientations to moral action are based in feelings of empathy, and a valuing of relationships that we learn from our earliest encounters in the social world. Feminist political theorists (Fraser 2001; Sevenhuijsen 1998) have suggested that the 'taken for granted', rational/emotional dichotomy among others (civilisation/nature, man/woman, white/black, mind/body) has not just constituted sets of individual differences, but forms part of a system of hierarchy, control and exclusion that affects human flourishing and particularly women's full development (Nussbaum 1995). While challenging the overly rational, technical modernist view of the human being, these scholars also posit a counter position to the postmodern view of the human being as a detached rational economic actor, rootless, unrestrictedly flexible and self-interested (Bauman 2003) and to the reductionism of overly rationalistic and bureaucratic perspectives on the teacher as a professional. This critical discourse suggests that, as teachers, we have a responsibility to recognise our own human vulnerability and interdependency and that of our colleagues and students, to value our embedded-ness as professionals within a complicated nexus of relationality. It also calls into question the notion of a compartmentalised professional identity and a profes-sional responsibility which is overly focused on teaching subjects or on learning outcomes in compliance with reductive and technical policies within education and the wider social context. Feminist moral, political and, more recently, psycho-analytic discourses, both theoretical and empirical (Benjamin 1998; Chodorow 1999; Hollway 2006), also challenge the postmodern view of the self-interested human subject, and suggest that it is rather our *innate capacity* for inter-relatedness and care that bring us into being as ethical subjects and that facilitate human flourishing. Moreover, this work challenges the traditional dichotomisation of a public/private sphere and its assumed naturalness. The questioning of a care divide and responsibility for caring in relation to traditional private familial and public spheres and institutions suggests a need to recognise human emotions and our capacity for relatedness as characteristic and inalienable to *all* human contexts and endeavours, including the educational context (see Chapter 2). The polarisa-tion of affect from rationality has been challenged as a false construction that facilitates the maintenance of hierarchies in all domains of life (epistemologically, experientially, discursively and in educational contexts), and restricts wellbeing and flourishing for individuals and for groups within society. Following these feminist challenges, a large body of interdisciplinary care scholarship continues to grow, informing new understandings of wellbeing that has significance for education and, in particular, the work of teachers. In light of these new ways of thinking, it is important to say something further about the relation between the concepts of affect, care and equality, as these form part of the larger landscape in which teachers' moral work and professional responsibility are located.

Equality, affect and care: constituents of professional responsibility

Radical egalitarian perspectives suggest that inequalities generated in the economic, cultural, political, affective and work and learning contexts inhibit human flourishing in particular ways. In the economic context, lack of resources, goods and services inhibit our flourishing, while in the cultural context, misrecognition of our identities as individuals and at the collective/group level prevent us from participating and create exclusions. Lack of voice and lack of access to power to act is experienced in the political context. The affective context is identified as one associated with feelings and relationships that, according to Baker et al. (2004) gives life meaning, and without which we cannot flourish as human beings. Psychoanalytic evidence (Benjamin 1998; Hollway 2006) and attachment theory and research (Bowlby 1988; Heard & Lake 1997) claim that our capacity for attachment and care giving is innate, and that in order to flourish we need to give and receive care at times of utter and inescapable dependency. Philosophical work (Fineman 2001; Kittay 1999; Nussbaum 1995) suggests that the measure of a 'good society' where humans can achieve flourishing is observed in the extent to which it cares for its weakest members. The affective context of life characterises our inter-relatedness and need for care and emotional connection.

The idea of living happily in poverty through our relations of care and connection is deconstructed in radical egalitarianism. While the capacity to care is thought now to be innate, car*ing* and lov*ing* are not magical relations that occur naturally, but are relationships that require effort, work and resourcing of various kinds. Emotional resourcing, for example, feeds relationships but it may not be sufficient for flourishing. In my work (O'Brien 2007, 2009) I have discussed how mothers' doing of care and emotional work in the interests of their children's schooling is shaped by their economic, cultural *and* affective resources. In the face of persistent economic insecurity and cultural exclusion because of their social class or ethnicity, mothers become worn down, and their emotional resources, which drive their care work for their children, become exhausted. While they still care deeply about their children's schooling and experience a moral imperative to continue their care, they may not be able to produce the particular efforts required for their children's educational flourishing (see also Reay 1998). Lynch et al. (2009: 1) in *Affective Equality* comment that love 'involves acting for those we care for not just feeling for them'. To facilitate affective wellbeing we have to be able to do as well as feel. However, as I have just suggested, the doing of care and acting in the interest of love, may be curtailed and unequally produced relative to other inequalities across life contexts. This means that the conditions for the doing of care relative to the particular contexts in which it is produced may impede or facilitate that effort to varying degrees. Thus, in order to discuss an ethics and practice of care in teaching, it will necessitate taking account of the specific local conditions of schooling and teaching, and the diversity and identities of groups of students being taught. Policy discourses and centralised policy interventions thus may further alienate or disadvantage populations they claim to serve and create frustrations and challenges for teachers in their daily work and responsibility for care of students.

are necessary to relational life across all contexts, given the interdependency of human beings and the significance of healthy affective states for human flourishing. In recent times, Noddings (2003) has argued most strongly that caring is a fundamental aspect of being an educator. She suggests that schooling and teaching without care are not education but rather a technical exercise with deeply unequal effects on different individuals and groups. The care responsibilities of an educator include care for oneself and intimates, caring about strangers, the planet (see Chapter 2) and about ideas and culture (the *manmade* world). It seems quite obvious from a care perspective that, if one does not care for oneself fully as a human being, one will not be capable of assessing the needs of others for their flourishing. To be truly learner/student centred, we must be both self-caring and heteronomous. I am not suggesting here that caring for students and their emotional needs as they present should replace or marginalise learning. Rather, the case that I am making is that student learning and good teaching turns upon an ethic of care that is fundamental to teachers' range of responsibilities to all their students. From an equality and social justice perspective, really caring about students may also involve redressing the distribution of care and teaching to students who are most vulnerable and require greater care for various reasons.

It would be foolish to underestimate the care challenges that teachers experience in trying to balance such a holistic perspective with demands for measurable learning outcomes that are generically stated and perhaps irrelevant, or even worse, perhaps damaging and not in the interests of some students. Freire (1970) rehearsed that argument much earlier in his attack on what he called 'banking education' in his seminal work *Pedagogy of the Oppressed*. In a context where formal didactic teaching had no relevance to the real needs of the population and their flourishing, Freire called for transformation through a radical education rooted in the expressed and spoken needs of the people/learners/teachers.[3] Noddings also argues for an alternative approach to education premised on an ethic of care that can bring about justice in a deeply unequal and exclusionary formal schooling system. Large bodies of sociological research indicate that classed, gendered, ethnic and racial inequalities are perpetuated through the middle-class, white, Western, educational system. Critical sociology of knowledge, which deconstructs privileged approaches to curriculum and what counts as knowledge and intelligence, also supports the kinds of arguments outlined by Noddings for a more caring and just educational system. While Freire calls for radical transformation through dialogical educational praxis, Noddings is no less radical in her call for care. Her work provides a template for care across contexts, neither privileging the school as a space for learning, nor ignoring the learning that takes place within the home and community. But in reality, we cannot make people care for others' ideas or the planet, in a formulaic or prescribed fashion, we cannot make them like or love, so as professional educators, we are still left with the question of how we bring about the work of 'a revolution of care' for wellbeing.

One of the challenges faced in this solidarity work is that teachers themselves may be somewhat uncomfortable with the term *care* in relation to their professional status as educators: they may not want to be categorised as 'educarers' (Lynch et al. 2007). The body of literature on the care aspects of teachers' work and identities, and on teaching as a caring profession, reflects diverse perspectives within this. In feminist sociological research, for example, Skeggs (1997) has discussed how feminised professions and particularly feminised care work with children, are seen as low status and misrecognised. Care, because it has been, and still is, associated with the feminine and mothering, is seen as natural and not given the same value as other forms of work or effort. For professionals for whom caring is an aspect of their professional practice, this poses a threat to their claim as professionals. In the current ideological context, to emphasise caring in teaching can be seen as a process of de-professionalisation and of losing hard-won ground. As Ball (2003) remarks, citing Seddon (1997), in globalised contexts teachers are de-professionalised and re-professionalised according to markets and a new ethic of self-interest. It is only recently, moreover, that the discourse and scholarship on care has gained respectability and status in the academy, being seen as an area worthy of serious consideration, and largely through the challenges of feminist scholars whose efforts have named care as a form of significant work and practice. Likewise, there is a slow but growing recognition and awareness for diverse forms of intelligence (Gardner 1987; Sternberg 1998) and particularly the interpersonal intelligences that facilitate our understandings of self, others and affective life. Schooling has emphasised the verbal mathematical intelligences and these are the ones that are still most valued and rewarded in education and credentialised for entry to higher levels of the labour market and the power and status accruing to varying positions within that. Teachers face these ideological and political challenges when they choose to value care, and to meet actively the real needs and foster the diverse talents of students.

Caring about justice and equality in schooling – caring about diverse 'others'

Pierre Bourdieu recognised the problems that dominant sets of values, largely those of the white middle classes, posed for those seeking to break ongoing cycles of social reproduction and inequality in education. The middle classes care deeply to continue a *habitus*,[4] a way of life and thinking that privileges them through the kinds of knowledge that are valued and cared about in the educational field, and through the social habits and distinctive practices that mark them as educated/cultured. This is not necessarily conscious, operating at the level of an unconscious habitus, but in schooling it is translated into curricula, codes of behaviour, dress and speech and extracurricular activities that mark out and reproduce the distinctions between individuals and the social groups to which they belong. The habitus, or ways of being, of the less dominant groups, mark them out for social, academic and affective exclusion. In the case of social and emotional connections, the very relationships we can engage in are regulated through the institutional practices of schools. For example, a great deal has been written in recent years about identities and sexualities in schooling, and many writers and researchers (Connell 1995; Mac an Ghaill 1994; Walkerdine, Lucey & Melody 2001) have demonstrated the affective injuries experienced by young people who do not fit with dominant heterosexual ways of being, both at the hands of teachers and students, under school systems that value the patriarchal order of traditional heterosexuality. In a pluralist multicultural and democratic society, teachers need to care about justice and equality and to have informed understandings of these concepts while engaging in a balancing act with the everyday routines of teaching a curriculum that provides relevant skills and concepts for students.

Cohen (2006) suggests that, to bring about respect and recognition in students, the goals of education need to be rebalanced to take account of the significance of social–emotional and character education. Indeed, he concludes that social–emotional education for democratic living is a human right, and thus must be provided for by teachers in public education as part of their professional practice. The *how* is something that Cohen discusses, and it is a thorny question, as to whether schools, as they stand, can do the job, given the need for teachers to be committed to and competent to teach in this area. Even Health Promoting Schools, which espouse similar types of goals, have been found in reality to be very poor on realising these worthy aims (Lynagh, Schofield & Sanson-Fisher 1997). Empirical research indicates that the emotional and social environment created by staff and teachers has a significant impact on wellness and health of students in schools (Anderson & Ronson 2005; Engels, Aelterman, Van Petegem & Schepens 2004). The case for engaging with students so they can participate and celebrate diversity in school and society is strong in the discourse, but it means that teachers need to reflect upon and understand their own praxis and ethical positions with respect to recognising and respecting the diversity of student identities they encounter.

Teachers' professional practice and critical/emotional literacy

I have been arguing in this second part of the chapter that teachers not only have a moral responsibility to care for their students, hands on and face-to-face (although that is, of course, important) and also exploring the territory that care theorists have termed 'caring about' as part of their professional responsibility as educators. Following Freire's critique of education and his assertion that students need the tools of critical literacy to name their world in order to understand it and transform it, critical cultural theorists in the US (Apple 1996, 2004, 2011, forthcoming; Giroux 1983, 2003) have written extensively on the need for critical literacy for students in US schools and, more generally, in the west. To care about students and the society they live in means developing in them the analytical, and I add, emotional resources to explore and critique the schooling they experience. Cohen (2006) argues that critical social–emotional education is a fundamental right for all, and when we consider that most students are in school under law, it seems reasonable to suggest that they have a right to express and evaluate how they feel, why they are doing things in particular ways and studying particular fields of knowledge.

Teachers need to be equipped for this kind of critical educational praxis through their own education, which should provide opportunities for critique, self-reflection and reflection on relationships (see Chapter 11). Responsibility for creating citizens that can live well in a democratic society means that teachers will require not only intellectual but also emotional resources to do this work. In this postcritical, neoliberal world, they will need to feel and reflect upon the commitment to caring about students as citizens. While it is important for educators to engage intellectually in the study of relationships in psychology or philosophy, it is also immediate and powerful to engage in reflection around our own practices. If teachers are to care about issues of justice, equality and wellbeing, they need to have reflected on issues of critical praxis before they are let loose in the classroom. Teachers who care about the impact of their work on the public good, the wellbeing of society, teachers who act to create the conditions of justice and equality in their own schools and classrooms, have been understood as public intellectuals by critical thinkers such as Freire (1970), Gramsci (1971), Apple (1996) and Burawoy (2005). In the critical tradition, their work has urged and encouraged teachers and other professionals (i.e. sociologists; see Burawoy 2005) to do critical, and what I argue is moral work, to look both within and beyond their own classrooms and educational contexts and to name and challenge the gross inequalities that impede human flourishing for 'subaltern' groups (Apple 2011, forthcoming), although Apple also suggests that a great deal of what passes as critical pedagogy is not radical and can range from a mere responsiveness to students to substantive reflexive processes that radically challenge exploitative relations. As such, these critical professionals extend their activity beyond a narrow instrumental professionalism that characterises much of what is regarded as teaching and learning today, towards a broader aim and a more public work that is concerned with the 'common good'. As I have suggested, this has implications for the initial education of teachers, and at the very least, it challenges teacher education paradigms focused on curriculum delivery and student learning outcomes that are overly rational and regulated by a metrics of technical performativity (Ball 2003). It necessitates dialogical and reflective engagements with 'becoming' teachers rather than static banking pedagogies, so as to encourage this kind of political and critical professional understanding and responsibility.

The challenges involved for teachers both personally and professionally in this type of engagement with students are sufficient to lift teachers out of their comfort zone and demand a willingness to dialogue in a very real way. It demands a capacity to be other-interested in a very genuine fashion, facilitating what the care theorists suggest is emotional attunement, a form of emotional literacy, a capacity for affective dialogue with the other, and not only with the face-to-face other but also with distant others (Hollway 2006). Focusing on critical/emotional literacy building in teachers also challenges traditional rational/emotional dualisms within teaching and the wider social sphere. Rational argument based in a justice approach alone may lead away from the call to act in the interests of another: it can lead to rationalisation (Freire 1970). In educational settings, policy rhetoric and social interventions may grant legitimacy to schooling processes that reproduce cycles of privilege and dominance, and let us as professional educators 'off the hook' of critical and affective engagement and action. However, when we feel compassion, anger or emotions of empathic quality, we are moved or encouraged to do the 'right thing' and to reach out to the 'other'. This 'affective critical approach' leads to action, that other expression of care, and enables us to move beyond the paralysis that may often be felt in times where global injustices seem so complex that at an intellectual level we do not know even where to begin.

Responsibility for caring for and about students and the distribution of care

In discussing teachers' professional praxis in relation to daily routines of *caring for* students, it is somewhat artificial to make a rigid distinction between caring for and caring about, but care theorists and the policy discourses on care often typify aspects of caring that are characteristic of different contexts. *Caring for* has more to do with meeting routine needs in a hands-on fashion, while *caring about* can be done from a social and geographical distance, as discussed above, in relation to ethical praxis and issues of equality and diversity. Caring for, of course, takes different forms relative to the particulars of the educational setting, the specific needs of students, and their capacities for self-care and their lack of or levels of maturity. One of the issues often raised by educators and that arises in the discourse is how to balance emotional caring for with caring about learning and future prospects of students. In a formal group setting such as the school, prescient and urgent wellbeing needs for emotional care and nurturing, such as affection, kindness, warmth and consideration, are difficult to meet. For teachers working in contexts and communities where young people and children have many unmet affective and physical, as well as learning needs, the demands may seem overwhelming. Research carried out in Ireland with primary and second-level teachers, working in some of the most disadvantaged schools in the country, found that teachers were very conscious of the conflicting positions they occupied as professional educators and their feelings of obligation to meet the basic care needs that students presented with on a daily basis (Farrelly 2009). In these schools, teachers' work was shaped by caring practices that were often supported at school level, to ensure students' overall wellbeing was facilitated. In the absence of such support, teachers felt the tasks and responsibilities of the educator were often too great and experienced frustration. While teachers in 'disadvantaged' schools also expressed satisfaction with the care they took of students in terms of meeting life *and* learning needs, they also felt comparatively disadvantaged in terms of meeting the academic demands of the school system. As Bourdieu has argued, the standards set in middle-class schools set the game for all students in a field where the conditions for success are deeply uneven. In terms of teachers' professional responsibility, is it reasonable to expect that those working in communities that have experienced inter-generational poverty and social disadvantage can expect the same learning outcomes and standards of achievement from students in schools where deeply unequal social and cultural conditions exist? Teachers' daily practices will be as Farrelly calls it 'a tightrope act' of trying to meet urgent care demands and the traditional demands of schooling. Teachers' narratives in Farrelly's research indicate that practices of 'caring for' students and the emotional resources of patience, courage, resilience, and in some cases 'love' were grounded in a value or ethic of care, of wanting to make a difference in people's lives. Although structures of pastoral care were in place in many schools, most teachers continued to feel and take responsibility for face-to-face care in their own classrooms. Moreover, teachers who had taught in more advantaged schools commented on the greater capacity and efforts for care that were characteristic of schools designated as disadvantaged. This study suggests that teachers working in areas of intense social challenge see care as an inalienably part of their daily practice and moral praxis as professionals. In other words, from their perspectives, their professional responsibility includes, in a strong way, the need to create time and energy for students whose most basic care needs require attention.

Concluding remarks

Readers may object to the arguments made here that teachers should be revolutionary care workers, facilitating student and societal wellbeing through caring for and caring about. The objection might be made on the basis that these aims are too idealistic and unfairly assigned as a burden of professional responsibility to teachers. We have, we believe, come a long way since people had to martyr themselves for their values and for the 'good'; but perhaps things have swung too far towards professional protectiveness and complacency in light of continuing gross injustices which schooling may itself perpetuate. Surely education and the work of teachers are about human flourishing and not about reproducing cycles of oppression and exploitation. Education should be about hope and possibility for all, not just those groups and individuals within society who are already positioned to benefit from the formal system. Those teachers who from day to day and year to year meet their students in dialogic caring practice, where those students are at, are the heroes and heroines of the profession and of the communities they serve. They compare to what Lynch and McLoughlin (1995) call the silent invisible armies of women in the community, carers putting bread on the table of emotional life and who ensure that communities and society function. In a world where rational self-interest is the assumed creed, teachers are not recognised or rewarded for what is a most significant aspect of their professional practice and what many understand as significant to their professional responsibility: their capacity to challenge intensifying neoliberal careless perspectives on the purposes and processes of education through their caring moral praxis.

Notes

1 Praxis is the term used by Freire and critical theorists and educators following him to refer to the dialectic between reflection and action. Educators move beyond a 'mere verbalism' in their practice in a constant cycle of reflection and action through dialogue with self and other.
2 Of course, postmodern discourses argue strongly against the idea of a metanarrative of a good, while dominant consumerist and economistic perspectives see the 'good' of society and happiness as defined by the individual's capacity to consume goods, defining the human as *homo consumeris*.
3 Freire also deconstructs dichotomisation of teacher/learner as a false one: teachers in relationship with students are learners and learners are teachers (Freire 1970).
4 Bourdieu (1977) describes the habitus as a set of psychological structures internalised by individuals and groups, a set of acquired patterns of thought, behaviour and taste, which is said to constitute the link between social structures and social practice.

References

Allardt, E. (1993) Having, loving, being : an alternative to the Swedish model of welfare research. In M.C. Nussbaum and A.K. Sen (eds) *The Quality of Life*. pp. 88–94. Oxford: Clarendon Press.

Anderson, A. & Ronson, B. (2005) Democracy – the first principle of health promoting schools. *Electronic Journal of Health Education* 8, 24–35. http://www.iejhe.org.

Apple, M. (1996) *Cultural Politics and Education*. New York: Teachers College Press.

Apple, M.W. (2004) *Ideology and Curriculum*, 3rd edn. New York: Routledge.

Apple, M. (2011, forthcoming) Paulo Freire and the tasks of the critical educator/scholar/activist. In A. O'Shea and M. O'Brien (eds) *Pedagogy, Oppression and Transformation in a Post Critical Context*. London: Continuum.

Baker, J., Lynch, K., Cantillon, S. & Walsh, J. (2004) *Equality from Theory to Action*. London: Palgrave.

Ball, S. (2003) The teacher's soul and the terrors of performativity. *Journal of Educational Policy* 18(2), 215–28.

Bauman, Z. (2003) *Liquid Love: On the Frailty of Human Bonds*. London: Polity.

Bauman, Z. (2004) *Liquid Love: On the Frailty of Human Bonds*. Cambridge: Polity Press.

Benjamin, J. (1998) *The Shadow of the Other: Intersubjectivity and Gender in Psychoanalysis*, London: Routledge.

Bourdieu, P. (1977) *Outline of a Theory of Practice*, R. Nice (trans.). Cambridge: Cambridge University Press.

Bowlby, J. (1988) *A Secure Base: Clinical Applications of Attachment Theory*. London: Routledge.

Burawoy, M. (2005) For public sociology. *British Journal of Sociology* 56, 259–94.

Chodorow, N. (1978) *The Reproduction of Mothering*. London: University of California Press.

Chodorow, N. (1999) *The Power of Feelings*. New Haven: Yale University Press.

Cohen, J. (2006) Social, emotional, ethical and academic education: creating a climate for learning, participation in the democracy and well-being. *Harvard Educational Review* 76(2), 201–37.

Collins, R. (1990) Stratification, emotional energy and the transient emotions. In T.D. Kemper (ed.) *Research Agendas in the Sociology of Emotions*. pp. 27–57. New York: State University of New York Press.

Connell, R.W. (1995) *Masculinities*. Cambridge: Polity Press.

Diener, E., Lucas, R. & Scollon, C. (2006) Beyond the hedonic treadmill. Revising the adaptation theory of well-being. *American Psychologist* May–June.

Devine, D., Grummell, B. & Lynch, K. (2010) Crafting the elastic self: gender and identities in senior appointments in Irish education. *Gender, Work and Organisation*, no. doi: 10.1111/j.1468-0432.2009.00513, February.

Engels, N., Aelterman, A., Van Petegem, K. & Schepens, A. (2004) Factors which influence the well-being of pupils in Flemish secondary schools. *Educational Studies* 30(2), 127–43.

Farrelly, M. (2009) *Care and performativity: walking the tightrope: A case study in an educationally disadvantaged setting*. Unpublished Ph.D. thesis, St Patrick's College, DCU, Dublin.

Fineman, M. (2001) 'Contract and care in symposium on the structures of care work, 76 Chi.-Kent. Rev. 1403', *Chicago Kent Law Review, Chicago Kent College of Law*, http://lawreview.kentlaw.edu/.

Fujita, F. & Diener, E. (2005) Life satisfaction set point: stability and change. *Journal of Personality and Social Psychology* 88(1), 158–64.

Fraser, N. (1997) 'After the family wage: a post industrial thought experiment', in *Justice Interruptus: Critical Reflections on the 'Postsocialist' Condition*. New York: Routledge, pp. 41–69.

Freire, P. (1970) *Pedagogy of the Oppressed*. New York: Continuum.

Gardner, H. (1987) *Frames of Mind: The Theory of Multiple Intelligence*. London: Fontana.

Gilligan, C. (1982) *In a Different Voice: Psychological Theory and Women's Development*, Cambridge, MA: Harvard University Press.

Giroux, H. (1983) *Theory and Resistance in Education*. Westport, CT: Bergin and Garvey.

Giroux, H. (2000) *Stealing Innocence: Youth, Corporate Power and the Politics of Culture*. New York: St Martin's Press.

Gramsci, A. (1971) *Selections from the Prison Notebooks*, trans. Q. Hoare and G. N. Smith. New York: International Publishers.

Hargreaves, A. (2000) Mixed emotions: teachers' perceptions of their interactions with students. *Teaching and Teacher Education* 16, 811–26.

Heard, D. & Lake, B. (1997) *The Challenge of Attachment for Care Giving*, London: Routledge.

Hollway, W. (2006) *The Capacity to Care: Gender and Ethical Intersubjectivity*. Sussex: Routledge.

Kittay, E. (1999) *Love's Labor: Essays on Women Equality and Dependency*. New York: Routledge.

Konu, A., Linoten, T. and Rimpela, A. (2002) Factors Associated with Schoolchildrens' General Subjective Well-Being. *Health Education Research* 17, 2.

Lynagh, M., Schofield, M. & Sanson-Fisher, R.W. (1997) School health promotion programs over the last decade. A review of the smoking, alcohol and solar protection literature. *Health Promotion International* 12(1), 43–60.

Lynch, K., Lyons, M. & Cantillon, C. (2007) Breaking silence: educating citizens for love care and solidarity. Invited paper for the *International Studies in Sociology of Education Journal*, 2007.

Lynch, K., Baker, J. and Lyons, M. (2009) *Affective Equality: Love, Care and Injustice*. London: Palgrave Macmillan.

Lynch, K. & McLoughlin, E. (1995) Love labour. In P. Clancy et al. (eds) *Irish Society: Sociological Perspectives*. pp. 250–92. Dublin: Institute of Public Administration.

Mac an Ghaill, M. (1994) *The Making of Men: Sexualities and Schooling*. Buckingham: Open University Press.

Mulcahy, D. (2008) *The Educated Person: Towards a New Paradigm for Liberal Education*. New York: Robert Littlefeld.

Nias, J. (1996) Thinking about feeling: the emotions in teaching. *Cambridge Journal of Education* **26**(3), 293–306.

Noddings, N. (1992) *The Challenge to Care in Schools: An Alternative Approach to Education*. New York: Columbia Teachers College Press.

Noddings, N. (2003) *Happiness and Education*. Cambridge: Cambridge University Press.

Nussbaum, M. (1995) *Women, Culture and Development: A Study of Human Capabilities*. Oxford: Clarendon Press.

O'Brien, M. (2007) Mothers' emotional care work in education and its moral imperative. *Gender and Education* **19**(2), 159–78.

O'Brien, M. (2008) *Well-being and Post Primary Schooling: A Review of the Literature and Research*. Dublin: NCCA.

O'Brien, M. (2009) Mothers, capitals and their impact on love and care work. In K. Lynch and J. Baker (eds) *Affective Equality: Who Cares? Love, Care and Solidarity Work*. pp. 158–79. London: Palgrave.

Opdenakker, M. & Van Damme, J. (2000) Effects of schools, teaching staff and classes on achievement and well-being in secondary school education: similarities and differences between schools and outcomes. *School Effectiveness and School Improvement* **11**(2), 166–96.

Reay, D. (1998) *Class Work: Mothers Involvement in their Children's Primary Schooling*. London: University of London Press.

Seddon, T. (1997) 'Markets and the English: rethinking educational restructuring as institutional design', *British Journal of Sociology of Education* **18**(2), 165–186.

Seligman, M. (2002) *Authentic Happiness: Using the New Positive Psychology to Realise Your Potential for Lasting Fulfilment*. New York: Free Press.

Sen, A. (2009) *The Idea of Justice*. Boston: A Lane and Harvard University Press.

Sevenhuijsen, S. (1998) *Citizenship and the Ethics of Care: Feminist Considerations on Justice, Morality and Politics*, trans. L. Savage. London, New York: Routledge.

Skeggs, B. (1997) *Formations of Class and Gender*. London: Sage.

Smerdon, B. (2002) 'Students' Perceptions of Membership in their Highschools', *Sociology of Education* 75, 287–305.

Sternberg, R. (1998) Abilities are forms of developing expertise. *Educational Researcher* **27**(3), 11–12.

Sugrue, C. (2004) *Curriculum and Ideology: Irish Experiences, International Perspectives*. Dublin: The Liffey Press.

UNICEF (2007) Innocenti Report Card 7, *Child Poverty in Perspective: An Overview of Child Well-being in Rich Countries*. Florence: Innocenti Research Centre.

Walkerdine, V., Lucey, H. & Melody, J. (2001) *Growing Up Girl: Psychosocial Explorations of Class and Gender*. Basingstoke: Palgrave.

4 Professional responsibility under pressure?

Tomas Englund and Tone Dyrdal Solbrekke

Introduction

Professional work is characterised by what might be called *discretionary speciali-sation* involving subjective judgement and tailored decisions to individual circumstances in which 'discretion of fresh judgment must often be exercised if they are to be performed successfully' (Freidson 2001: 23). What we focus upon in this chapter is how that kind of professional performance is situated in a field of force between the judgements made by professionals and public instances controlling and evaluating this performance. We are also interested in how this discretionary specialisation is established in different professional formation processes and we argue that there is an essential aspect of discretionary specialisa-tion that has been somewhat neglected in previous research, namely the *different meanings* given to *professional responsibility*. It is not only a matter of *how* profes-sional responsibility is practised, but also one of *what* is given priority in the rhetoric of professionalism. Our intention in this chapter is to contribute to a discussion of these questions. By bringing to the fore the concepts of (professional) 'responsibility' and 'accountability', we identify a tension between the two concepts and more insight is gained into the different logics, and implications of 'responsibility' and 'accountability' regimes.

The tension between professional responsibility and accountability

Our research interest is prompted partly by the increased concern among professionals over calls for external accountability (e.g. Green 2009; Hoyle & Wallace 2009), and partly by conclusions from research (or the lack of) on the focus on professional responsibility in professional preparation and practice (e.g. Benner et al. 2010; Strain et al. 2009; Sullivan & Rosin 2008).

We use the professions of nursing and teaching as a reference to illustrate our arguments. Teaching and nursing are as much defined as professions as the clas-sical occupations of law, medicine and religion (Evetts 2003). Thus, nurses and teachers are formally coupled to the public sphere of being collectively oriented rather than self-oriented (Brint 1994), what Talcott Parsons (1951: 434) termed 'the normative obligation of professions'. We find these professions particularly interesting in that they play an important role as gatekeepers of the welfare state. Despite obvious differences, they are also both characterised by a face-to-face relationship with clients and a moral obligation to serve social as well as individual interests. Nurses and teachers administer huge public resources, interpret regulations, distribute goods and intervene in people's lives (Eriksen, Grimen & Molander 2008), and they 'not only meet personal needs; they are at the core of our relationship as citizens to our government and they also reflect the ways we think about ourselves as citizens in society' (Gross Stein 2001: 4).

Social trustee professionalism in a field of conflicting forces

Current use of the terms profession, professionalisation and professionalism includes a rich variety of occupations and connote different meanings (Solbrekke 2007). The term 'professionalisation' is understood as a sociological project, relating to the authority and status of the profession, 'a manifestation of the historical and social ambition of an occupational group to achieve status and a position in society' (Englund 1996: 76; cf. Hoyle 2001: 146). 'Professionalism' implies qualifications and capacities; the competencies for discretionary speciali- sation that are required for successful responsible performance. It is the latter dimension that is foregrounded in this chapter.

Without indulging in feelings of nostalgia for the traditional ideas of profes- sionalism, we argue that it is worth revisiting such classical ideas to remind ourselves of values such as civic engagement and social responsibilities, whereby professional responsibility gains a specific meaning. It implies a commitment to a body of knowledge and skills, both for the profession's own sake *and* for use in the service of its clients and in the interests of society (Grimen 2008), safe- guarding democracy by acting as mediators between the state and individual citizens (Durkheim 2001). According to this ideal, the work of professionals should have a moralising effect by upholding purposes and motives beyond the utilitarian goals of the marketplace (Turner 2001). These purposes have been recognised as the moral and political dimension of professionalism, and charac- terised by Steven Brint (1994) as 'social trustee professionalism', by William Sullivan (2005) as 'civic professionalism' and Ronald Barnett (1997) as 'critical professionalism'.

However, it has been argued also that the responsibility of professionals for civic engagement has declined. Brint (1994), for example, argues cogently that most professionals' conceptions of professional responsibility, as well as their understanding of the purpose and societal role of their professions, have narrowed considerably to purely cognitive and technical dimensions of profes- sional work. According to him there has been a historical transformation of the concept of professionalism, with implications for professional responsibility: from a professionalism that is more social and collective-oriented ('social trustee professionals'), to more self-oriented and utilitarian considerations, where the basis of professionalism is the expertise of technical knowledge (see Solbrekke, 2007, for further elaboration). As a consequence of such a shift, which is recognised in most Western countries, delivering safe and efficient technological services to the public has become paramount in professional practices. Time-consuming activities, such as caring for elderly people or young students, have increasingly tended to be neglected or given less status (Gross Stein 2001).

Additionally, in recent years, a demand for greater privatisation of public services in health care and education has received considerable impetus from policy-makers (Heggen & Wellard 2004; Svensson & Karlsson 2008). There is a stronger political emphasis today on ensuring innovation and economic growth in society than on the moral and social dimensions of work – a tendency also recognised in the global rhetoric of accountability in professional education, as can be seen in the rhetoric of European higher education. The Bologna process, beginning with the 1999 declaration on the purpose of creating a common European higher education area, uses a language that emphasises the need for more transparency and for comparable and compatible standards, in order to ensure economic strength and competitiveness through the production of expertise and flexible skilled workers (Karseth 2008). These new trends give prominence to a technified, utilitarian and economic purpose of professional work and education which may be at odds with the moral implications of 'social trustee professionalism'.

Another significant pressure on the ideas embedded in 'social trustee profes-sionalism' is related to the current 'public control regimes' that have evolved in the last 20–30 years. Deregulation of the market has led to the promotion of a policy which encourages devolution of decision making and responsibility down to the local level, away from central government. This new method of steering in the public field, introduced by the ideas of neo liberalism two to three decades ago, is often described as *New Public Management*. However, this devolution of decision making to the professions has frequently been accompanied by goals and standards of quality defined by politicians, resulting in demands for greater 'oversight', 'transparency' and 'accountability' (Svensson 2008). For the purpose of regulating and auditing the efficiency of the delivery of public goods such as public health care and education, states (politicians and bureaucrats) have developed more restrictive demands in terms of greater externally prescribed accountability: means of governance – 'systems of accountability' – to ensure that professionals are loyal to predefined political and economic goals. The underlying idea is to gain better control over professionals' work by making it more transparent through accountability mechanisms.

However, while there is a need for public accountability as a means of ensuring good-quality public services and building/maintaining public trust, it is also necessary to be aware of the risks of possible malpractices in the mechanisms of accountability in today's societies. The drive to measure 'efficiency' in terms of 'cost effectiveness' has, together with the demands of evidence-based prac-tices, created a new vocabulary of accountability, in which there is little room to ask the necessary questions: for what purpose and for whom are the services effective? (Gross Stein 2001). Thus, it seems necessary to revitalise what Becher et al. (1979) underlined in their analysis of accountability in schools: a programme of public accountability must balance external and comparable indicators of efficiency, for example, with internal standards defined by the profession. If not, 'constitutional measures would thus be likely in the end to defeat its own object – to reduce standards by undermining teachers' morale rather than to esteem them by building up professional self-esteem' (Becher et al. 1979: 37).

We argue, therefore, that more insight is needed into how professional responsibility and accountability are conceived by politicians, bureaucrats and academics educating for professional work. By digging into how these concepts seemingly play out in today's governance of professions, we provide an analytical frame for getting a better understanding of the intertwined complexity of professional responsibility and accountability in practice. In our view, there is merit in investigating the potential of 'social trustee' professionalism at a time when logics such as managerialism, entrepreneurship and market-oriented thinking have increasingly intruded into the field of professions (Brint and Levy 1999). These issues are related to the question of the role of professions in society, and of the overall purpose to which professionals should be dedicated. Consequently, we have to analyse how current conditions for professional work, linked to the growing demands of external and public/private accountability, challenge and play out in relation to the moral and societal dimensions of professional responsibility. With these considerations in place, it is appropriate to articulate the purpose of this chapter as an attempt to revitalise a broader and stronger conception of *professional responsibility*, by focusing attention on and elaborating the concepts of 'accountability' and 'responsibility' in relation to each other.

An underlying question is: 'Has "accountability" gradually come to overthrow the concept of 'professional responsibility' in the current governance of professionals?' (Svensson 2008). And, if so, is there a shift in how professional responsibility is enacted in practice? The following questions have guided our approach.

- What are the origins and etymological meanings of the concepts of professional responsibility and accountability?
- How can we understand the use of these concepts in current practices?
- What can be learned from making a conceptual distinction between professional 'responsibility' and 'accountability'?

Methodological and analytical approaches

The approach we adopt in order to clarify *responsibility* in a climate of *accountability* is inspired by pragmatism, in the sense that we attempt to expose the ongoing struggle over, and shifting meanings of, the two concepts yet do not search for precise and definite meanings. Rather, because concepts are understood as historically, socially and culturally constructed, they suggest different connotations contingent on the types of logic and implications generated by their use in current managerial and professional practices. Our aim is to point to the possible consequences and challenges embedded in the concepts by showing how they are embedded and located over time, and accorded different meanings in different contexts (Cherryholmes 1988; Englund & Quennerstedt 2008; Skinner 1988, 1999). Conceptual analyses seldom take sufficient account of the contradictory ways in which concepts can be used, and conceptual semantics remains insufficient if it does not analyse the pragmatic contexts in which the concepts are used, contexts where concepts are given a performative function, implying that the language used not only describes but also evaluates and creates. All concepts, Skinner (1988) argues, gain their meaning from the place they occupy within pragmatic contexts, and when the meaning of a concept is changed, its relationship to an entire vocabulary is also altered. This may mean, with regard to the increased use of accountability and its logic – what can be called the climate of accountability – that the top-down meaning embedded in managerial accountability as interpreted and practised in the logic of new public management regimes has triumphed over the meaning of professional responsibility, within both practice and research in the field. If our anticipation is plausible, current policies and the current language and practical use of accountability have put the moral and social aspects of responsibility in jeopardy.

In our search for the different meanings within this 'vocabulary struggle', we have also noticed that there is a specific use of accountability in connection with public accountability, as elaborated and given meaning by political scientists in particular (Bovens 2005). According to our interpretation, the meaning implicit in public accountability is reminiscent of, or at least connotes, the meaning of 'social trustee professionalism' as evident in the classical texts on professionalism, but not in the recent regimes of new public management and accountability. Below we will elaborate the analysis and we intend to show how the two concepts have different origins and have developed within different traditions and contexts, giving them different meanings.

Professional responsibility

Professional responsibility is a concept which, on a normative and general level, appears to be relatively unambiguous. It embeds the responsibility for professionals' discretionary specialisation with regard to both individual clients and the public interest, and it requires professionals to base their judgements in both science- and experience-based knowledge and professional ethics. This means that the tasks and their outcome are believed to be so indeterminate 'as to require attention to the variation to be found in individual cases. And while those whose occupation it is to perform such tasks will almost certainly engage in some routines that can be quite mechanical, it is believed that they must be prepared to be sensitive to the necessity of altering routine for individual circumstances that require discretionary judgement and action' (Freidson 2001: 23).

In practice, however, 'professional responsibility' is given different meanings, depending on cultural differences, political priorities and the interests of the stakeholders defining it (Valor 2006). Typical examples are the possible disagreements between government and the individual practitioner about what is 'best practice'. A very common experience in teaching and nursing is the conflict between forms of accountability that necessitate spending time reporting on classroom activities and students' results, and the form of professional responsibility that entails engaging with and teaching the students (Becher et al. 1979); or, in the case of nurses, between reporting about the procedures of caring and actually being with and caring for the patient. Pressures to deliver efficient treatment for more patients compete with the need to provide a good caring situation for the person who is sick, and often thrust professionals into making decisions that may conflict with their primary professional responsibility (Vike et al. 2002). (See Chapter 10 for an illustrative case of how the practice of professional responsibility may change.) For teachers, a similar situation may arise in the conflict between producing the best results in international comparative tests with the values of inclusion, equivalence and participation for all students in education.

Evidently, then, while 'professional responsibility' appears to be a relatively clear normative mandate at a general level, it becomes more complex in 'real-world' settings (Solbrekke & Heggen 2009). To act in a professionally responsible manner becomes a multifaceted matter, not only because of the demands of efficiency and competitiveness, but also because society is characterised increasingly by value pluralism, with a 'jungle' of expectations and conflicting ideas about how to deliver the best service to each citizen. Enacting responsibly means handling dilemmas between individual and collective concerns, considering multiple interests – also those of external stakeholders (Barnett 1997; Sullivan 2005). Contesting claims on professionals will always create a tension between what is evaluated as good and efficient in terms of '*(ac)countable*' and '*economic*' priorities and what is good and 'efficient' in terms of *morally responsible* actions (Gross Stein 2001).

Accountability

'Accountability' connotes 'good governance' in the sense of being responsible for delivering good and efficient services and being accountable to the public (Becher et al. 1979). In modern political discourse, 'accountability' holds promises of fair and equitable governance and can be seen as a 'social relationship in which an actor feels an obligation to explain and to justify his or her conduct to some significant other' (Bovens 2005: 184).

However, the development and function of strategies deployed by the 'accountability movement' seem to emphasise efficient practices, which to a minor extent comprise the practice of a holistic and complex professional responsibility, in which proximity, attention and waiting (Biesta 2010) are central. An important function of the system of accountability is to reduce the ambiguity of professional practice. According to this logic, the necessary means are to oblige professionals to adhere to, and be accountable against, prescriptive policy standards of quality and to make their judgements and work transparent to the public (Hoyle & Wallace 2009). But, while it is a legitimate aspiration to make professional work as transparent as possible, there is also a risk that too great a focus on performativity, efficiency, flexibility and transparency will reduce accountability to a set of technical and managerial requirements at the expense of the moral dimensions of public accountability (Bovens 2005).

Within current practices of public management of professions, we find an increased focus on accountability in order to make practices transparent with the help of external standards (Svensson 2008). Collegial standards defined by the professions have been replaced by control of in-service performance in accordance with criteria predefined by politicians or other stakeholders outside the profession. In view of this, it is the politics of the new forms of accountability that challenge the moral implications of professional responsibility. To find support for this argument, we need to ask why the concept of accountability has become problematic with regard to acting in a professionally responsible manner. To this end, we elaborate further on the distinctions between 'responsibility' and 'accountability'.

Distinctions between 'responsibility' and 'accountability'

Dictionaries provide some helpful nuances of meaning for the two concepts. In the online Thesaurus Digital Library, key synonyms for 'responsibility' are trustworthiness, capacity, dependability and reliability, trust, capability, judgement and choice. In contrast, key definitions of 'accountability' include answerability, blame, liability and obligation (Thesaurus 2009). From this it seems reasonable to conclude that 'accountability' emphasises the *duty to account* for one's actions and concerns what is rendered to another, while 'responsibility' is a *moral obligation* assumed by oneself, or bestowed upon a person to be used for another. 'Responsibility' as a concept assumes a proactive attitude and an approach in which a professional *voluntarily* takes responsibility for 'the other' by involving his or her capacity to act responsibly from a moral perspective (Martinsen 2006).

If the proposed distinction is persuasive, professional responsibility in teaching and nursing presupposes that teachers and nurses are given the opportunity to act responsibly *for* their students and patients, by allowing them time and space for moral action and 'room' in which professional discretion may be exercised. In other words, a teacher or nurse must be able to listen to and have the capacity to see the needs of his or her students or patients – though within a broader perspective, in a balanced interplay between the needs of the individual and collective concerns, and between internal responsibilities and external accountability claims. Such a notion of professional responsibility relies on *mutual trust* and respect between the one who *has taken responsibility for* the other (the professional agent) and the one who *is being taken responsibility for.*

'Responsibility' in this sense relies on trust in the professional agent, for instance, the teacher or nurse, being qualified for discretionary specialisation willing to handle dilemmas and having the freedom to deliberate on alternative courses of action. He or she is expected to be able to justify his or her decisions in the specific setting from a professional point of view, based in science- as well as experience-based knowledge and in moral reasoning (Benner et al. 2010). However, the actions taken cannot always be predicted and their 'outcomes' are not always measurable in terms of clear and predefined descriptors or indicators. Exercising such a responsibility goes beyond the limits of accountability and is linked to a sense of freedom, because professionals are *trusted,* yet also *committed,* to act in the interests of others (Sullivan 2005) – and the greater the freedom, the greater the responsibility.

'Accountability', on the other hand, implies quite different notions. As we have seen, it relates to concepts such as counting and to legal, economic and organisational actions (Svensson 2008). It is bound to a contractual obligation, and emphasises the duty to answer for your actions to others or to society. In such a relationship, the professional agent's actions are to be controlled by evaluating them against predefined measures. Consequently, the practices of 'accountability' are oriented towards control rather than trust. Within this logic 'good services' are guaranteed by means of measuring and 'accounting' instruments, rather than by relying on professional discretion.

Conscious of the risk of oversimplifying, nevertheless, in Table 4.1, we have summarised the two concepts, indicating their logics and implications in use. For the purposes of analysis and our ongoing discussion, we construct two categories which are analytically polarised, yet not to be comprehended as static and final definitions. They should be understood, rather, as evolved and evolving, more fluid and fluctuating in different systems of logic that are re-configured over time. It is this type of difference between the meanings of these concepts and the logics of how they are used in today's practices that we find particularly useful in

Table 4.1 Types of logic and implications of professional responsibility and accountability

Professional responsibility	Professional accountability
Based in professional mandate	Defined by current governance
Situated judgement	Standardised by contract
Trust	Control
Moral rationale	Economic/legal rationale
Internal evaluation	External auditing
Negotiated standards	Predetermined indicators
Implicit language	Transparent language
Framed by professions	Framed by political goals
Relative autonomy and personally inescapable	Compliance with employer's/politicians' decisions
Proactive	Reactive

order to understand the shift on a more normative level, too. What is seen as 'good' within the logic of accountability differs from what is conceived as 'good' in the logic of 'responsibility'. This is also what constitutes the challenging interplay in discretionary specialisation.

On the basis of these distinctions between professional responsibility and accountability we approach the implications for professional work. The distinctions are useful in analysing the implications for professional discretion and professional education, where the different meanings of the two concepts give rise to different practices. 'Responsibility' implies proactive action, an action which the professional initiates and voluntarily takes responsibility for in accordance with the commitments embedded in the purpose of his or her profession. Within this pattern, professionals are entrusted with space to use their professional discretion in deciding what is 'best' for their client and for society. 'Accountability', on the other hand, is about reactive action; an action initiated as a result of the demand from others to report on actions and results. The rationale underlying accountability in this sense is that 'mechanisms' are, of necessity, based on clear descriptors and a simplified 'transparent' language, and easily understood by all users of professional services. This is a logic based on the belief that clear points of reference will ensure and enhance the quality of work and hence of the service to the public as customers (Dubnick and Frederickson 2009). It is a form of political/public management based on measuring and accounting through control instruments, rather than relying on professional judgement. However, in this kind of governance there is a tendency to neglect the dimensions of responsibility that are not easily articulated or measured. There is a risk therefore that, for example, actions such as those based in tacit knowledge and a moral sensitivity to 'the other' (cf. Martinsen 2006) will be undervalued.

Challenging and unavoidable kinds of readiness for action

As the above discussion indicates, acting responsibly requires professionals who can manage the demanding task of handling the tension between internal responsibilities and public accountability. However, acting in accordance with the ideals of professional responsibility is demanding. In addition, professionals who are characterised as 'responsible' tend to be more unpredictable than those who are merely 'accountable', because 'responsibility' does not imply 'blind loyalty' to predetermined standards defined by an employer. Rather, professionally responsible actions are dependent on professional deliberation and professional judgements. They are less 'true' to common agreements and rules, unless these are in accordance with what they consider to be their primary professional commitment. (see Chapter 9 for examples of principals bending and breaking rules in order to behave professionally responsible). In contrast, professionals who are impeccably accountable are recognised by their concern to act in accordance with predefined standards and not to deviate from what has been agreed upon, or rather, what has been stated in one way or another. In other words, there is less flexibility in relation to the circumstances surrounding their agreed-upon actions. They are predictable in the sense that they will most probably follow the rules, rather than use their 'professional discretion' to consider how to respond to the needs of an individual or society.

By this reasoning we are not arguing for a nostalgic view of the autonomy of professions, with professionals held in awe for their special knowledge and not required to account for their actions or outcomes (Leraci 2007). Professional work requires competent agents who are able to deliberate and negotiate the claims of responsibility and accountability (see Chapter 1 for an elaboration on legitimate negotiations). It also requires professional associations that encourage social trustee values, and a willingness to impose sanctions if their members do not live up to the standards of their profession. This implies both actively made personal choices in accordance with a knowledge and moral base, *and* reporting to the public and to individual clients. Such responsible actions depend on the possibility of openly deliberating on what is good practice. In addition, there is a need to make professional practices as transparent *as possible*. Transparency may be laudable when understood in the sense that patients or students and their relatives are allowed to question the practice and services of a professional nurse or teacher. It is legitimate to ask for efficient health care or teaching methods. However, such characteristics are rendered problematic if public accountability is reduced to merely what is measurable and possible to articulate in common and clear answers (Svensson 2008). Professional values of 'respect', 'personal regard', 'competence' and 'professional integrity' (indispensable to the exercise of professional judgement) can then very quickly become compliance, conformity and passivity to predetermined standards, rather than proactive professional agency (cf. MacBeath 2002; Solbrekke & Sugrue, forthcoming). Such practices are more often characterised by 'technicisation' or 'instrumentalism', and the reduction or elimination of professional discretion and judgement (Svensson 2008).

However, there is evidence from a variety of professions that professionals are reacting to the increased use of 'audit systems' (Power 1997), which in many respects feel alien to traditional professional practices (Freidson 2001). When 'accounting' systems only involve reporting data which are perceived as not meaningful or productive for the purposes of professional practice, 'accountability' becomes a concept that is met with scepticism (Hoyle & Wallace 2009). Many professionals claim that the mechanisms of accounting take up too much of their working time. It is questionable, therefore, whether the externally driven accountability agenda provides the most efficient means of enhancing the quality of professional work in the public interest. If accounting for what is 'economically measurable' becomes privileged over social and moral politics, and professional responsibility and ethics are reduced to 'efficiency', the willingness of the professional to act responsibly may be jeopardised. This is perhaps understandable, yet indefensible according to the claims of 'social trustee' professionals.

Conclusion – and possible implications for professional practice

In this chapter we have brought to the forefront the different logics and their implications generated by the language use of the concepts of professional responsibility and accountability. By deconstructing the two concepts, we have drawn attention to some crucial distinctions between them, as presented in Table 4.1. In particular we have problematised what is happening under the current public management regimes and rhetoric of accountability, in which the moral aspects of professional responsibility appear to be diminishing in significance. We have also pointed to the fact that professional responsibility requires an ability to handle multiple conflicts in day-to-day work, a discretionary specialisation which in turn requires knowledge and awareness of the different types of logic underlying responsibility and accountability. This may be helpful in enabling us to understand *why* professionals make the priorities they do in their daily work.

In the endeavour to help students and practising professionals to develop a repertoire for enacting responsibly, we need to relate issues of responsibility and accountability to the purpose of professional work, and how it may be played out in the different contexts of professions such as nursing and teaching. Inspired by research on nursing education undertaken by the Carnegie Foundation (e.g. Benner et al. 2010), we support the view that it is necessary to develop spaces and strategies that encourage the formation of moral and practical reasoning and a capability to act in accordance with a conscious awareness of professional responsibility (Sullivan & Rosin 2008). Such spaces must be established in order to help students and professionals develop the ability to deliberate on different alternatives, try them out in practice, and reflect upon their practices (Englund 2008; Solbrekke 2008; see Chapter 7 on professional formation). To be trusted by others as a competent, professionally responsible actor, the individual requires an ability to act in certain approved ways, based on his or her capacity to make moral and self-reflective choices that relate to other people's needs and interests. This means that professionals have to learn the 'means of representation': the norms and values that work as instruments in the making of responsible practices (Shotter 1984: 28).

Professional responsibility is not learned and encouraged by merely transferring predefined authoritative and standardised rules. It is not the traits of professions, formal structures or status; *their professionalisation* that guarantee professionally responsible behaviour. Professional codes of conduct are useful as a starting point, but they have to be enhanced with issues of civic responsibility and ideas of how these codes are to be lived out in practice, confronted by plural discourses embedded in varied situated and cultural practices (Barnett 1997; Sullivan & Rosin 2008). Therefore, implications of professional responsibility and accountability should be articulated and critically deliberated on in education and social practices; examined, de-constructed and reconstructed on the basis of the moral implication of current professional mandates and an 'interrogation' of one's own motivation and personal interest (Englund 2002). Such practices have potential to become a catalyst for sustained dialogue regarding ongoing professional learning in and beyond the workplace, as well as in the academy. They may re-shape and re-invigorate aspects of professional practice and make issues of professional responsibility a communal matter and not only a responsibility left to the individual professional. Furthermore, because 'social and moral responsibility is much more a matter of responsiveness to others in need than it is a matter of rule-following' (May 1996: 1), it is important both to understand and to investigate professional responsibility as moving beyond merely accountability performance, situated both as part of a relationship between professionals and clients and as part of a broader societal responsibility.

Deliberating on different alternative ways of acting, trying them out in practice and reflecting upon them may be a useful start when it comes to developing practical reasoning that can help professionals to reach 'legitimate negotiated compromises' (May 1996) in the complexity of daily work. As professionals we all need to dwell with and imagine the quandaries we encounter at work, and how to balance demanding and possibly conflicting interests in everyday situations. We need to articulate and discuss what is meant by *professional* expertise, what it means to be loyal to the moral obligations of the professional demand to use knowledge to serve others – both the individual client and the public. 'Externally' defined norms are undoubtedly important in preventing unlawful or unethical conduct, but blind loyalty to such rules may diminish the capacity of the individual professional to make reflective judgements (Colnerud 2009). Inspired by John Dewey (1983), we must understand professional responsibility as part of the morality and identity construction embedded in the reflective process that evolves when reflecting upon practice; what actually happens and what one think should happen, who one is, and who one wishes to become, while also reflecting upon one's personal contribution within a larger societal context. The stimulation of such a reflective process may help professionals to develop the capability to understand professional responsibility as a relational and social responsibility while also enabling them to evaluate critically the authorised professional ethics of their individual profession: *their professionalism*. It includes a capacity to cope with tensions between societal concerns and individual clients' interests, and also an ability to balance commitments in private life with the diverse and multiple requirements of working life (May 1996; see also Chapter 2).The ability to act in such a way is what characterises responsible professionals. Finally, 'bringing professional responsibility back in' means allowing the moral and societal mandate to become the driving force for professional practice, while technical accounting systems function as a useful tool supporting the main normative dimension of professional work. This means that 'responsibility must precede and supersede accountability' (Hargreaves & Shirley 2009: 101). Professionals must be supported and encouraged to keep up proactive responsible practices, and not simply lapse into reactive reporting. This is a claim that should concern *all* professionals, including the academics responsible for educating professionals in higher education, with a view to creating a moral base for professionals that can serve as a navigator (Taylor 1989) in a more and more 'accountable' and complex working life. We must constantly remind ourselves that professional responsibility implies more than mere accountability. It invokes degrees of autonomy for the professional to exercise professional judgement in the interests of individuals and civil society – a most important premise for professionally responsible practice – and a most crucial reminder for faculties where professional programmes are provided.

References

Barnett, R. (1997) *Higher Education: A Critical Business*. Buckingham: SRHE and Open University Press.

Becher, T., Eraut, M., Barton, J. & Canning, T. (1979) *Accountability in the Middle Years of Schooling. An Analysis of Policy Options*. Final report of the East Sussex LEA/ University of Sussex Research Project.

Benner, P., Sutphen, M., Leonard, V. & Day, L. (2010) *Educating Nurses: A Call for Radical Transformation*. San Francisco: Jossey-Bass Publishers Inc.

Biesta, G. (2010). *Good Education in an Age of Measurement. Ethics, Politics, Democracy*. Boulder & London: Paradigm Publishers.

Bovens, M. (2005) Public accountability. In Ferlie, E., Lynne, L. and Pollitt, C. (eds) *The Oxford Handbook of Public Management*. pp. 182–208. Oxford: Oxford University Press.

Brint, S. (1994) *In an Age of Experts*. Princeton: Princeton University Press.

Brint, S. & Levy, C.S. (1999) Profession and civic management. In Skocpol, T. and Fiorina, M.P. (eds) *Trends in Rhetoric and Practice 1875–1995*. pp. 163–210. Washington, D.C.: Brookings Institution Press.

Cherryholmes, C. (1988) *Power and Criticism. Poststructural Investigations in Education*. New York: Teachers College Press.

Colnerud, G. (2009) *Colleagues' misconduct as ethical dilemmas*. Paper presented at the annual conference of the Nordic Educational Research Association, 8–10 March, Trondheim, Norway.

Dewey, J. (1983) Ethics. In Boydston, J.A. (ed.) *John Dewey. The Middle Works 1899–1924*, Vol. 5, Carbondale. IL: Southern Illinois Press.

Dewey, J. (1988) The public and its problems. In Boydston, J.A. (ed.) *John Dewey, The Later Works 1925–1953*, Vol. 2. pp. 235–372. Carbondale, IL: Southern Illinois Press.

Dubnick, M. and Frederickson, H.G. (2009) Accountable agents: federal performance measurement and third party government. *Journal of Public Administration Research* **20**, 143–59.

Durkheim, E. (2001) *Professional Ethics and Civic Morals*. London: Routledge.

Englund, T. (1996) Are professional teachers a good thing? In Goodson, I. and Hargreaves, A. (eds) *Teachers' Professional Lives*. pp. 75–87. London: Falmer Press.

Englund, T. (2002) *The university as a place for deliberative communication? An attempt to apply Habermas' discourse theory on higher education*. Paper presentation at the American Association for the Study of Higher Education (ASHE) 27th Conference, 20–24 November, Sacramento, USA.

Englund, T. (2008) The university as an encounter for deliberative communication – creating cultural citizenship and professional responsibility. *Utbildning & Demokrati – tidskrift för didaktik och utbildningspolitik [Education and Democracy – journal for didactics and educational policy]* 17(2), 73–96.

Englund, T. & Quennerstedt, A. (2008) Linking curriculum theory and linguistics: the performative use of 'equivalence' as an educational policy concept. *Journal of Curriculum Studies* 40(6), 713–24.

Eriksen, E.O., Grimen, H. & Molander, A. (2008) *Making welfare state professionals accountable: The problem of discretion.* Paper presented at the 5th Interim Conference of the International Sociological Association: Sociology of Professional Groups. Challenges to professionalism. Limits and benefits of the professional model, 12–13 September. Centre for the Study of Professions, University College of Oslo, Norway.

Evetts, J. (2003) The sociological analysis of professionalism – occupational change in the modern World. *International Sociology*: http://iss.sagepub.com/cgi/content/abstract/18/2/395.

Freidson, E. (2001) *Professionalism: The Third Logic.* Cambridge: Polity Press.

Green, B. (ed.) (2009) *Understanding and Researching Professional Practice.* Rotterdam: Sense.

Grimen, H. (2008) Profesjon og profesjonsmoral [Professions and professional ethics]. In Molander, A. & Terum, L.I. (eds) *Profesjonsstudier [Studies of professions].* pp. 144–60. Oslo: Universitetsforlaget.

Gross Stein, J. (2001) *The Cult of Efficiency.* Canada, CBC Massey Lectures Series: Anansi.

Hargreaves, A. & Shirley, D. (2009) *The Fourth Way: The Inspiring Future for Educational Change.* Thousand Oaks: Corwin, Sage.

Heggen, K.M. & Wellard, S (2004) Increased unintended patient harm in nursing practise as a consequence of the dominance of economic discourses. *International Journal of Nursing Studies* 41, 293–8.

Hoyle, E. (2001) Teaching: prestige, status and esteem. *Education Management Administration & Leadership* 29(2), 139–52.

Hoyle, E. & Wallace, M. (2009) Leadership for professional practice. In Gewirtz, S., Mahoney, P., Hextall, I. and Cribb, A. (eds) *Changing Teacher Professionalism*, pp. 204–14. London: Routledge.

Karseth, B. (2008) Qualifications frameworks for the European higher education area – a new instrumentalism or 'much ado about nothing'? *Utbildning & Demokrati – tidskrift för didaktik och utbildningspolitik* 17(2), 51–72.

Leraci, S. (2007) Responsibility versus accountability in a risk-averse culture. *Emergency Medicine Australasia* 19, 63–4.

Martinsen, K. (2006) *Care and Vulnerability.* Oslo: Akribe.

May, L. (1996) *The Socially Responsive Self. Social Theory and Professional Ethics.* Chicago: University of Chicago Press.

Parsons, T. (1951) *The Social System.* New York: Free Press.

Power, M. (1997) *The Audit Society: Rituals of Verification.* Oxford: Oxford University Press.

Shotter, J. (1984) *Social Accountability and Selfhood.* Oxford: Basil Blackwell.

Skinner, Q. (1988) Language and social change. In Tully, J. (ed.) *Meaning and Context. Quentin Skinner and His Critics.* pp. 119–32. Cambridge: Polity Press.

Skinner, Q. (1999) Rhetoric and conceptual change. *Finnish Yearbook of Political Thought* **3**, 60–73. Available online at: http://www.jyu.fi/yhtfil/rediscriptions/articles1999. htm (accessed 9 April 2008).

Solbrekke, T.D. (2007) *Understanding conceptions of professional responsibility.* Ph.D. dissertation, University of Oslo.

Solbrekke, T.D. (2008) Educating for professional responsibility – a normative dimension of higher education. *Utbildning & Demokrati – tidskrift för didaktik och utbildnings- politik [Education and Democracy – Journal for Didactics and Educational Policy]* **17**(2), 73–96.

Solbrekke, T.D. & Sugrue, C. (In press) Learning from conceptions of professional responsibility and graduate experiences in becoming novice practitioners. In Mc Kee, A. & M. Eraut, (Eds.) "Learning Trajectories, Innovation and Identity for Professional Development". Springer.

Solbrekke, T.D. & Heggen, K.M. (2009) Sykepleieansvar – fra profesjonelt moralsk ansvar til teknisk regnskapsplikt? [A nurse's responsibility – from professional moral responsi- bility to technical accountability?] *Arbejdsliv* **11**(3), 49–61.

Strain, J., Barnett, R. & Jarvis, P. (2009) *Universities, Ethics and Professions.* London: Routledge.

Sullivan, W.C. (2005) *Work and Integrity. The Crisis and Promise of Professionalism in America.* San Francisco: Jossey-Bass Publishers Inc.

Sullivan, W.M. & Rosin, M.S. (2008) *A New Agenda for Higher Education. Shaping a Life of the Mind for Practice.* San Francisco: Jossey-Bass Publishers Inc.

Svensson, L. (2008) *Professions and Accountability. Challenges to Professional Control and Collegiality.* Paper presented at the 5th Interim Conference of the International Sociological Association: Sociology of Professional Groups. Challenges to professional- ism. Limits and benefits of the professional model. Centre for the Study of Professions, 12–13 September, Oslo University College, Oslo.

Svensson, L. & Karlsson, A. (2008) Profesjon og organsisasjon [Profession and organisation]. In Molander, A. and Terum, L.I. (eds) *Profesjonsstudier [Studies of Professions].* pp. 130–41. Oslo: Universitetsforlaget.

Taylor, C. (1989) *Sources of the Self: The Making of Modern Identity.* Cambridge: Cambridge University Press.

Thesaurus Digital Library. http://thesaurus.reference.com/browse/ responsibility (accessed 5 July 2009).

Turner, B.S. (2001) Preface to second edition of Emile Durkheim (1957/2001), *Professional Ethics and Civic Morals.* London: Routledge Sociology Classics.

Valor, C. (2006) Corporate social responsibility and corporate citizenship: towards corporate accountability. *Business and Society Review* **110**(2), 191–212.

Vike, H., Haukelien, H., Bakken, R., Brinchmann, A. & Kroken, R. (2002) *Makt- og demokratiutredningen 1998–2003. Maktens samvittighet: om politikk, styring og dilem- maer i velferdsstaten* [The power and democracy study, 1998–2003. The conscience of power: On policy, governance and dilemmas in the welfare state]. Oslo: Gyldendal Akademisk.

5 Teaching, integrity and the development of professional responsibility

Why we need pedagogical phronesis

Bruce Macfarlane

Introduction

The possession of a doctorate has long been seen as a sufficient qualification to teach at university coupled with the received wisdom that teachers are born, not made. These assumptions have tended to retard efforts to raise the status of teaching in higher education. Over the last 20 years, there has been an exponential growth in professional development for academic faculty in response to the massification of higher education and increasing competition between institutions for students, both nationally and internationally (Knapper 2010). This period has also seen the introduction of a wide range of reward and recognition schemes to promote interest in, and respect for, the teaching role. Considerable efforts have been made to promote the scholarship of teaching and learning in the wake of Boyer's influential work (Boyer 1990). Yet, international survey data indicate that the proportion of university faculty whose primary interest is in teaching has actually fallen since 1992, while those indicating their primary interest is in research has risen by 9 per cent (Locke 2008). This is indicative of a shifting set of priorities that have important implications for the notion of professional responsibility.

Halsey and Trow's study of British academics during the 1960s found that only 10 per cent were interested in research and a mere 4 per cent regarded research as their first duty (Halsey & Trow 1971). Writing in the late 1970s, Wilson asserts that the majority of American academics considered 'teaching to be more important than research' (Wilson 1979: 234). Hence, the prioritisation of research over teaching is a relatively recent trend and might appear strange, or even perverse, given the need to raise professional teaching standards in a modern mass system. This attitude, though, is consistent with the increasing fragmentation of the academic profession into the para-academic functions associated with teaching, research and service (Macfarlane 2011a). It is partly a result of the expansion of the higher education system worldwide and the increasing division of labour among academic faculty that has accompanied it. The proportion of faculty employed in 'teaching-only' positions has increased and the unbundling of the role means that academic life is now more differentiated into the 'haves' and 'have nots'. Crudely, the 'haves' work in elite institutions, do research and spend comparatively little time teaching. The 'have nots' work in access-based institutions, do little or no research and spend most of their time teaching and assessing students (Sikes 2006).

The growth of higher education has split the academic profession more starkly than ever before. In this context, professional responsibility is under severe pressure, particularly in relation to teaching as a relatively disesteemed activity despite institutional efforts to reward good practice at the margin. Here it is important to note that such efforts rarely displace the pre-eminence of research and may even lower the status as a result of tokenism and the strengthening of bifurcation (Macfarlane 2011b). Faculty at elite institutions, in particular, are being encouraged to become enterprising income-generators committed to increasing their citation rating rather than professional and responsible teachers.

In this context, this chapter will focus on the role and function of initial professional development courses for academics with a teaching role and the importance of incorporating a focus on ethical issues in academic practice. It will explore the centrality of ethical issues to professional teaching practice and how integrity may be developed through a focus on practice dilemmas linked to virtue theory. This approach to professional ethics contrasts with compliance-oriented codes of practice. Drawing on an Aristotelian approach, I will argue that the most important quality of a 'good' teacher is pedagogical *phronesis* (McLaughlin 1999), one of several key intellectual and moral virtues – including fairness, authenticity, collegiality and humility – which are central to acting in a professionally responsible manner.

The growth of professional development

There has been a significant growth in initial professional development courses for teachers in higher education since the late 1990s across a number of national contexts. In the UK alone, over 100 such programmes have been accredited by the Higher Education Academy. Demands for higher professional teaching standards among academic faculty are growing. National professional teaching standards for higher education have already been developed in the UK and a recent government-backed report on university funding has recommended that all new academics with teaching responsibilities should take a teaching training qualification (Browne 2010).

In constructing the curriculum, teaching and learning certificate programmes face an uneasy tension between pressures to induct participants into institution-specific procedures and policies as opposed to more theoretically driven critical analysis of pedagogical practice, informed by the wider research literature. The academic interests and professional instincts of educational developers who organise and teach such programmes tend to lean towards the latter objective but significant institutional pressures can exist for greater attention to be paid to the advocacy and inculcation of policies and mission statements. Programmes are also predominantly based on a 'psychologised' understanding of teaching in higher education and draw on concepts such as deep and surface learning, reflective practice and learning styles. The philosophy, sociology and history of (higher) education (Peters 1964) is largely excluded from this curriculum while there is a significant 'pedagogic gap' (Malcolm & Zukas 2001) between professional preparation programmes and the complex, uncertain and 'messy' reality of *being* a higher education teacher. Developing a theoretical and practical understanding of the ethical issues of academic practice is a part of developing a strong sense of professional responsibility. If practitioners can be encouraged to do so, this is one way of closing the pedagogic gap between teaching and learning theory and actual practice.

Postgraduate certificates in learning and teaching in higher education[1] are now offered by nearly all UK and Australian universities as a mechanism for ensuring that new academic faculty are prepared for the teaching role. Universities in other parts of the world, such as Hong Kong, also provide a range of 'introductory' or induction-type courses of between a day and a week in duration. While shorter in duration, these programmes face similar challenges in balancing content between academic and institution-specific purposes. Many postgraduate certificates were derived from former induction programmes where the main focus was on inculcating policies and procedures rather than a broader form of professional development. They also derive from the largely practical focus of early educational development units in the 1960s (Land 2004). The work of the UK Staff and Educational Development Association and the Higher Education Research and Staff Development Association of Australasia has helped to support the gradual spread of such programmes from the early 1990s.

In the UK, a fresh impetus was given to the professional development of faculty in the late 1990s with the publication of the Dearing report on higher education which recommended, *inter alia*, the need to raise the status of teaching (NCIHE 1997). The report also led to the creation of the Institute for Learning and Teaching in Higher Education, which became an accrediting body for postgraduate certificates in learning and teaching at UK universities. By 2007, the newly re-branded Higher Education Academy had accredited 168 such programmes (Kandlbinder & Peseta 2009). A series of similar reforms have been introduced in Australia, including the establishment of the Australian Learning and Teaching Council (formerly the Carrick Institute for Learning and Teaching in Higher Education) in 2004 and a Learning and Teaching Fund designed to incentivise institutions to improve the quality of the student 'experience'.

Therefore, initial professional development for academic faculty has moved firmly into the mainstream in the space of little over ten years. In the UK, a range of system-wide forces contributed to this rapid growth including further massification, the introduction of professional teaching standards for higher education in 2006 and the increasing benchmarking of university standards through quality assurance measures and the publication of market-sensitive data on student satisfaction levels. In Australia, similar pressures exist with new academic standards for universities currently under development led by the Australian Learning and Teaching Council.[2] The rapid emergence of professional development programmes for academic faculty in these contexts has taken place against the backdrop of a number of suppositions.

Underpinning assumptions

Training as teachers, not academics

Professional development programmes for academics are almost entirely concerned with their preparation as 'teachers' in higher education rather than academic practitioners who also research and perform service tasks (Blackmore & Blackwell 2006). While sometimes these courses are referred to as 'academic practice', this phrase tends to be interpreted quite narrowly and in reality focuses almost exclusively on teaching and student learning. Where 'research' is included in the aims and objectives of such courses, this tends to be about encouraging participants to undertake research into their own teaching practice otherwise known as 'pedagogical research'. Curiously, the nature of this commitment can potentially conflict, or lead to a change of focus away from, subject-based research more likely to benefit the career development of academic faculty (Stierer 2007).

Therefore, programmes of 'professional development' for university teachers that focus on the teaching role look increasingly out of kilter with the emergence of research expectations in 'new' as well as 'old' universities (Sikes 2006). Increased competition among institutions for research funding in the wake of research audit exercises in the UK, Australia and New Zealand are having a significant effect on the re-shaping of academic practice but this is yet to be substantially reflected in the way postgraduate certificates are constructed. While the successful completion of a Postgraduate Certificate is often an espoused condition of probation at UK universities for inexperienced faculty, there is little evidence that this requirement is enforced in practice. In other words, while institutions are formally committed to new faculty becoming 'competent' teachers, their career chances are really shaped by a broader set of considerations increasingly focused on their research, publication and income-generation activities.

Moreover, professional development courses in teaching are more firmly established in institutions that are predominantly teaching rather than research led. While this might appear consistent with institutional mission, faculty working in such institutions are more likely to possess a strong teaching background, possibly as a result of having previously worked in the schools or post-compulsory education sector rather than coming from a research background. The professional development needs of faculty in teaching-led institutions tend to coalesce around research rather than teaching. It follows that faculty working in research-intensive institutions may require relatively more teaching development provision, although their personal and professional objectives are unlikely to identify such needs.

The domesticating curriculum

Many postgraduate certificates originated as induction courses and expanded over a number of years until some form of formally accredited programme emerged (Land 2004). This background means that there is still an often unspoken tension between, on the one hand, induction into institutional procedures, cultures and modes of working, and, on the other, a more critical engagement with an academic body of literature concerned with learning and teaching in higher education. While most programmes seek to traverse these two aims, there is almost always an uneasy tension between them.

The role of postgraduate certificates in enculturalisation is reflected in the way that universities tend to regard educational development units as agents of institutional change and consequently link or align them closely with human resource and central management functions as a result (Bath & Smith 2004; D'Andrea & Gosling 2001). Most are located as part of central support services rather than in academic faculties. This location creates a tension between different types of course aims.

Postgraduate certificates are, by definition, a masters' level qualification prompted in large part by the need to demonstrate that such an award for teaching has academic status. This status necessitates, or perhaps justifies, the construction of aims and objectives that are academic in nature and connected with examining a body of theoretical knowledge and associated ideas critically. Yet, in practice, another set of institution-specific aims tend to exist alongside these academic objectives. These are associated with inducting 'students' (who are often, in effect, colleagues) into institutional practices and ensuring that they conform to a variety of connected values. This can include their preparation to teach according to localised (and sometimes amateurish) definitions of 'good practice' assessed through observation by often untrained but 'experienced' senior faculty, and a preparedness to internalise and express implicit or explicit support for prevailing university policies and strategies. Indicative of this latter orientation is where programmes focus strongly on the inculcation of policies concerning, say, student diversity and inclusivity, and course approval and quality assurance processes with 'expert' teaching contributions from organisational postholders in these various areas. Hence, the institutional status and location of postgraduate certificates tends to result in a competing, and often conflicting, set of aims. This type of programme may be labelled as postgraduate but much of the learning can, in the worse cases, be essentially about the internalisation of organisational practices.

Such practices are connected to what Trowler and Cooper (2002) would characterise as teaching and learning 'regimes' exacting, in the process, a substantial influence over the formation of academic identity in the context of teaching and learning programmes. Their analysis also draws on the distinction made by Agyris and Schön (1974) between espoused versions of these regimes and how they really operate in practice to argue that the extent to which the curriculum is open to negotiation on the basis of practitioner needs is questionable (Trowler & Cooper 2002).

A strong institutional focus calls into question the extent to which such programmes are genuinely critical and academic in nature rather than a narrower form of context-specific training. The credibility of programmes can be adversely affected where they focus too heavily on seeking to disseminate institutional policies and priorities, particularly among faculty who see themselves as 'cosmopolitans' rather than 'locals' (Gouldner 1957). These 'cosmopolitans' identify more strongly with their discipline than the organisation, tend to be more research-active and engaged with communities of colleagues beyond, rather than within the institution. In this context, participation in and completion of a postgraduate certificate is about 'toeing the line' and possibly fulfilling a probationary requirement (Macfarlane & Gourlay 2009). Such programmes are predominantly aimed at young and inexperienced faculty who are rarely in the position to challenge the intellectual focus or the need to comply if they wish to fulfil their probationary requirements. In terms of professional responsibility, this means that such courses take as their main point of reference the institution rather than the profession. As a result, professionalism is presented through a narrow prism. While the espoused emphasis of such courses is often on the importance of critical engagement and contestation, the hidden curriculum is about domestication and the inculcation of institutional norms and values.

The 'psychologised' curriculum

Another underpinning assumption of postgraduate certificates is their theoretical basis. Most are heavily focused on a limited number of key concepts drawn principally from the psychology of education. According to a recent survey undertaken by Kandlbinder and Peseta (2009), the five most dominant concepts in such programmes are:

- reflective practice derived mainly from the work of Schön (1983);
- 'constructive alignment' derived from the work of Biggs (1996);
- deep and surface learning derived from the work of Marton & Säljö (1976);
- the scholarship of teaching and learning derived from Boyer (1990) and others;
- assessment-driven learning derived from the work of Gibbs and Simpson (2002).

These concepts are listed in order of their influence with reflective practice the most dominant. This finding corresponds with the similarly dominant role of reflective practice as the 'underlying philosophy' of teacher education for the school sector over the last 20 years (Whitty et al. 1992: 297). Arguably only the first three of the ideas identified by Kandlbinder and Peseta represent theoretically grounded concepts, with the final two (the scholarship of teaching and learning and assessment-driven learning) embodying a broader grouping of socio-political stances, notably the 'scholarship of teaching and learning', which has been criticised for its anti-intellectualism and conceptual confusion (Boshier 2009). What the survey reveals is the dominance of what Malcolm and Zukas (2001) have identified as the psychologised curriculum for higher education teachers. Here, psychological approaches to teaching and learning tend to predominate, resulting in a reductive and more limited conceptualisation of pedagogy as an educational 'transaction' between individual learners and teachers, and an asocial construction of the learner. While the psychology of education has always represented an important strand of educational scholarship, it comprises only a small proportion of educational research as a whole (Crozier 2007). Thus, novice higher education faculty are only being inducted into a small segment of the relevant literature, which might more broadly include the sociology of the discipline (e.g. Becher & Trowler 2001), the history of higher education in the relevant context, and the aims of higher education (Barnett 1990). Nor do such courses introduce faculty to their potential wider social role as public intellectual acting as critics, commentators and advocates of particular causes (Said 1993). Here there is a tradition, particularly in some national contexts such as France, for academics to work in trying to influence attitudes in society drawing them into contestation beyond their own immediate academic specialism. To echo Trowler and Cooper (2002), there is a need for postgraduate certificate courses to 'move beyond' the psychological approach to one which more strongly encompasses sociological persepectives.

The evidencing of practice

A fourth underpinning assumption of postgraduate certificates is their mode of assessment. Most adopt some form of 'reflective portfolio' consisting of a mixture of evidence gathering and more academically oriented engagement with the literature. Portfolios are becoming increasingly popular as a means of evidencing the professional learning of a wide range of professions (Baume & Yorke 2002). In the UK, portfolios are often organised to demonstrate explicitly compliance with national professional standards. This makes it relatively straightforward for such courses to meet accreditation requirements because their learning outcomes are identical, in effect, to the professional standards.

However, assessment by portfolio raises a number of concerns around authenticity. Portfolios often purport to provide a mechanism for professionals to connect their working practice with theory but can encourage a compliance-based approach to values requiring participants to 'evidence' the way in which they meet these expectations. This tends to result in a defensive, anodyne and sometimes inauthentic description of critical incidents, where new professionals feel they must demonstrate their commitment to particular values such as 'diversity' or institutional managerial objectives, such as the use of a prescribed university virtual learning environment. Requiring participants to scratch around for evidence of their 'competence' or 'goodness' in this way is both embarrassing and fundamentally flawed as a means of professional preparation. Even if encouraged to do so, participants will rarely reveal a great deal in such documents about their failures (or doubts) as a teacher preferring instead to focus on successes that demonstrate that they have 'met' various required standards. Such behaviour is about conforming with performative expectations rather than engaging meaningfully with the concept of professional responsibility. This raises a fundamental question about the extent to which assessing teaching development in this way can be considered authentic. The fear is that participants, who are often already skilled academic writers in their own right, may simply play the 'assessment game' (Stocks & Trevitt 2008).

The neglect of values

In the UK, the representation of evidence in reflective portfolios will often mirror the accreditation requirements of the Higher Education Academy, which identifies a series of areas of professional knowledge, areas of activity and professional values, the latter of which are expressed in the following terms (The Higher Education Academy 2010):

1   respect for individual learners;
2   commitment to incorporating the process and outcomes of relevant research, scholarship and/or professional practice;
3   commitment to development of learning communities;
4   commitment to encouraging participation in higher education, acknowledging diversity and promoting equality of opportunity;
5   commitment to continuing professional development and evaluation of practice.

In the context of the preparation of a higher education faculty, professional values are seen, in practice, as subsidiary to the areas of 'knowledge' and 'activities' which serve to define the professional capacities of a higher education teacher in the UK. Yet the portfolio method of assessment means that novice teachers are often required to evidence that they have 'met' or in some sense conform with this set of values. This can lead to statements, for example, that the novice teacher has taken particular measures to accommodate the needs of students with disabilities or sought to encourage greater integration of international students within class activities. While such initiatives are important, the requirement to report such activities in such self-justificatory terms is of dubious value. Furthermore, the teaching-only nature of postgraduate certificate programmes makes it difficult for practitioners to develop an understanding of ethics and values connected to academic practice and identity more broadly.

Ethics and values in relation to professional practice more generally are often seen to be 'covered' by reference to a written code or set of principles or values. When such codes are used as the sole basis of professional development, this tends to encourage compliance rather than an engagement with values. Moreover, the UK has adopted a set of professional values, which, while generally non-contentious, have limited specific relevance to teaching in a *higher* education environment as opposed to any other. Elsewhere I have suggested that commitments such as protecting student academic freedom or understanding the needs of adult learners would have had more resonance for many faculty members working in higher education than this set of general teaching values (Macfarlane & Ottewill 2005).

Another difficulty in depending on a written code of practice is that, while such documents invariably contain a praiseworthy set of sentiments, they are often too generalised and de-contextualised to be of much value to the practitioner. Faced with a real, often complex situation, a professional academic would rarely find much comfort or use in relying on a code of practice. In teaching professionals about ethical issues, such codes tend to be arid, prescriptive documents that take little account of the 'messy' reality of practice. An alternative approach is to think of the ethics of academic practice as connected with everyday moral 'virtues'. These refer to excellences of character that are required by professionals to carry out their role as teachers. The idea of virtue goes beyond the idea of 'skills' or techniques associated with being an effective teacher such as how to give a lecture or classroom control (Carr 2009). For Aristotle, virtues were things like courage, generosity and truthfulness (Aristotle 1906).

Virtues do not provide a step-by-step guide to action in the manner of an ethical algorithm, as they are essentially concerned with personal identity rather than action, although the assumption is that 'good' people are more likely to do 'good' things. Learning about virtue takes place on a continuous basis and is refined through experience and influenced by others, notably professional role models. This means that someone never really 'acquires' a set of virtues but spends their life striving to become a better person, a notion which fits comfortably with the modern mantra about professional self-improvement. Virtue theory also recognises that emotion and human desires play an important role in the way people behave rather than trying to describe a rational and theoretical ethical position in the manner of utilitarianism or Kantianism (van Hooft 2006).

Pedagogical phronesis

Understanding the centrality of virtues in the everyday decision making of academic faculty members is critical to engaging teaching professionals. This is not the same as simply 'going through the code of practice'. Such an approach fails to engage with the values which professionals hold as individuals, depending on their background and experience, and offers little context for meaningful discussion, which is generally accepted as essential for the teaching of ethics. Furthermore, postgraduate certificates tend to pay limited regard to the departmental or discipline context. This is the real arena in which professional values are formed, and the role of senior academics as role models is critical in shaping them.

A number of writers have identified lists of moral virtues connected with life in general and teaching more specifically. Virtues represent the mean position between extremes of behaviour. Courage, for example, lies between the extremes of cowardice and recklessness. Aristotle understood excellence of character in terms of sincerity, right ambition, modesty and liberality among other virtues. In relation to the teaching role, Hare (1993) identifies courage, humility, impartiality, open-mindedness, empathy, enthusiasm, judgement and imagination. Elsewhere, I have argued that a relatively similar set of virtues can be detected from the application of practical reason (Macfarlane 2004). These include respectfulness towards students; (proper) pride in relation to preparation for teaching; courage to innovate; fairness particularly in connection with the assessment role; restraint in taking theoretical and ideological stances; collegiality in working with colleagues and students; and openness in evaluation of our teaching.

Clearly, however, there is a risk in simply presenting learners with a 'list' of virtues. A more effective approach is to promote discussion of real life or real-to-life scenarios where fundamental virtues can be identified and applied. Yet, it is important to stress that appropriately complex professional scenarios rarely lend themselves to 'right' answers. The ultimate 'answer' is in developing teachers with the disposition to act with care and thoughtfulness in any particular situation (Pring 2001). Such scenarios should reflect ordinary, everyday situations, such as a student requesting an extension for an assignment rather than 'extreme' situations. The latter approach to case study design in the teaching of business ethics runs the risk of reinforcing attitudes that unethical practice is rife and also often fails to connect to more ordinary, everyday dilemmas.

It might not be immediately obvious though how a list of virtues, with which few would probably disagree, might translate into something real or concrete by way of professional actions and responsibilities. A way forward in understanding the link to practice is provided by Nixon (2008). He connects the virtuous dispositions of truthfulness, respect, authenticity and magnanimity in academic life with what he terms 'virtuous orientations' (Nixon 2008: 110). These relationships of virtue, as Nixon terms them, mean that the virtue of magnanimity, for example, implies the virtuous orientations of autonomy and care. He argues that the possession of a strong sense of professional identity or autonomy is a precondition for someone to be able to 'reach out' to others, 'accommodating, what is unknown, strange and radically different (Nixon 2008: 99). Similarly, he explains the virtue of authenticity as about exercising courage in relation to one's own agency and compassion in the role of 'other-as-agent'. At the heart of Nixon's analysis is the concept of capability. Here he is strongly influenced by the 'capabilities' approach advocated by Sen (1999) and Nussbaum (2000) who shows how the capabilities approach has a particular resonance for women. As Sen argues, if someone is poorly educated, or perhaps illiterate, they will never really be able to exercise fully their political freedoms since they will not enjoy the capability to participate fully. Practical wisdom or *phronesis* is an essential capability and a teacher in higher education who does not possess this quality will be less effective as a result. Without such a capability, anyone would struggle to function as a professionally responsible teacher.

Understanding what it means to teach 'with integrity' requires an integration of various virtues in professional practice; however, these might be defined or identified. Most lists of virtues though are long and demanding. This creates a challenging proposition as personality differences between individuals means that teachers tend to be naturally disposed towards some virtues but not necessarily others. Some virtues are instrumental in nature and concerned with 'getting things done', such as courage or resoluteness, while others, such as respectfulness or sensitivity, are essentially non-instrumental (Pincoffs 1986). In other words, these virtues are about forming relationships with others and the exercise of softer interpersonal skills. Practitioners with strong non-instrumental virtues, for example, might be considered to make good personal tutors. A higher education teacher needs a combination of instrumental and non-instrumental virtues, although most will be aware of their own strengths and weaknesses in achieving such a balance. Promoting self-awareness in this way is helpful in preparing practitioners for the challenges they will face in their teaching role.

Here, it might be argued that equipping higher education faculty members as 'reflective practitioners' provides an adequate means of preparing them for the moral and ethical challenges they will face as teachers. Yet, being able to reflect does not necessarily connect with action meaning that a reflective teacher is not automatically a good one (McLaughlin 1999). Despite the intuitive appeal of reflective practice, it does not quite so easily translate into establishing better or more appropriate actions as a teacher.

What is often lacking from the notion of reflective practice is judgement, or what Aristotle termed *phronesis* or practical wisdom. In many ways *phronesis* is a better means of understanding the challenges of being a teacher than reflective practice since it connects values with actions. While craft knowledge or skills, what Aristotle called *techne*, can help in responding to a limited number of specific situations, *phronesis* is about deciding what to do more broadly. It demands some conception of what it means to live a good life and, crucially, the capacity to do so (Nixon 2008). Yet, more generally, practical wisdom must be applied in handling the large range of challenges thrown up by managing a group of students. Techniques, in other words, will never be enough. Pedagogical *phronesis* is about having good judgement as a teacher. It is what ultimately makes a good teacher rather than technique or even, to some extent, knowledge, and takes a lifelong and sustained commitment. Technique and knowledge are necessary but they are not sufficient.

Relationships of virtue stretch well beyond the teaching role. They also determine how a teacher might meet a range of other professional responsibilities in relation to the research role, as a public intellectual or as an academic citizen more generally. Applying virtues to teaching does, however, sharply highlight connections with other areas of professional practice in higher education, such as research or service work. There are several virtues that are common to being a teacher and a researcher. Examples might include respectfulness towards students and research subjects, respectively, or courage to innovate in classroom practice and in tackling unfashionable or highly challenging research questions. Practitioners in higher education are also faced with difficult 'trade offs' between the extent to which they devote time to research activities and in preparing for teaching. Similarly, offering students support beyond formal teaching duties, such as via personal tutoring or assessment feedback, rarely results in reward or recognition beyond personal conscientiousness. Here, the use of time spent on such service tasks might be more rationally spent on developing research, publication or income generation opportunities. Hence, choices in the use of time as an academic demand an ethical judgement. This is about maintaining an ethical balancing exercise between meeting the needs of students and developing a career where the rewards lie principally in individual achievement for research and scholarship. Such ethical issues are not easily resolvable.

Conclusion

The assumptions and dominant principles underlying the preparation of higher education practitioners are narrowly constructed in terms of a psychologised curriculum that rarely connects with the dilemmas of teaching practice. What we have, in effect, is a curriculum for the preparation and development of academics as teachers that is too oriented towards knowledge and skills and neglects the development of their practical wisdom or pedagogical *phronesis*. The politics of postgraduate certificates is impacted by the politics of institutional ownership and often results in insufficient attention to broader aspects of the study of what it means to *be* a higher education practitioner.

What is needed is a curriculum for the preparation of new academic faculty that reflects a much broader conception of their role in all elements of practice including research, service activities as well as teaching. 'Professional responsibilities' exist in relation to each of these roles, not just teaching. In relation to the research role, it is unfortunate that ethical matters are seen as part of the increasingly bureaucratic project-approval process. This tends to militate against a genuine engagement with professional responsibilities in research. Understanding professional responsibilities in teaching in the same procedurally driven manner will only serve to undermine genuine engagement. In the age of the unbundled academic, it is important that we do not lose sight of the responsibilities that traverse the functions of academic life.

Notes

1 This phrase is intended to incorporate a range of similarly titled postgraduate programmes which aim to prepare academics predominantly for their teaching role. They will be subsequently referred to as 'postgraduate certificates'.

2 The Australian government announced their intention to close the Australian Learning and Teaching Council in January, 2011.

References

Argyris, C. & Schön, D. (1974) *Theory in Practice: Increasing Professional Effectiveness.* San Francisco: Jossey-Bass Publishers Inc.

Aristotle (1906) *The Ethics of Aristotle: the Nicomachean Ethics*, trans. G.H. Lewes. London: Walter Scott.

Barnett, R. (1990) *The Idea of a Higher Education.* Buckingham: Society for Research into Higher Education/Open University Press.

Bath, D. & Smith, C. (2004) Academic developers: an academic tribe claiming their territory in higher education. *International Journal of Academic Development* 9, 9–27.

Baume, D. & Yorke, M. (2002) The reliability of assessment by portfolio on a course to develop and accredit teachers. *Studies in Higher Education* 27(1), 7–25.

Becher, T. & Trowler, P. (2001) *Academic Tribes and Territories: Intellectual Enquiry and the Culture of Disciplines.* Buckingham: Society for Research into Higher Education/ Open University Press.

Biggs, J. (1996) Enhancing teaching through constructive alignment. *Higher Education* 32(2), 347–64.

Blackmore, P. & Blackwell, R. (2006) Strategic leadership in academic development. *Studies in Higher Education* 31, 373–87.

Boshier, P. (2009) Why is the scholarship of teaching and learning such a hard sell? *Higher Education Research and Development* 28(1), 1–15.

Boyer, E. (1990) *Scholarship Reconsidered: Priorities of the Professoriate.* Princeton, NJ: The Carnegie Foundation for the Advancement of Teaching.

Browne, J. (Chair) (2010) *Securing a Sustainable Future for Higher Education: An Independent Review of Higher Education Funding and Student Finance.* Report of the Independent Review of Higher Education Funding and Student Finance. Available at http://hereview.independent.gov.uk/hereview/report/

Carr, D. (2009) Revisiting the liberal and vocational dimensions of university education. *British Journal of Educational Studies* 57(1), 1–17.

Crozier, W.R. (2007) Capacity and methodology in university education: psychology of education as a case study. *Higher Education Review* 39(2), 25–41.

D'Andrea, V.-M. & Gosling, D. (2001) Joining the dots: re-conceptualising educational development. *Active Learning in Higher Education* 2(1), 64–80.

Gibbs, G. & Simpson, C. (2002) Does your assessment support your students' learning? *Learning and Teaching in Higher Education* 1, 3–31.

Gouldner, A.W. (1957) Cosmopolitans and locals: toward an analysis of latent social roles – I. *Administrative Science Quarterly* 2(3), 281–306.

Halsey, A.H. & Trow, M.A. (1971) *The British Academics.* London: Faber and Faber.

Hare, W. (1993) *What Makes a Good Teacher: Reflections on Some Characteristics Central to the Educational Enterprise.* London, Ontario: The Althouse Press.

The Higher Education Academy (2010) *The UK Professional Standards Framework for teaching and supporting learning in higher education.* Available at http://www.heacademy.ac.uk/ourwork/universitiesandcolleges/accreditation/ukpsf

Kandlbinder, P. & Peseta, T. (2009) Key concepts in postgraduate certificates in higher education teaching and learning in Australasia and the United Kingdom. *International Journal for Academic Development* 14(1), 19–31.

Knapper, C. (2010) Plus ça change ... educational *development past and future. New Directions for Teaching and Learning* 122, 1–5.

Land, R. (2004) *Educational Development: Discourse, Identity and Practice*. Buckingham: Society for Research into Higher Education/Open University Press.

Locke, W. (2008) *The Changing Academic Profession in the UK and Beyond*. London: Universities UK.

Macfarlane, B. (2004) *Teaching with Integrity: the Ethics of Higher Education Practice*. London: Routledge Falmer.

Macfarlane, B. (2011a) The morphing of academic practice: unbundling and the rise of the para-academic. *Higher Education Quarterly* 65(1), 59–73.

Macfarlane, B. (2011b) Prizes, pedagogic research and teaching professors: lowering the status of teaching and learning through bifurcation. *Teaching in Higher Education* 16(1), 127–130.

Macfarlane, B. & Gourlay, L. (2009) The reflection game: enacting the penitent self. *Teaching in Higher Education* 14(4), 455–9.

Macfarlane, B. & Ottewill, R. (2005) A 'special' context?: Identifying the professional values associated with teaching in higher education. *International Journal of Ethics* 4(1), 89–100.

Malcolm, J. & Zukas, M. (2001) Bridging pedagogic gaps: conceptual discontinuities in higher education. *Teaching in Higher Education* 6(1), 33–42.

Marton, F. & Säljö, R. (1976) On qualitative differences in learning: outcome and process. *British Journal of Educational Psychology* 46, 4–11.

McLaughlin, T.H. (1999) Beyond the reflective teacher. *Educational Philosophy and Theory* 31(1), 9–25.

NCIHE (National Committee of Inquiry into Higher Education) (1997) *Higher Education in the Learning Society*. London: HMSO.

Nixon, J. (2008) *Towards the Virtuous University: The Moral Bases of Academic Practice*. New York/London: Routledge.

Nussbaum, M.C. (2000) *Women and Human Development: The Capabilities Approach*. Cambridge: Cambridge University Press.

Peters, R.S. (1964) *Education as Initiation, Inaugural Lecture*. London: Harrap

Pincoffs, E. (1986) *Quandaries and Virtues: Against Reductivism in Ethics*. Kansas: University Press of Kansas.

Pring, R. (2001) The virtues and vices of an educational researcher. *Journal of Philosophy of Education* 35(3), 407–21.

Said, E. (1993) *Representations of the Intellectual*. London: Vintage.

Sen, A. (1999) *Development as Freedom*. Oxford: Oxford University Press.

Schön, D.A. (1983) *The Reflective Practitioner*. New York: Basic Books.

Sikes, P. (2006) Working in a 'new' university: in the shadow of the Research Assessment Exercise? *Studies in Higher Education* 31(5), 555–68.

Stierer, B. (2007) HE Lecturers researching HE issues: a problematic element of contemporary academic practice. Paper presented at the *Annual Conference of the Society for Research into Higher Education: Reshaping Higher Education*, 11–13 December, 2007, Brighton, UK.

Stocks, C. & Trevitt, C. (2008) Signifying authenticity: how valid is a portfolio approach to assessment? Paper presented at the *Irish Conference on Engaging Pedagogy*, Griffith College, Dublin.

Trowler, P. & Cooper, C. (2002) Teaching and learning regimes: implicit theories and recurrent practices in the enhancement of teaching and learning through educational development programmes. *Higher Education Research and Development* **21**(3), 221–40.

van Hooft, S. (2006) *Understanding Virtue Ethics*. Chesham: Acumen.

Whitty, G., Barrett, E., Barton, L., Furlong, J., Galvin, C. & Miles, S. (1992) Initial teacher education in England and Wales: a survey of current practices and concerns. *Cambridge Journal of Education* **22**(3), 293–306.

Wilson, L. (1979) *American Academics: Then and Now*. New York: Oxford University Press.

Part 2
Professional responsibility
From practice to theory

6 Risk, trust and leadership

Peter Gronn

Introduction

In an education policy environment of high-stakes school reform and accountability, it goes without saying that the risks associated with school leadership, especially for principals and headteachers, will escalate and that the need for calculated strategies of risk assessment and management is magnified significantly. Likewise, with the ever-present looming threat of public humiliation (and even dismissal) for school leaders, due to their schools' inability to attain performative targets, trust and the ability of school leaders to be able to build and sustain relationships of trust, assume an increasingly high priority. Curiously, however, until recently, discussion of risk and trust in school leadership has been limited or even rare. Apart from the recent contributions of Gronn (2009) and Thomson (2009), consideration of risk, for the most part, has been conspicuous by its absence, although in the realm of trust the picture has been slightly more encouraging, in both the UK (e.g. Bottery 2003) and the USA (e.g. Bryk & Schneider 2002). With regard to trust, this school leadership situation contrasts with that of the general leadership field, where Dirks and Skarlicki (2004: 20–1), for example, assert that trust has been acknowledged by scholars for over four decades as an important issue for leaders. On the other hand, Luhmann (1988: 94) claims that trust 'has never been a topic of mainstream sociology' and, in the social sciences more generally, Kramer (1999: 570, 581) is equally insistent that scholarly interest in trust accelerated only as recently as the 1990s, a view with which Hardin (2008: 1) broadly concurs – due mainly to the foregrounding of the benefits of trust for societies in the writings of such scholars as Putnam (1993) and Fukuyama (1995). Even so, this explanation still begs the question of why such benefits may have become of interest only in this recent period. Despite this rather patchy picture, trust and risk, as is shown below, are key elements in what it means to be a professionally responsible school leader. Knowledge of the parts they play and how they function in schools is required for enhanced understanding of the leadership of learning.

These lacunae in school leadership are odd because – quite apart from the fact that they contribute significantly to the complexity of what it means to be a leader – risk and trust are intrinsic to what it means to be able to live a life, not to mention a professional life. Thus, to take a mundane illustration, whenever as a pedestrian I cross a road in the presence of an oncoming vehicle in the distance, I am exposing myself to potential danger and taking a risk, so that if, for example, I slip over or miscalculate the gap between the driver and myself, as well as the car's speed, I am trusting that the approaching driver is not inebriated, possesses a current driving licence, is insured, is alert to my plight and has the good sense (and ability) to slow down and avoid me. Sadly, mundane or not, media reporting highlights the all-too-frequent tragedy lurking in this illustration. As is indicated in the next three examples (taken from UK media reports during 2007), however, there is very little difficulty in identifying the risks associated with decision making for school leaders. In the first, a Scottish secondary headteacher was suspended by a local authority after having allowed students to sit their Standard Grade exams in S3 rather than S4. His suspension followed a critical inspectorial report in 2006, which had taken issue with this practice, on the grounds that there was insufficient time to prepare pupils properly, and after the inspectors had described the school's curriculum as weak. The school in question had dropped its early presentation policy in December 2006, but (in the eyes of HMIE[1]) the school and the head had apparently still not made sufficient progress in implementing an action plan. While the head's suspension in this case appears to have occurred due to the inadequacy of the school's action plan, rather than the S3 presentation, he was punished for having taken that initiative and was forced to dispense with it. In accountability terms, presumably, his action was deemed to have been irresponsible.

In the second example, for which the newspaper headline read 'Battle of a wee laddie's Twix' (February 2007), a Scottish primary head, with the backing of the school's board, developed an innovative strategy with which to tackle the problem of childhood obesity and yet he too fell foul of the local authority. The head imposed a ban on children bringing sweets with them from home to school so that, whenever these were smuggled in, they were confiscated until the end of the school day at which time they were returned. In this case, in the face of some parental objections, the head was instructed by the local authority that he was not authorised to implement the measure and that he should rescind it. The photograph which accompanied the newspaper account of this episode portrayed a mother (solidly built, it has to be said) and her two wee ladies (one of them decidedly chubby looking) each standing outside the school fence and gleefully brandishing packets of sweets. A clear message of defiance was communicated by this image, as was evident in the thin-lipped smirks on the three faces and the tone and sub-text of the article, which could be surmised by readers as: Who do these people think they are? How dare they try to dictate to my children! The resulting negative impact of the head's climbdown on his authority is surely self-evident. Moreover, in this instance compliance with external control undermined the head's professional judgement. For this reason, the example raises the question of how far leaders might be prepared to go in exercising their discretion as professionals.

Finally, in October 2007, an article entitled 'Head fined after boy's fatal fall' appeared on the website of the BBC. This item reported that the headteacher and owner of a small private school in Wales was fined and ordered to pay costs – in all, about £20,000 – when, tragically, a pupil playing 'Batman' apparently jumped off a set of steps, fell and died as a result of the head injuries incurred. The child, it seems, had been permitted unsupervised access to the steps. This head's legal team commented that the judge's verdict 'would affect schools the length and breadth of the country', which was code for saying that the heavy fine would send shock waves throughout the profession. This head's personal liability is indicative of the risks associated with the exercise of his legal responsibilities, and the legal redress sought by the parents after the tragic loss of their child is testimony to their view that professional trust had been breached and that responsibility had not been exercised with due diligence.

In light of the knowledge gap highlighted at the outset, and the poignancy of these three examples, this chapter discusses some dimensions of risk and trust, both of which are integral to professional responsibility, and the interplay between the two concepts. It also shows how and why trust and risk are inherent in leadership practice; and it considers the significance and the consequences (intended and unintended) of the impact of decision-making environments for school leaders that are characterised simultaneously by high risk and low trust. Slightly more emphasis is given to trust than risk. There are two reasons for this. First, while risk and trust are conceptually distinct, exposure to risk forms part of what it means to trust – as trust 'presupposes a situation of risk' (Luhmann 1988: 95; and see Frowe 2005: 37) – and most forms of trust entail some degree of risk-taking. Thus, in rational choice theory, for example, trust is viewed as a 'calculative orientation toward risk' (Kramer 1999: 573). The second reason is because, based on the important findings of Bryk and Schneider (2002), trust-building is increasingly acknowledged to be a key capability for professionally responsible school leadership (see Gronn 2010; Robinson 2010).

Risk

Risk, according to Breakwell (2001: 2), is 'the probability of a particular adverse event occurring during a stated period of time'. The idea of probability, which denotes likelihood, introduces a calculus that, perhaps in its most extreme form, is manifest in the statistical exactitude of the work of actuaries, whose calculations and projections provide the basis for underwriting premiums for various forms of insurance against loss. Adversity entails exposure to hazard or harm. The potential for hazard, in turn, dictates the need for precaution which opens up two closely associated dimensions of risk: perception (or identification) and assessment (and evaluative notions of severity and weighting). These operations are followed by risk management (strategies of anticipation, protection, mitigation, etc.) Would that these steps in the above logical sequence were that simple, for each one entails individual and collective judgements which, because they are subjective, are prone to human error and miscalculation and are also complicated by the unpredictable intervention of accident and chance. Such a rational calculative approach to risk, of course, begs questions concerned with teachers' professional value judgements about learning, such as: What pedagogical actions or initiatives might be in the best interests of a particular child or group of children?

The opening three examples of school leaders display varying degrees of risk and hazard: loss of face and humiliation in the first two instances, perhaps, along with moral censure and sizeable immediate material loss and possible future loss of livelihood (as a school proprietor) in the third. The examples prompt the question: On a comparative scale of high to low risk, just how risky is the work of a school leader, in particular the role of a headteacher? The answer to this question is complicated by two features of occupational classification. First, some work and activities (and pastimes, for that matter) are clearly and self-evidently identifiable as inherently more risky than others. National defence force personnel, emergency service workers, mountaineers and rock-climbers, for whom potential loss of life and limb is likely, are obvious examples. Furthermore, these four instances highlight the second feature: there are people who, for a variety of motives, are voluntarily and deliberately attracted to, or choose to pursue careers in, high-risk 'edgework' (Lyng 1990). In such realms, knowingly exposing oneself to risk becomes a preferred way of life. If such high-wire edgework entails 'a clearly observable threat to one's physical or mental well-being or one's sense of an ordered existence' (Lyng 1990: 857), then for the majority of school leaders the likelihood of high vulnerability and exposure to extreme hazard has to be reasonably low. Taken at face value, then, the first two examples of school heads (certainly the first, probably the second) illustrate the potential for leadership hazard when attempting to be innovative and entrepreneurial in a school system in which, ostensibly, norms of challenge and support govern the relations between schools and local authorities. That is, on the one hand, there is the assumption that schools (while by no means fully autonomous) are encouraged to devise their own solutions to a range of student learning-related problems (i.e. they are challenged), while on the other, as units within a local authority jurisdiction, they have access to a range of advice, personnel, services and resources to assist them in fostering learning improvement (i.e. they are supported). From the first two examples, however, the likely lesson to be drawn by fellow and potential heads is: be risk averse; strike out on your own and you are likely to be hung out to dry. In short, the dark side of the experience of schools being left to their own devices in making decisions is, in some cases, to risk the experience of abandonment. It is small wonder, then, to take another leadership-related example, that when they select their senior personnel, the pressures on schools to play safe (by choosing from within, rather than without, dependable, groomed and known candidates) are often strong (see Gronn & Lacey 2006: 116–19) – the triumph, it would seem, of prudence over hazard.

What about a historical perspective: is reasoning about risk a distinctively modern phenomenon and are there grounds for claiming that contemporary societies may be inherently riskier than their pre-modern forebears? Scholarly opinion on these questions remains divided. For Luhmann (1988: 97–9), as a way of framing expectations about contingent and unfamiliar events, 'risk' entered European discourse only as recently as the invention of the printing press and the diffusion of literacy, and its discursive passage was facilitated by the freedom of choice afforded by the emerging doctrine of liberalism. The argument about the greater intrusiveness of risk as part of modernisation – much of which is owed to the unforeseen consequences of scientific discoveries and a technological legacy – originated with Beck (1992). It attains its apogee in claims about the need for reflexive, prudential and responsible behaviour by individual subjects. In the absence of 'compelling measures of risk in earlier times and today', however, Hardin (2008: 28), for one, is wary about such thinking, which he views as a tendency towards golden age reasoning.

Trust

The link between risk and trust is a perception of vulnerability, which is 'derived from individuals' uncertainty regarding the motives, intentions and prospective actions of others on whom they depend' (Kramer 1999: 571). Considered in relation to Luhmann's (1988) distinctions between familiarity, confidence and trust, the significance of this claim becomes clear. When Luhmann says that an individual is able to take for granted the realm of the familiar, he means that she or he has little or no reason to experience any event or thing as surprising or unexpected. When confronted by unfamiliar circumstances or contingencies, however, the frame of mind with which that same individual responds may be one of either confidence or trustfulness. While Luhmann's attempted conceptual delineation between these two modes of attributing self-assurance is thinly drawn, his distinction turns on the perception of risk (and the experience of vulnerability): 'if you do not consider alternatives (every morning you leave the house without a weapon!), you are in a situation of confidence' (Luhmann 1988: 97; and see Dasgupta 1998: 32, note 2). Seemingly, if we are confident then we have hope. In the event that a person has weighed the alternatives, however, a feeling of want of confidence in another person or an institution has probably provided grounds for deeming her, him or it to be a risk and consequently unworthy of trust. Here, the relevance of Hardin's (2006: 28) suggestion about the pointlessness of trusting a person also becomes clear: it makes no sense to say that you trust someone 'unless there is some risk of your suffering a loss if that someone does not fulfil your trust after you have acted on that trust to their initial benefit'. In this respect, as the three initial examples of school heads indicate, ongoing responsible relations among working professionals always retain a degree of vulnerability.

Trust and trustworthiness (the belief that persons or institutions merit trust because they are expected to act in beneficial, or at least non-detrimental, ways; Gambetta 1988: 217) are anchored in reciprocity – a norm which has been defined as 'a mutually contingent exchange of benefits between two or more units' (Gouldner 1960: 164). When this norm is internalised by both of the parties to an exchange or transaction, it 'obliges the one who has first received a benefit to repay it at some time' – a claim, incidentally which endorses Luhmann's point about confidence as a reasonable expectation. Why? By providing realistic grounds for 'the one who first parts with his valuables, that he will be repaid', with the consequence of 'less hesitancy in being the first and a greater facility with which the exchange and the social relation can get underway' (Gouldner 1960: 177). On the other hand, there is a range of modes of reciprocation and by no means all of these fulfil the complementary equivalence expressed by Hardin (2006: 8) as: 'I do something for you because I trust you to reciprocate'. Thus, in exchanges there may be disparities between recipients and donors, for example, and differences between those who exercise rights and those who fulfil obligations, along with varying degrees of dependence and indebtedness experienced between the parties. Exchanges take a number of forms. Two of the most common are professional service provision and market transactions, with a contrast between the two usually drawn along the following lines: the relationship of professional service provider and client is characterised as one of *credit emptor* (let the person trust), as distinct from the relationship between buyers and sellers as one of *caveat emptor* (let the person beware). The contractual flipside of *credit emptor* is that a professional person or group (i.e. the entrusted party) reciprocates by utilising their skills and knowledge in service of the interests of a client. Both modes of exchange, however, may be either explicitly or implicitly contractual, with trust being 'central to all transactions' (Dasgupta 1988: 49) including markets.

One should be wary of discussing 'trust' in an undifferentiated manner, for there are, *inter alia*, different sources of trust and bases on which people trust one another (see Tschannen-Moran & Hoy 2000: 558–64), different levels and degrees to which they trust one another (Gambetta 1988: 218–20, 232), different types of trust, and varying ways of measuring the incidence of trust and distrust. With respect to types and degrees of trust, time and distance are key distinguishing criteria. One trust type is what Meyerson, Weick and Kramer (1996) refer to as swift (or fast) trust. Specifically, temporary or short life-span work groups and organisations are what these authors have in mind (as when experts are assembled to work on a project), although there are numerous other more mundane examples. These include travelling in a taxi, eating fast food or banking over the Internet. In each instance, if I as a consumer act or decide quickly – because I would not normally undertake a comprehensive risk assessment in such everyday instances – I expose myself to potential hazard. What if the taxi driver has limited road-handling ability and equally poor geographical knowledge? Suppose the fast-food ingredients are not fresh and nutritious? What happens if the personal account details I transmit over the internet are not adequately protected? In each of these instances of fast reliance on other people, one of the few guarantees on which I might be able to rely is reputation. This is because in numerous daily exchanges there is a strong incentive for the parties to safeguard each other's interests (Gambetta 1988: 222). As Hardin (2006: 19, original emphasis) notes, in the three-part relation he proposes between a Truster, a Trusted and a matter at stake, my trust (as the Truster) depends not on the interests of the Trusted, but on 'whether my own interests are *encapsulated in the interests of the Trusted*, that is, on whether the Trusted counts my interests as partly his or her own interests'. A (perhaps, the) key factor which provides an incentive for trust in fast (and not so fast) trust situations is the reputation of the Trusted. Because a reputation is valuable and hard won, there is likely to be an incentive to behave in ways that sustain, rather than prejudice, that reputation (Gambetta 1988: 233; Hardin 2006: 24). Professional reputations, in particular, stand or fall on such relational trust.

Assurance additional to that provided by reputations may come from accumulated information on the part of the Truster. Indeed, if the contractual parties to an exchange were to be 'blessed with an unlimited computational ability to map out all possible contingencies enforceable in contracts' (Gambetta 1988: 218), there would be no need for trust. On the other hand, the potential advantage conferred by increased knowledge is by no means unequivocal. While on the one hand, the acquisition of relevant knowledge may help reduce dependence of the Truster on the Trusted, the logic of relations with the providers of professional services tends to point in the opposite direction. After all, my limited capacity to acquire the necessary esoteric knowledge (e.g. medical, legal) that comprises the defining attribute of professional occupations is usually the very factor that prompts me to seek their advice in the first place. Moreover, that specialist knowledge provides the foundation on which those professional groups' claims to moral legitimacy rest and is the basis on which I put my trust in them (Frowe 2005: 43) – although reputation can also work to my advantage here: if, having judged my previous experience with a professional person to be adverse, in future I may choose to engage another person.

In contrast with swift trust, the development of trust in organisational leaders may provide an instance of slow trust. As with risk, there is a perceptual and attributional basis to trust determination by a Truster. For this reason, the referents to whom employees as Trusters turn when framing their trust judgements are crucial. Direct engagement with a variety of hierarchically positioned and informally dispersed leaders is likely to be one significant perceptual influence. When the exigencies of distance or location preclude this option, however, or when leadership access may be restricted, then of equal (or possibly even more) importance is the mediating influence provided by co-workers. Such influence is likely to be paramount in cases in which colleagues depend on one another to complete their work (Dirks & Skarlicki 2004: 32). Failing either of these options, one may to be able to put one's trust in a role, rather than in a person. In this connection, Meyerson, Weick and Kramer (1996: 181) invoke a distinction between role-based interaction and person-based interaction to hypothesise that, at least in the case of swift trust temporary systems, the former interaction mode facilitates more rapid development of trust than does the latter. Apart from the question of whether it makes any sense to try to relate to an impersonal role, regardless of the person who inhabits it, there are two other factors that complicate leadership relations generally in enduring organisational arrangements: these are the Švejk problem (see later) and the control paradox (Miller 2004), with both compounded in schools by circumstances of external adversity or hostility (Staw, Sandelands & Dutton 1981).

Trusting school leaders

Central to the definition of professional work, and the element which differentiates a professional worker from an employee who carries out an instruction, is the concept of discretionary power. Frowe (2005: 44) defines this as the exercise of 'personal judgment about what courses of action are appropriate in particular situations' and says that it arises from the knowledge base that underpins professional practice. As advocates of professional school leadership capability point out (e.g. Gronn 2010) that knowledge base includes an ethical dimension. This claim to some degree of autonomy is the very antithesis of circumstances, as Fox (1974: 19) refers to them, of 'trained obedience to specific external controls'. In this connection, it is a moot point whether, with the adoption by governments of regimes of inspectorial accountability and audit – which are designed to limit severely or even undermine teachers' exercise of discretionary power (Frowe 2005: 51) – teaching can ever hope to be thought of as a profession, particularly when these selfsame governments continue to insist on instructing teachers on what and how to teach.[2]

In an early investigation of trust in the workplace, Fox (1974) compared the dynamics of trustful and distrustful relations in high and low discretion forms of employment. In contrast with the hallmarks of low discretion employment, which takes the form of control in close supervisory relationships and the achievement of standardised performance through compliance with imposed bureaucratic rules, the defining attributes of high discretion employment are more likely to comprise investment of personal identity through moral commitment to collective ends and purposes, self-discipline, a degree of decision-making latitude, and relations based around problem-solving (Fox 1974: 25–37). The reality of high discretionary employment, however, need not necessarily be aligned with mutually experienced high trust relations, nor need low discretionary employment equate with low trust relations. Indeed, while both low discretion–low trust and high discretion–high trust combinations may be historically common industrial relations patterns, sets of circumstances which combine high discretion with low trust, and low discretion with high trust, are possible. Fox (1974: 97) construed the critical determinant of the commensurability of level of trust with form of work to be the question of whether hierarchically positioned superiors and subordinates feel constrained to acquiesce in the imposition of the other party's definition of their work roles. Implicit in this idea of acquiescence, of course, be it constrained or consensually bestowed, is a relationship of bargaining, and therefore of power.

These distinctions between high and low trust go some way to help explicate the difficulties faced by leaders in schools, especially when the external policy environment may be conducive to low trust. This is the case, for example, when, as part of their role responsibilities for learning improvement, they endeavour to build collective decision-making trust among teachers who have been socialised to expect to exercise a significant degree of discretionary power in relation to teaching and learning. On this latter point, there is no need simply to take Frowe's (2005) word for the eclipse of teachers' discretionary power and their feelings of low trust, because Daly's (2009) recent survey of US teachers in schools identified under federal legislation as 'program improvement' (PI) schools, for example, provides some solid empirical evidence. PI status means that 'a series of progressive sanctions is set into motion, ultimately resulting in the reconstitution of the school, in its restructuring, or in the state's takeover' (Daly 2009: 169). The data highlight the greater extent to which PI teachers perceive evidence of threat-rigidity within their own schools along with diminished feelings of trust, when compared with the responses of a control group sample of non-PI teachers (Daly 2009: 191). Threat-rigidity refers to the detrimental effects (e.g. reduced information flow and processing, increased anxiety and behavioural rigidity, loss of cohesion) that typically result from perceived external threats (Staw, Sandelands & Dutton 1981: 516–20). More generally, it has been argued that the coerciveness implicit in threat-rigidity is counterproductive: with the burden of risk-sharing being increasingly shouldered by employees, coercion and the threat of sanctions stimulating resentment, and diverting resources away from the completion of tasks and into surveillance and information gathering, and weakening incentives to cooperate (Gambetta 1988: 220–1). In particular, coercion and threatened sanctions are not satisfactory answers to the Švejk problem and they fail to deal with the control paradox.

By the Švejk problem,[3] Miller (2004: 101) means the inclination employees may have to work to rule when completing tasks either singly or collectively. Because of the inherent limitations of employment contracts (due to their inability to specify through mechanical elicitation all the requirements of tasks in advance of their completion), the adoption by employees of a strategy of minimal compliance with rules and orders risks bringing organisations to a standstill. Awareness of this possibility no doubt accounts in part for the interest among management theorists in such recent phenomena as psychological contracts in the workplace and organisational citizenship behaviour. Švejkism is a form of disengagement and antithesis of the exercise of professional judgement. In that sense, such judgemental minimalism may be considered the antithesis of what it means to act professionally. On the other hand, Švejkism also represents a weakening of commitment, and for that reason it can be understood as a response to feeling devalued and being treated unprofessionally by superiors or leaders. Mere articulation of this Švejk possibility, however, and the potential impact of collective working to rule, should not be taken as evidence of the likelihood of its occurrence. This is because professional workers (especially those among the helping professions such as teachers) are probably morally disinclined to be thorough-going Švejks. Were they to respond, Švejk-like, to circumstances which they experience as uncongenial or even punitive, then their strategising is likely to be low level. Thus, while active resistance may be one possible line of response to threats of negative sanction, a more likely strategy by people who enter teaching with a strong motivation to serve the interest of their student, is to disengage by refusing to embrace change, retreating to a psychological comfort zone and being unwilling to apply for leadership roles. Whatever the response, evidence of the incidence of some degree of Švejkism in a school offers a useful indicator that overall levels of trust may be veering towards the low end of a high–low continuum. What, then, might a school leader do to foster a high trust work environment?

As part of their role accountability, school leaders are required to monitor their staff. While such monitoring may take a number of forms (e.g. observation of performance, annual appraisal) and may vary in the degree of its tightness or looseness, the requirement to monitor has to be reconciled with the need to secure cooperation. After all, the idea that organisations are cooperative systems and that it is the job of administrators to find ways of inducing employees to cooperate was the core of the argument advanced by Barnard (1982 [1938]) in his classic book, *The Functions of the Executive*. If Miller's (2004: 121) articulation of successful monitoring as part the control paradox is broadly correct (i.e. that, as part of what he views as a gift exchange, compliance-inclined Švejks might be motivated to work harder with less monitoring), then his claim has important implications for securing cooperation and sustaining leadership trust. What is at stake here is perceptions of monitoring and their purpose, and their impact on trust relations. If Miller's representation of reciprocity as a gift exchange is correct, then monitoring perceived as heavy (e.g. regular surveillance or high-stakes inspection), as distinct from forms viewed as light-touch (e.g. annual performance reviews) may be more likely to induce mere compliance (or even forms of Švejkism). To be able to shift the basis of the negotiated equilibrium from one of constrained to voluntary acquiescence, however, especially in the face of ill-supportive external circumstances, requires calculated strategies of trust-building. Such negotiation is both possible and legitimate. Much is likely to depend on a leader's ability to display benevolence, reliability, competence, honesty and openness (Tschannen-Moran 2001: 314), as well as teachers being able to predict a leader's behaviour, to be assured of the consistency of her or his responses and to be able to point to evidence of a leader's integrity (Tschannen-Moran & Hoy, 2000: 571). And yet, if Gambetta (1988: 223) is correct in asserting that securing cooperative behaviour 'does not depend on trust alone', then the achievement of voluntary compliance may also require a willingness to be vulnerable as part of calculated risk-taking by leaders. In return for teachers providing evidence of high-quality teaching practice, this could enshrine a combination of capacity-building measures, including: regular internal talent spotting and the creation of opportunities for young and inexperienced teachers to exercise senior level leadership; the periodic rotation of a range of portfolio responsibilities to broaden colleagues' decision-making experiences and skills bases; generous provision of learning outcome targeted professional development; the re-direction of budgetary resources to permit the recruitment of learning support staff to work intensively with teachers; intensive mentoring and coaching; and the offer of remuneration above pay-scale base rates.[4]

But what is the likelihood of the achievement of such a gift exchange? Empirical endorsement of the battery of initiatives just listed is found in Cosner's (2009) investigation of 11 US principals' successful strategies for the promotion of collegial trust. Strong support is also found in Tschannen-Moran's (2009) survey of well over 2000 teachers in 80 US middle schools. Her data corroborate the earlier findings of Bryk and Schneider (2002), which were derived from research in the Chicago public school system. What these two authors showed was that, when survey results on levels of trust (between teachers–teachers, teachers–parents and teachers–principals) were compared with students' results on annual standardised tests, there was a direct relationship between trust and improvement. In particular, the authors were able to demonstrate that 'much higher levels of trust, on average, were reported in schools that eventually would be categorised as academically improving than for those categorised in the nonimproving group'. Three years later these differences were found to persist, so that in the case of non-improving schools, there were still about three-quarters of them 'offering negative reports on the composite indicator of trust' in reading and mathematics (Bryk & Schneider 2002: 110). The conclusion was that 'the composite trust measure is highly predictive of school productivity trends' and that where trust was high it 'functioned as a substitute for the rigid enforcement of rules' (Bryk & Schneider 2002: 111). In Tschannen-Moran's case, she also found that where trust was high it 'functioned as a substitute for the rigid enforcement of rules' (Tschannen-Moran 2009: 239–40); that principals 'set the tone for the quality of relationships among adults in the building', such that when a culture of trust prevailed among a school's faculty, 'students may benefit as the recipients of this trust' (Tschannen-Moran 2009: 240). Equally strong endorsement of the significance of trust relations was found in Tschannen-Moran's (2001) earlier survey of nearly 900 teachers in 45 US elementary schools, which measured the contribution of various forms of interpersonal collaboration in fostering trust in principals. One lesson here for leadership would seem to be that, if and when professionals trust one another, and are trusted, the potential scope for discretionary judgement expands and the incentives to accept responsibility are strengthened.

Conclusion

Echoing the observations with which this chapter commenced, as recently as a decade ago, Tschannen-Moran and Hoy (2000: 547) noted how educational researchers knew 'very little about the nature of trusting relationships in a school once the children arrive and the doors are shut'. Hopefully, the discussion in this chapter will have demonstrated how that description is no longer accurate, so much so that cumulative knowledge findings have begun to build over the intervening decade. In relation to professional leadership responsibility and its role in school improvement, for example, the centrality of trust and the fostering of trust are no longer merely 'on the agenda', so to speak, but have begun to deliver robust, tangible returns in respect of adding value by fostering and sustaining processes conducive to student learning. Moreover, hopefully it has also been demonstrated that such gains are possible even when external circumstances are ill-conducive to the genesis and maintenance of trust. Likewise with risk: if only as a result of recognition of its close relationship with trust, there are now signs of increased acknowledgement of risk as a phenomenon intrinsic to leadership and awareness of what it means for leaders to be able to take risks, and with some sense of the consequences. While there may still be much to learn about both concepts, if I may paraphrase Gambetta (1988): for leaders to trust in or bank on trust, is a risk that is well worth taking. To risk trust is likely to enhance professional responsibility, and requires courage rather than defensiveness.

Notes

1 Her Majesty's Inspectorate in Education.
2 This occurred in the 2010 general election in the UK, when at least one of the political parties promoted a particular approach as the preferred way to teach reading in primary schools.
3 Derived from the novel *The Good Soldier Švejk*, by Jaroslav Hašek, in which the main character, Private Josef Švejk, succeeds in constantly frustrating the orders of his superiors by interpreting them literally.
4 As observed, for example, in one of the schools participating in the University of Cambridge 'Spotlighting School Autonomy' project.

References

Barnard, C.I. (1982[1938]) *The Functions of the Executive*. Cambridge, MA: Harvard University Press.

Beck, U. (1992) *Risk Society*. London: Sage.

Bottery, M. (2003) The management and mismanagement of trust. *Educational Management, Administration & Leadership* 31(3), 245–61.

Breakwell, G.M. (2007) *The Psychology of Risk*. Cambridge: Cambridge University Press.

Bryk, A.S. & Schneider, B. (2002) *Trust in Schools: A Core Resource for Improvement*. New York: Russell Sage Foundation.

Cosner, S. (2009) Building organizational capacity through trust. *Educational Administration Quarterly* 45(2), 248–91.

Daly, A.J. (2009) Rigid response in an age of accountability: the potential of leadership and trust. *Educational Administration Quarterly* 45(2), 168–216.

Daspugta, P. (1988) Trust as a commodity. in Gambetta, D. (ed.) *Trust: Making and Breaking Cooperative Relations*. pp. 49–72. Oxford: Basil Blackwell,

Dirks, K.T. & Skarlicki, D.P. (2004) Trust in leaders: Existing research and emerging issues. In Kramer, R.M. and Cook, S. (eds) *Trust and Distrust in Organizations: Dilemmas and Approaches*. pp. 21–40. New York: Sage.

Fox, A. (1974) *Beyond Contract: Work, Power and Trust Relations*. London: Faber & Faber.

Frowe, L. (2005) Professional trust. *British Journal of Educational Studies* **53**(1), 34–53.

Fukuyama, F. (1995) *Trust: The Social Virtues and the Creation of Prosperity.* Harmondsworth: Penguin.

Gambetta, D. (1988) Can we trust trust? In Gambetta, D. (ed.) *Trust: Making and Breaking Cooperative Relations.* pp. 213–37. Oxford: Basil Blackwell.

Gouldner, A.W. (1960) The norm of reciprocity: a preliminary statement. *American Sociological Review* **25**(2), 161–78.

Gronn, P. (2009) Emotional engagement with leadership. In Samier, E. and Schmidt, M. (eds) *Emotional Dimensions of Educational Administration and Leadership.* pp. 198–211. London: Routledge.

Gronn, P. (2010) Leadership: its genealogy, configuration and trajectory. *Journal of Educational Administration and History* **42**(3), 405–35.

Gronn, P. & Lacey, K. (2006) Cloning their own: aspirant principals and the school-based selection game. *Australian Journal of Education* **50**(2), 102–21.

Hardin, R. (2006) *Trust.* Cambridge: Polity Press.

Kramer, R.M. (1999) Trust and distrust in organizations: emerging perspectives, enduring questions. *Annual Review of Psychology* **50**, 569–98.

Luhmann, N. (1988) Familiarity, confidence, trust: problems and alternatives. In Gambetta, D. (ed.) *Trust: Making and Breaking Cooperative Relations.* pp. 94–106. Oxford: Basil Blackwell.

Lyng, S. (1990) Edgework: a social psychological analysis of voluntary risk taking. *American Journal of Sociology* **95**(4), 851–86.

Meyerson, D., Weick, K.E. & Kramer, R.M. (1996) Swift trust and temporary groups. In Kramer, R.M. and Tyler, T.R. (eds) *Trust in Organizations.* pp. 166–95. Thousand Oaks: Sage.

Miller, G.J. (2004) Monitoring, rules, and the control paradox: can the good soldier Švejk be trusted? In Kramer, R.M. and Tyler, T.R. (eds) *Trust in Organizations.* pp. 99–126. Thousand Oaks: Sage.

Putman, R.D. (1993) *Making Democracy Work: Civic Traditions in Modern Italy.* Princeton, NJ: Princeton University Press.

Robinson, V.M.J. (2010) From instructional leadership to leadership capabilities: empirical findings and methodological challenges. *Leadership and Policy in Schools* **9**(1): 1–26.

Staw, B.M., Sandelands, L.E. & Dutton, J.E. (1981) Threat-rigidity effects in organizational behavior: a multi-level analysis. *Administrative Science Quarterly* **26**(4), 501–24.

Thomson, P. (2009) *School Leadership: Heads on the Block.* Abingdon, Oxford: Routledge.

Tschannen-Moran, M. (2001) Collaboration and the need for trust. *Journal of Educational Administration* **39**(4), 308–31.

Tschannen-Moran, M. (2009) Fostering teacher professionalism in schools: the role of leadership orientation and trust. *Educational Administration Quarterly* **45**(2), 217–47.

Tschannen-Moran, M. & Hoy, W.K. (2000) A multidisciplinary analysis of the nature, meaning, and measurement of trust. *American Educational Research Journal* **70**(4), 547–93.

7 Teaching professional responsibility

A clash of approaches in both legal and nursing education

Molly Sutphen and William M. Sullivan

Introduction

Professions represent more than an organised deployment of expertise to solve problems. Such a view would illustrate a purely technical, narrow understanding of professionalism, one that misses the public and ethical significance of professionals and what they do. Professions at their best are organised around values of integrity in work and responsible service to the community. Professional values are vital to highly effective organisations in fields ranging from law to engineering to education and health care. Indeed, the provision of expert services with a high degree of integrity and social responsibility is the fundamental promise of civic professionalism. Moreover, professions provide not only competent service but, for practitioners, a sense of calling to work that confers dignity and recognition because it supports valuable common purposes and social solidarity. With their collegial forms of organisation, professions continue to provide modern societies with inspiration for work lives that diverge from those driven primarily by market or managerial imperatives (Sullivan 2005).[1]

Authentic, civic professional values are still vital, serving many of the most respected members of the professional communities as sources of moral identity and motivations to competence and responsible service. However, today many fields, including both law and the health professions of nursing and medicine, find themselves under increased pressure from market competition and bureaucratic governance that threatens a collegiality and sense of purpose for many professionals. In both the US and in Europe, professionals are routinely subjected to the criteria of return on investment capital and technical 'efficiency' at the expense of professional norms of expertise and collegial purposes. These trends threaten to deform authentic professionalism in a narrowly technical, even economic, direction. This can mean that the goods internal to a practice – service to society, integrity or other such characteristics that professionals agree upon as touchstones of their profession – may be compromised for economic ends or in the name of narrow goals of efficiency imposed by employers. This stance may not only undermine the morale of professionals, robbing them of their autonomy as practitioners in a profession but it can have negative effects on the wellbeing of those whom professionals serve (Gardner, Csikszentmihalyi & Damon 2001).[2]

These trends raise important questions for professional education. How can the institutions in which future professionals are prepared for practice best respond to the challenges presented to civic professionalism by these destructive tendencies? Given the importance of what is at stake – which is nothing less than the future of professionalism – what sorts of approaches to developing professional responsibility are likely to prove effective in equipping students to enter the challenging new worlds of professional practice as effective champions of the traditions of service and responsibility that define their professions?

Our aim is to argue for the importance of focusing through all the phases of preparation for a profession upon the formation of identity and to nurture a sense of professional purpose, especially when explicitly addressing issues of ethics and professional responsibility. To this end, we start with a discussion of a series of studies of professional education in the US undertaken over the past decade by the Carnegie Foundation for the Advancement of Teaching. We draw on these studies to contrast two ways of teaching professional responsibility that are currently employed in American law schools and programmes in nursing education. One approach, widespread in law though also present in nursing, emphasises an understanding of how to follow the 'rules of the game'. Students are taught professional responsibility as only rules they must abide by, which can limit strategic thinking and decision making. The other, opposing, approach focuses upon professional responsibility as a dimension of the formation of professional identity. In this, students learn professional responsibility through an approach we have dubbed teaching the 'integrity of the practice'. In doing so, teachers teach the rules of practice as well as alert students to the responsibilities they have to their profession, society and individuals, including colleagues and patients or clients. They help students notice and then make decisions about all sorts of ethical questions or quandries that are inherent to any practice situation, instead of just following rules.

We start with a brief overview of the Carnegie Foundation studies on the preparation for the professions. Then, drawing on data collected over the course of the Carnegie Foundation National Nursing Education Study, we provide a detailed description of the two approaches – teaching the integrity of practice and teaching the rules of the game – in nursing education and then contrast them with a sketch of how they are used in legal education.

The Carnegie Foundation's comparative studies of professional preparation

Over the course of the first decade of the century, the Carnegie Foundation for the Advancement of Teaching has studied the educational practices used to prepare lawyers, engineers, clergy, nurses and physicians through a programme of comparative studies called the Preparation for the Professions Program (Benner et al. 2010; Cooke, Irby & O'Brien 2010; Foster et al. 2005; Sheppard et al. 2008; Sullivan et al. 2007).

These studies conducted extensive inquiry into the curricula, pedagogies and assessment used to support learning in each profession. This research has given rise to a common framework for understanding and comparing the different approaches to education across these diverse professional fields. Despite differences, each profession addresses three dimensions of professional training, with different emphases and approaches. The three dimensions, designated formative 'apprenticeships' to underscore their ability to shape the thinking and dispositions of students who enter the professions, are: first, intellectual or academic training to learn the academic knowledge base and the capacity to think in ways that are important to the profession; second, a skill-based apprenticeship of practice: the craft know-how that marks expert practitioners of the domain; and, third, an apprenticeship to the ethical standards, social roles and responsibilities of the profession, grounded in the profession's fundamental purposes (Sullivan 2005: 207–10).

This framework categorises the student's experience of professional education into three forms of professional apprenticeship. These reflect contending emphases within all professional education. They thereby make possible comparison across the different fields. Although professional education in all fields includes some attention to all three apprenticeships – the knowledge base, the complex skills of practice and the ethical standards, social roles and responsibilities – each field frames the central features of the apprenticeships differently, and each uses different strategies for accomplishing them. American legal education, for example, emphasises the first, or intellectual, apprenticeship, taught in classrooms through a distinctive style of 'Socratic' pedagogy, almost exclusively during the 3 years of graduate legal education. Nursing, by contrast, has always emphasised the second apprenticeship of practice, centring much of its preparation on the clinical experience, although it includes substantial emphasis upon the first apprenticeship in the form of instruction in the disciplinary knowledge important to the profession.

Not surprisingly, the way legal education has tended to approach the teaching of professional responsibility reflects its inherited pattern of emphasis on the first apprenticeship, with didactic classroom instruction the typical 'default' choice. Nursing, with its heritage of rich clinical instruction might be expected to approach the issue of professional responsibility from the angle of providing students with mentored entry into the practice. However, as we shall see, this is not always the case. For in all fields, the first, intellectual apprenticeship holds a certain primacy because of its superior prestige within academic settings. This presents a major challenge to achieving what the Carnegie studies call the third apprenticeship, the development of a sense of being a professional who has internalised the purposes and standards of the profession.

The third apprenticeship describes those efforts in professional preparation that strive to bring together expert knowledge and skill with ethical purpose and motivation for responsible use of professional powers. The way issues of ethical deportment and professionalism are approached in the education of lawyers and nurses is critically important for encouraging students to take seriously the development of both an understanding of and a mature commitment to responsible professional practice. This is the educational goal of great importance if students are to be prepared for the ethically challenging practice environments they are likely to encounter.

We turn now to two approaches to teaching professional responsibility in nursing observed over the course of the Carnegie National Nursing Education Study.

Teaching the rules of nursing

Nursing students must learn to practise in often large and always complex institutions of health care, where they must care for patients as well as meet the administrative requirements of the health care agency and many government agencies. To teach students to practise within the requirements of these agencies, faculty members can end up narrowing their focus to a set of skills to meet administrative needs and a bounded set of rules or regulations. At risk are other dimensions of practice, including professional responsibility and civic duty. An example of teaching in a maternal/child nursing course at one school illustrates some of these tensions and the pitfalls of narrowing professional responsibility to a set of rules and skills.

In one course on maternal/child nursing observed in conducting research for the Carnegie National Nursing Education Study, the teacher devoted an entire class – all 4 hours of the class meeting – to teaching nursing diagnosis, which is a form of documentation designed to serve as a standardised communication tool for nurses.[3] The class consisted of the teacher showing dozens of PowerPoint slides with a nursing diagnosis on each one and asking what words were missing, or whether there were too many words. Except for the occasional aside by the teacher describing in a few words a clinical situation she had seen or a brief recitation by a student about a diagnosis in a patient she had seen, there was little discussion about patients in particular situations and the appropriate nursing care for that situation. Instead, the class discussion resembled an oral multiple-choice examination on the rules for writing a correct nursing diagnosis. The teacher concentrated her teaching almost exclusively in only one of the apprenticeships, that of skilled know-how – the skill of writing a nursing diagnosis – though she devoted brief periods to teaching in the apprenticeship for nursing knowledge. As for teaching professional responsibility, the teacher missed many opportunities to discuss, for example, such matters as trust or truth telling in documentation.

There was a distinct legal cast to this class, where the teacher emphasised the rules of a hospital and the laws nurses were subject to, emphasising the language that would hold up in a court of law. Another teacher on the team responsible for delivering the course echoed this legal stance when she answered the question of what she considered was essential for the preparation of nurses in this course:

> Well, they're beginning to understand the role of the nurse in terms of legal responsibilities. The charting [and] documentation responsibilities and the liabilities, the necessary safety issues, medication administration, all those kind of foundations are going to be built on as they go on and if they have to develop more and more independence later on. There's a lot of emphasis on safety.[4]

This teacher touches on areas covered in the observed class that are of course crucial to nursing: nurses do have considerable legal responsibilities; must know the appropriate charting documentation; have liabilities; be knowledgeable about medical administration; and well-versed in patient safety for the sake of their patients and for the sake of the bureaucratic governance of health care institutions. Granted these are professional responsibilities, but what is striking is the emphasis on safety, liabilities and legal responsibilities, all of which meet the administrative needs of a health care agency. What is missing is any specific reference to the practice of maternal/child nursing. Missing are patients and their families or a nurse's colleagues and the professional responsibilities that arise in the course of working with colleagues who are caring for patients

The students of these teachers also felt there was much missing. When interviewed about the class, one highlighted what she saw as her school's over-emphasis on skills – such as the skill of writing a nursing diagnosis – and too little attention to other domains of nursing practice: 'It's a dual reality ... We're learning what we don't know, the intricacies of being a nurse, but they don't teach us how deal with the doctor, how to deal with the nurses, interpersonal conflicts, and actually being a nurse is more holistic than the skill sets that we're developing'. For this student, there is more to nursing than the sum of the skills she has learned. She bemoans what she believes she has missed from her teachers, ticking off examples of where she needs guidance in professional responsibility.

Several other students gave further evidence of missed opportunities to teach professional responsibility and they show what effect it has on their formation as nurses. According to several students interviewed from the class observed, they were not allowed to give women shots of Depo-Provera, an injection for birth control, because their nursing instructors had decided that the doctors involved had not given patients enough information about possible side-effects of the injections. One student commented:

> our nursing instructors, well they wouldn't tell us, 'Don't say anything', and they wouldn't say, 'Tell 'em'. They just said, 'You're not going to give depo shots', and it was kind of left at that.

And another elaborated:

> But it was kind of like an unspoken understanding that, 'Just don't say anything. You're students. Just don't start any trouble with the hospital deal, with the liability of it. And just kind of ride below the radar'. That's the impression that I felt like we were given from the instructors. That's not what they said, but.

As this student relates, it seems far better to learn to fly under the radar rather than raise questions about informed consent. When pressed about feeling the need 'to ride below the radar' and whether a nurse should take a different tack, the student answered:

> Once you have your own license, you have your independence. I think you could make more decisions that may not be the accepted norm, and get away, not get away with it, but feel more comfortable doing so than you do when you're a student. When you're a student, ... I'm not trying to speak for everybody, but I wouldn't want to stir up anything. I would have never said anything about the depo, one way or the other, because I wouldn't want it to get [anyone] in trouble. Even if I thought it was better for the patient, as a student I wouldn't have said anything.

The student's comment speaks to the low position of a student in the overall hierarchy of practice in that clinical setting as well as to being ill-prepared for coping with the power differences in that hierarchy.

The message this and the other students reported was they should not raise questions about ethical concerns, in part because they had so little power, and they should fear questions that might 'stir up anything'. The students understood equally the message from their instructors that they needed to keep silent and their professional responsibility to inform patients of possible side-effects from a medical intervention, yet none reported that they upheld that responsibility. None reported even raising questions with their instructors about the ethics of informed consent in this particular situation, although it is possible that a student in the class did. The value of silence about the alleged wrongdoing and keeping silent about the actions of doctors trump the responsibility of bearing witness to wrongdoing. These students acknowledge that professional norms – here of being able to raise the possibility that a patient has not been informed of possible side-effects – are sacrificed in the name of expediency for nurse educators unwilling to allow students to question an entrenched hierarchy of physicians and nurses.

Teaching for the integrity of the practice in nursing

Given that students need to learn how to practise in agencies that are large bureaucracies with entrenched hierarchies and often constrained by economic pressures, how can students be taught differently? One approach is not to separate the apprenticeships, as faculty did in the maternal/child course, and instead integrate them throughout all of their teaching. This can best be accomplished when teachers and students alike narrow the gap between clinical and classroom education. Thus, regardless of the setting, teachers ask students to draw on their nursing knowledge, skilled know-how and professional responsibility in the course of their care of patients or discussions about caring for patients.

Simulation is one approach that allows teachers to integrate the apprenticeships and can provide the opportunity students to further reflect on experiences they have had in the clinical setting or create new opportunities for experiential learning. Likewise, when a teacher provides cases or narrative accounts of patients in order to demonstrate how a nurse might reason about a patient's care, situation and experience across time. One student explained how her teachers deepen her experiential learning through such discussions:

> Our instructors encourage us to make connections between the classroom materials and the clinical experiences. They help increase our knowledge and facilitate our learning by helping us think through any tough situations with our patients and their diagnosis. They also encourage our peers to become involved, which increases the brainstorming and enriches the experience that each student gets to have.

This last point speaks to an important element in this approach to teaching professional responsibility: students hear from the teacher and each other about what they might do or what areas they may need to investigate. Both simulation and case studies provide the means for the teacher and students to reason out loud about the clinical, social and nursing details of a case. By posing different scenarios or starting with 'what if' questions (such as 'what if the patient begins to slur their words?' or 'What if the patient loses the ability to speak?), the teacher then can help all the students imagine the myriad possibilities of how that patient's clinical trajectory, situation and nursing may change in the future. The development of a clinical imagination or the ability to imagine many possible scenarios helps students anticipate situations and better prepare for them. Practice is never predetermined – indeed it is underdetermined – which means that nurses be able to interpret situations, use their judgement to decide how to act, and have a facile ability to anticipate many possible outcomes for their patients (Benner et al. 2010: 143–53). As the student who worried that she was not being taught how to cope with interpersonal conflicts shows, students cannot just master a set of skills or regulations and follow them doggedly. The skills she learned are a poor substitute for what the practice demands.

In the following part we discuss legal education, where teaching the 'rules of the game' is more common than in nursing education.

Law schools: 'legal ethics without ethics'

Everywhere in the US, the bar examination admits students to practise tests students on their knowledge of the legal profession's ethical code, an elaborate set of regulations, based in case law, known as the Model Rules. Law schools accordingly require students to take one or more courses with titles of legal ethics or professional responsibility. These courses introduce students to ethical issues basic to their future practice lives, including how to recognise ethical issues involved in the confidentiality of the attorney–client relationship, conflicts of interest and conflicts among obligations, such as those to promote clients' interests versus those to tell the truth. This is important knowledge. The form of such courses, commonly called 'law of lawyering' courses, focuses on legal cases of violations of the Model Rules. Teachers often approach this material, and students work with the cases, in much the way they do other areas of case law: they apply techniques of analytical reasoning to parse out in which instances and for what reasons courts have held practitioners in violation of the Rules and how they have been sanctioned.

As far as it goes, this approach is useful and obviously of immediate practical value to students facing examination on the Model Rules. The drawback, as critics of the approach such as the legal educator Deborah Rhode have pointed out, is that such teaching can – and often does – separate these legal issues from questions of right and wrong.[5] Since they restrict attention to the analysis of cases and code, the relation of the rules to the complex pressures of actual practice gets pushed into the background. This is a disadvantage of teaching professional responsibility primarily through the first, academic apprenticeship. Too often, the result is that, by default, professional responsibility becomes defined privately as modes of practice that safely avoid rule violations and sanctions: 'ethics without the ethics'.[6] The larger unintended consequence is that legal ethics and professional responsibility courses can convey the notion that ethical considerations matter chiefly as potential threats to individual success as a lawyer rather than as aspects intrinsic to the very identity and responsibility of the lawyer as professional.

Exploring professional identities in law school

However, the 'law of lawyering' is not the only form of teaching professional responsibility in American law schools. For the past decade and more, there has been increasing recognition of a need to present ethics in a more positive light, indeed to infuse ethical thinking 'pervasively' into courses. Equally important, there have been significant developments of a whole alternative approach to teaching legal ethics, one that recognises the need to connect students' thinking about right and wrong, pressing them to think about how their obligations as lawyers intersect with their wider responsibilities as citizens and as persons.

For example, consider a course entitled 'Advanced legal ethics' developed for students who will soon graduate. Students read and discuss not only case law, but also essays on legal practice and education, as well as professions more broadly. Practitioners and other professionals participate in the course as speakers and students are required to undertake research projects designed to provide insight into a variety of dimensions of practice, including forming connections with practitioners, as a way of reflecting on the complex demands, ethical and personal, of legal practice. Results from such experiments suggest that students find such courses help them to reclaim and clarify their sense of purpose in seeking a career in the law (Sullivan 2005: 154–6). These courses build upon the traditional strength of the legal academy in the domain of the first apprenticeship, but they reach more deeply than is typical into the formative dimension of the second and third apprenticeships in order to expand and enrich the students' grasp of the actual nature of legal practice. By bringing together analytical acuity and wide-ranging intellectual perspectives on the practice of law with personal encounters with the demanding nature of practice situations seen as sites for responsible engagement, this approach models as well as probes the meaning of responsibility in the legal profession.

Such an approach directly links the academic approach typical of law school with experience of the second apprenticeship of practice. By drawing students' attention to the often conflicting pressures that beset contemporary practice of the law, the aim is to provide students with coaching in anticipating such problems and then working out strategies for addressing them. The goal of this approach to teaching ethics can rightly be called achieving integrity in practice.

Conclusion: widening the pedagogical lens towards reflection

We have contrasted two approaches to teaching in two fields: teaching the 'rules of the game' and teaching integrity of a practice in nursing and legal education. In the first, more limited approach, the goal of teaching is to make students aware of what will catch them up or get them into trouble in their practice. In many law schools, for example, courses on 'professional responsibility' present ethics as 'the law of lawyering', where the purpose is to show 'how far one can go' in aggressively pursuing client interests. Similarly in nursing schools, topics that have a moral valence, such as documentation and charting of nursing practice, are often taught as administrative regulations and rules. In such approaches teachers teach the practice as though it were only an instrument to a particular end, such as winning cases or protecting the professional from legal challenge. By teaching with such an approach, teachers miss opportunities to point out those goods intrinsic to a practice and their intrinsic motivations. In the example we gave of the nursing students, the goods of and motivations for the practice were not even mentioned: truth telling; how a record should be a nuanced understanding of what a patient is experiencing; or even the whole point of documentation which is first to keep an accurate record of a patient's situation in order to better care for them over time. Such an approach, as we argue, is too limited to foster a deep engagement with responsible practice and does not help students develop the habit of imagining different outcomes and thus preparing for them.

Compared with teaching the 'rules of the game', teaching the 'integrity of the practice' involves a different stance on the part of the teacher. The point is to help students capitalise on the experiential learning they undertake in simulated or actual practice situations. These experiences help students anticipate how possible outcomes, contingencies or situations that might arise in their practice and may influence any or all of those for whom they are responsible. The overall aim, therefore, is to enable students to see in their mind's eye how a situation might unfold. Helping students decide what they will need in several domains of practice as a case or situation unfolds points towards the need to stimulate students towards developing their imagination to envision the many different possible situations, outcomes or difficulties that might emerge from their actions.

The approach to teaching professional responsibility that emphasises the 'integrity of practice' grows directly out of a concern for forming professional identity and the formation of practitioners who will be engaged with improving their practice throughout their career. Its emphasis is upon gradual student engagement with the full ethical complexities of practice compared to the artificial simplifications typical of the 'rules of the game' approach. While more common in nursing than in legal education, both fields provide valuable examples of the richer, more developed, 'integrity of practice' emphasis.

The examples of teaching for the integrity of legal and nursing practice share common characteristics: teaching and learning in all three apprenticeships occurs; students and teachers reason out loud about possible consequences or concerns; and teachers guide students in imagining possible situations and then help them anticipate what they will need as a situation unfolds. As students become lawyers or nurses, part of their formation includes learning to see possibilities or obstacles in situations that a lay person would not perceive (Benner et al. 2010:166–67). They must also be able to conceive of situations in their widest context, where documentation is not merely a routine nurses undertake to satisfy administrative needs and regulations, but a testament to their integrity and truth telling.

At the least, nursing and law students must also have the opportunity to discuss the impact of all parts of their practice, from the daily and seemingly mundane practices of keeping track of papers to the more dramatic and life-changing impact they may have on individual patients or clients and society more generally. It is through the experience of reflection that they may be able to see their practice as a whole and their education as preparation for upholding the values of integrity in work and responsible service to the public, even as they come to see what these will mean in their day-to-day practice.

Notes

1 The contrast between technical and civic professionalism, as away of understanding and organising professional practice, is developed in detail in Sullivan (2005).

2 Gardner, Csikszentmihalyi & Damon (2001) provide an analysis of the effects of such developments, as well as strategies for countering such 'misalignment' between the guiding purposes of the professions and the organisational contexts in which they work.
3 Developed by the organisation formerly known as the North American Nursing Diagnosis Association (NANDA), nursing diagnosis is supposed to describe a patient's situation according to a nurse's clinical judgement, using a formal statement of the diagnosis, aetiology and the indicators for the nurse's clinical judgement. See http://www.nanda.org/ (accessed 19 October 2010).
4 All quotations in this part are from interviews conducted by the research team from the Carnegie Foundation National Nursing Education Study with informants from one of the nine schools studied.
5 Deborah L. Rhode has written extensively on ethical instruction in law schools. See, for example, Rhode (2001).
6 For elaboration and development of these points, see Sullivan et al. (2007: 148–54).

References

Benner, P., Sutphen, M., Leonard, V. & Day, L. (2010) *Educating Nurses: A Call for Radical Transformation*. San Francisco: Jossey-Bass Publishers Inc.

Cooke, M., Irby, D. & O'Brien, B. (2010) *Educating Physicians: A Call for Reform of Medical School and Residency*. San Francisco: Jossey-Bass Publishers Inc.

Foster, C.R., Dahill, L., Golemon, L. & Tolentino, B.W. (2005) *Educating Clergy: Teaching Practices and Pastoral Imagination*. San Francisco: Jossey-Bass Publishers Inc.

Gardner, H. Csikszentmihalyi, M. & Damon, W. (2001) *Good Work: When Excellence and Ethics Meet*. New York: Basic Books.

Rhode, D. (2001) The professional responsibilities of professions. *Journal of Legal Education* 51, 158–66.

Sheppard, S., Macatangay, K., Colby, A. & Sullivan, W. (2008) *Educating Engineers: Theory, Practice, and Imagination*. San Francisco: Jossey-Bass Publishers Inc.

Sullivan, W.M. (2005) *Work and Integrity: The Crisis and Promise of Professionalism in America*, 2nd edn. San Francisco: Jossey-Bass Publishers Inc.

Sullivan, W.M., Colby, A., Wegner, J., Bond, L. & Shulman, L. (2007) *Educating Lawyers: Preparation for the Profession of Law*. San Francisco: Jossey-Bass Publishers Inc.

8 Professional responsibility

Persistent commitment, perpetual vulnerability?

Geert Kelchtermans

Introduction

Over the past two decades, education and schooling have fallen under the spell of performativity, which Ball defines as:

> a technology, a culture and a mode of regulation that employs judgements, comparisons and displays as means of incentive, control, attrition and change – based on rewards and sanctions (both material and symbolic). The performances (of individual subjects or organisations) serve as measures of productivity or output, or displays of 'quality', or 'moments' of promotion or inspection.
>
> (Ball 2003: 216)

Schools have to prove that they 'perform' well and this, in essence, has come to mean: showing that they produce the desired learning outcomes in their students. Effectiveness and efficiency have become the main or even the only valid criteria to evaluate education. It is beyond the scope of this chapter to discuss extensively the pervasive impact the performativity discourse (and the way it has been materialised in policy rules, quality control procedures, evaluation tools, etc.) has on schools and teachers (see Englund & Solbrekke, Chapter 4; Kelchtermans 2007). One aspect of that impact was that education and schooling, as well as the relationships they involve, have been fundamentally framed in economic terms, with schools and teachers being conceived of as the producers on the one hand and students/parents the consumers on the other. This economic, contractual relationship is reflected in a particular sense of the concept 'accountability' that has widely spread in educational discourse and practices: teachers and schools have to account for their professional practice by showing that they indeed produced the outcomes that were demanded by the predefined goals or standards. It appears that accountability in this economic and technical sense has come to dominate or even replace the meaning of the traditional educational concept of responsibility.

In this chapter I explore what has been lost sight of, what has become irrelevant, negligible or neglected since accountability has filled up the conceptual space of responsibility. Furthermore, I will link this to an idea of teacher professionalism, arguing that we need to maintain or restore a broader idea of what makes teachers 'professional', beyond the technical knowledge and skills that 'work' to produce certain learning outcomes in students.

My favourite teacher

To build and begin my argument, I draw on a content analysis of a column that ran between 2006 and 2008 on a biweekly basis in one of the main Belgian newspapers, *De Standaard*, and was called 'My favourite teacher'.[1] Publicly well-known people (e.g. artists, radio or television hosts, politicians, clergy) were asked to pay a brief tribute to their favourite teacher by describing him or her and to elaborate on the reasons for their appreciation. What made him/her their favourite teacher? Of course, these autobiographical evaluations are done in retrospect and reflect the author's actual ideas about himself or herself rather than provide historical facts on characteristics of effective teaching. But they also reveal what is considered to be at stake in an educational relationship that is seen as valuable, meaningful, powerful, influential and – in a broad sense of the word – effective. In other words, the data in these articles help us to document and understand what it may mean if teachers take up responsibility in education rather than be accountable for particular student outcomes.

In the answers to the question what has made somebody a favourite teacher, I distinguish three broad sets of reasons, although in the individual cases they were often found in combination.

Passion for the subject

Firstly, the favourite teachers were people with a strong personality, who took a stance, and stood for something (Bullough 2008). Quite often, that 'something' was their subject discipline: they were well-informed and knowledgeable about their subject as well as passionate and fascinated by it. They had something to say about it and cared about the subject, as much as they cared about contaminating their students with their own passion and interest. Metaphorically speaking, one could say they were really 'somebody', not just 'anybody' (Kelchtermans & Hamilton 2004), while at the same time 'incarnating' a 'body' of knowledge and engaged in a relationship with their students through that knowledge and because of it. They felt responsible for bringing about knowledge of and interest in their subject in the students. However, whether the latter was achieved, was not so much a question of instrumental pedagogical effectiveness, but rather had to do with the fact that the subject had become intertwined with the person they were. In that sense the word incarnation is to be understood almost literally: they represented history, French, mathematics, Latin … 'in the flesh'. Some examples are the traditional, old school, bourgeois-looking literature teacher impressed and puzzled his students by getting tears in his eyes when reading aloud particular poems and did not try to hide his emotions, since they were part of what literature meant to him (2008-06-09). Or the later radio host, who recalls her Latin teacher, a man who was passionate about and dedicated to the subject:

> mythology of the gods of antiquity, but I have also taken up a genuine interest in the language as such, and pursued the pleasure of unravelling complicated texts... (2007-09-17).

Or a university administrator (with a degree in engineering) who recalls one of his former professors:

> thanks to him the laws of thermodynamics really came to life. (...) he emphasised problem solving. Yet, he argued that in order to perfectly solve a problem one would need endless amounts of time and money and since that is not possible, problems can never be solved 100%. In an imperfect world, an engineer needs to keep that in mind, he argued. So if a particular solution to a problem is not socially relevant, it is not a good solution, even if, from a theoretical point of view, it is the best one .... (2006-09-25)

This last example illustrates how a personal stance towards one's subject and its meaning for society makes the difference. By taking a stance, explicitly demonstrating and living up to particular values and ideas, those teachers implicitly (or explicitly) invited their students to join them in their choices or at least reflect on them and develop a personal stance themselves. As such, those teachers were not just accountable, but demonstrated a much broader, holistic view of responsibility for their subject and their students.

Another example comes from a later writer-philosopher who recalls one of his professors arguing that:

> a philosopher must tell the truth, even if that brings him to the stake. That was really a revelation. Until then the main message in schools had been to walk within the lines and now I was challenged to do the opposite, to think critically (2006-12-04).

Making a difference in students' lives

A second characteristic of favourite teachers was the teachers' ambition to actually achieve something in the students' lives. Essential for this category is the dedication and the willingness to have impact, to make a difference. The goals and aims for the dedication were in a sense predefined (e.g. by the curriculum), but never exclusively. Those teachers developed an openness and sensitivity for the unforeseen, the accidental and managed to develop a sense of seizing the opportunities when they showed up. Their dedication to achieve results went beyond what was prescribed or even predictable. In the retrospective accounts describing them, their former students primarily used the verbs stimulating, encouraging, inviting, challenging, questioning, etc.

In their pedagogy, those teachers often deviated from the well-trodden paths, creating opportunities for exploration and learning that contained some risks and had no guarantee for success. Their actual teaching reflected courage, since they were pushing the boundaries of what was assumed proper teaching in a manner consistent which what they thought as fit, even if it exposed them to the risk of being questioned or criticised by others. For example, having students make a movie instead of the traditional assignments for French (bringing in all the organisational, technical, social dynamics on top of the strictly linguistic issues) (2006-09-11). Yet, sometimes they managed to use their – even traditional – pedagogy in ways that worked differently. The later mayor of an important Flemish city recalls a literacy teacher 'who made us see things we didn't see before' (2006-12-18). Or similarly, a later copywriter and publicity agent, refers to the revelation he felt when his former literacy teacher once stopped the class when reading the sentence in a novel by Multatuli:

> 'And man created God to his likeness' and asked 'what does that mean? Did the author just make a mistake or did he do it on purpose?' I can still recall that moment vividly, because I thought it was incredible: by twisting around two words, the author had created multiple layers in the text. I'd never seen or understood anything like that... (2008-06-09).

Commitment in an educational relationship

The final characteristic, which applied to most cases, was a particular quality of the educational relationship. In these cases the teacher engaged in that relationship as a person and this personal commitment made all the difference. These are the examples of teachers who related to individual students in ways that nurtured their self-esteem, built self-confidence and stimulated them to make authentic choices, even if that was against the mainstream values or the particular hopes the parents had for their son or daughter. For example, a later novelist recalls the teacher who helped her with mathematics, a subject she neither liked, nor was particularly good at:

> Her patience made all the difference. She was passionate about her subject, but at the same time had a very broad interest in other things. Basically she was a caring and wise woman. That was crucial for me, because I didn't feel very happy in High School. She also understood that someone who had problems with 'her' subject, could still be intelligent. That's why I didn't feel like a loser with her and that definitely made studying a lot easier... (2006-11-06).

By building the relationship with the student on respect and dignity, this teacher had managed to enhance the student's self-esteem. This was not necessarily a predefined outcome, nor linked to a particular instrumental intervention at some point in time, but rather a constitutive characteristic of her relating to her students.

Even this relatively superficial analysis of the newspaper column shows that there is a lot more at stake in an educational relationship than what can be captured by accountability or performativity. Obviously what these former customers of education valued in retrospect is not simply the effectiveness with which predefined goals had been achieved. They do not hold their former teacher accountable as clients do towards a firm or an entrepreneur about a product or service they had delivered. Framing the experience in terms of economical accountability implies that we blind ourselves to what is really at stake and important. It is obvious that the former students have valued the outcomes of the process, yet those outcomes are more complex than a list of specific cognitive or affective objectives that have been achieved. Of course, one cannot state that the idea of effectiveness in education (in the sense of achieving valued objectives) is without legitimacy. The concern to bring all students to a proper mastery level in reading, writing, mathematical understanding, sciences, foreign languages, and so on remains a justified educational purpose and a key task of the professionals involved in schooling, even if only for reasons of social justice. Yet, when conceived of as merely or primarily instrumental 'means to an end' relationships, the interactions and dynamics between teachers and students are deprived of much of their educational meaning. There is definitely more to responsible teaching than the technical production of outcomes.

Professional responsibility

Key to understanding the interactions in teaching and learning (as well as their actual meaningfulness in retrospect) is the fact that the educational relationship involves and develops between human beings. Because educational relationships involve different human beings, they are not economical or instrumental but ethical in nature (Fenstermacher 1990). In education the teacher or educator engages in a relation of care with the student/child (Noddings 1984). And it is this relationship of moral commitment, personal engagement and care that is captured in the traditional concept of responsibility.

The etymological roots of responsibility encompass the idea of answering somebody (cf. in French the word *répondre*: to answer). Yet, this answering is more than recognising a particular need and fixing it by providing the right answer or solution. Rather, it puts teachers in a receptive or even passive position: even before enacting whatever purposeful pedagogical project to bring about changes in their students, teachers find themselves facing students that have been entrusted to them. Through their mere presence, those students incarnate a call for care and attention. Attention, openness, sensitivity towards the students precedes intentions and goal-driven actions by the teacher. Responsibility is taken up as an answer in a relationship the teacher finds himself or herself in as if she or he owed it to the students. And this is not in the sense of paying off some kind of debt or returning a loan, but rather feeling morally compelled or obliged. She or he engages to answer a call, a question, a need that is explicitly or implicitly sent out by the students. It is the presence of the students that makes the teacher a teacher, rather than what she or he does to the student. In that sense, teachers are exposed to their students.

Understanding educational responsibility this way implies that teachers' professionalism and professional duties ('responsibilities') are not mere technical (instrumental 'means to an end' connections to produce a particular result), but also moral (ethical). They involve value-laden choices in the attempt to do justice to the pupil that has been entrusted to one's care (and therefore one's responsibility). Furthermore, this doing justice is not something that is clearly defined and identical for all students, but on the contrary needs to be identified and decided upon time and time again in the myriad of day-to-day interactions in schools.

Engaging in this relationship is not without risks, since one always engages as a person, as somebody (Kelchtermans & Hamilton 2004). Teachers bring themselves in and expose themselves, and this often triggers intense emotions (see e.g. Nias 1996). Apart from the deeply personal character of the involvement, the risk in teachers' professional commitment (or responsible action) stems from the fact that one can never fully predict what will happen, what the results will be or whether they will be desired or not. Students are not passive recipients of education, but are by definition actively involved in an educational relationship, making sense of what they see and experience, and this eventually makes them learn. This was illustrated in the different categories of favourite teachers. What the students' perception, appreciation and learning will look like or entail can never be fully predicted. And teachers have to live with that. This brings me to the idea of vulnerability as a structural characteristic of teaching.

Vulnerability as a structural characteristic of teaching

The issue of 'teacher vulnerability' arose from my work on teachers' professional biographies over the last two decades. The different studies involved repeated life history interviews to collect extensive narrative accounts of teachers' own career experiences (Kelchtermans 1993, 1996, 2005, 2009). All these narratives revealed critical incidents (Measor 1985), demonstrating that teachers often felt powerless, threatened, questioned by others (principal, parents) without being able to defend themselves properly, etc. Yet, linked to it were also accounts of not being in full control of the processes and tasks they felt responsible for as teachers. Borrowing a term from Blase (1988), I referred to this dimension in teachers' job experience as 'vulnerability' (Kelchtermans 1996, 2005, 2008, 2009).

On the basis of the career stories, I concluded that the

> basic structure in vulnerability is always one of feeling that one's professional identity and moral integrity, as part of being 'a proper teacher', are

questioned and that valued workplace conditions are thereby threatened or lost. Coping with this vulnerability therefore implies political actions aimed at (re)gaining the social recognition of one's professional self and restoring the necessary workplace conditions for good job performance.

(Kelchtermans 1996: 319)

Vulnerability in that sense is not so much to be understood as an emotional state or experience (although the experience of being vulnerable definitely triggers intense emotions), but as a structural or inherent characteristic of the teaching job.

Vulnerability in this sense helps us to better understand the meaning of responsibility in education. Put differently, the actual meaning and content of educational responsibility is closely connected to vulnerability as an inherent characteristic of teachers' work.

There are at least three elements that make up vulnerability in teaching. A first element lies in the fact that teachers are not in full control of the conditions they have to work in (e.g. regulations, quality control systems, policy demands). Teachers' working conditions are to a large extent imposed on them: they work within particular legal frameworks and regulations, in a particular school, with a particular infrastructure, population of students, composition of staff. Furthermore, teachers and students most often do not choose each other, they simply find themselves being assigned to each other. Teachers taking up professional responsibility do so in conditions that they have not chosen or even may disagree with.

Secondly, vulnerability refers to the experience that, only to a very limited degree, teachers can prove their effectiveness by claiming that pupils' results directly follow from their actions. All teachers acknowledge that student outcomes are only partially determined by their teaching. Equally or sometimes even more decisive are personal factors (motivation, perseverance, etc.) or social factors, that are often very hard to influence, change or control. It is not only difficult to prove the extent to which a teacher can claim credit for students' results, but it is equally difficult to determine or predict when a result of teachers' actions possibly might occur and become visible at all. Very often teachers are not in a position to witness when the seed of their efforts finds fertile ground to develop. Many of the aforementioned favourite teachers will probably only have found out about the impact they had had when they read the newspaper in which the column was printed. All too often students never tell or have the chance to tell a former teacher that she or he had been so significant in their lives. That is why quality control systems, based only or primarily on students' test scores (in line with performativity and accountability), are felt by so many teachers to be an unfair evaluation of their work, doing injustice to the essential characteristics of their job and working conditions, as well as the responsibility that goes with it.

Finally, and this is the most fundamental meaning of the concept of 'vulnerability', teachers cannot but make dozens of decisions about when and how to act in order to support students' development and learning, but they don't have a firm ground on which to base their decisions. Even when the justification for teachers' decisions can be explicitly stated, with reference to a certain idea (argument) of good education in general and good education for this pupil here and now, in particular, that judgement and decision can always be challenged or questioned (Kelchtermans 1996). Several examples of the favourite teachers were people who had the courage to make thoughtful decisions on curriculum and pedagogy that deviated from what was usual or even what was imposed. It is the thoughtfulness, commitment and responsibility that turned these teachers into favourites, yet their actions and choices remained vulnerable to criticism and questions.

Responsible vulnerability and vulnerable responsibility

Without the different forms of vulnerability, teaching could be a strictly technical job of establishing the appropriate 'means to an end' relationships, monitoring processes and registering the outcomes. If there were a fully transparent understanding of the particular working conditions and their influence on students' learning, if the specific impact of teachers' actions could be identified exactly and if there were certainty regarding the best actions in every situation, then teachers would not feel vulnerable. Nor would they need to take up responsibility, but could rather just confine themselves to performing their roles technically. An extreme illustration of this ambition and belief can be seen in the so-called 'scripted curricula', where teachers are supposed to literally follow and enact the detailed prescriptions in the script-like course materials to produce the desired outcomes, which will eventually be evaluated by standardised testing (Kelchtermans 2007). In this system teachers do not take up responsibility or, more precisely, they are forbidden to do so, because they are not considered professional or qualified enough to judge particular educational situations and act on them properly. Achinstein and Ogawa (2006), for example, have documented and analysed the dramatic and disastrous effect these working conditions have on the motivation, commitment and sense of professional identity of new teachers, who tried to enact their professional duties from an educational responsibility perspective.

Therefore if we do not want to go down this path of attempting to eliminate both vulnerability and responsibility by reducing teaching to purely technical knowledge and skills production – assuming that it would be possible at all and ignoring the devastating emotional and intellectual consequences for both students and teachers – then we will have to face the complexity of this vulnerability and responsibility as being two sides of the same coin. They presuppose and constitute each other. It is only because of the complexities, uncertainties, multidimensionality and unpredictability characterising educational situations that the need for careful judgement, interpersonal commitment and eventually responsible action emerges. If one is questioned on these judgements and decisions, one cannot account for them in a technical, economical way, but only answer, take a stance, argue, make explicit one's considerations and, by doing that, take up responsibility.

In education, vulnerability and responsibility are fundamental conditions teachers find themselves in. Vulnerability therefore implies the inevitable element of passivity and exposure that characterises teaching. It is not something one makes happen. Although in most educational research, training and analysis the emphasis is on acting, planning and designing, it needs to be acknowledged that there is also a passive dimension of undergoing surprise, puzzlement and powerlessness, as well as the uncertainty of never knowing for sure whether one's actions and attempts were educationally right.

In line with this reasoning, there are two basic attitudes to cope with vulnerability: enduring and embracing it. Since vulnerability is inherently part of education and teaching, one has to live with it. Endurance is a more negative stance. It demands mental strength, stamina, dedication and courage. Yet, a more positive – and possibly even more realistic – attitude would be to understand vulnerability as having intrinsic educational value and to embrace it. It is precisely in the enactment of committed judging and caring that a kind of educational space opens up in the relationship between teachers and students. In that relationship not everything is fixed, roles and positions are not fully defined or prescribed, and careful judgement can be wrong, etc. But exactly for that reason, new and unforeseen developments become possible and can start to unfold.

A consequence of this reasoning is that professional and responsible teaching implies living with a fundamental *paradox*: on the one hand one has to engage in knowledgeable, thoughtful, purposeful action in order to achieve predefined goals in the best way possible, while on the other hand this committed and purposeful action allows things to happen, events to literally take place, educationally meaningful experiences to appear for students, without them being envisaged. To put it differently, in teaching there is at the same time always both more and less happening than one had planned for. Acknowledging this is not an alibi for lousy lesson plans, careless interventions or technically bad teaching performance. On the contrary, only carefully prepared and professionally enacted teaching allows one to be alert for and aware of the educationally meaningful that happens unexpectedly.

The passivity that characterises the educational relationship is thus also a positive reality and as such something that needs to be *embraced*. It is because not everything can be planned for in the educational relationship that authentic interactions between people can take place. Furthermore, that interaction can have deeply meaningful educational value just because it 'happened', it 'took place'. Again, the stories of the favourite teachers amply demonstrate this.

As a consequence, when thinking about responsibility in teaching, this dimension of passivity, of exposure and vulnerability should be acknowledged and thoughtfully conceptualised. Being a responsible teacher implies that one incarnates the paradox of taking a stance, speaking out on normative ideas and values and, in line with this, designing educational conditions that are intended to help students learn and develop their individual capacities and identities as much as possible, while at the same time knowing that this purposeful action does not fully capture, direct or predict what will happen.

Responsibility and reflection

The idea that embracing vulnerability demands alertness and openness to the unforeseen has consequences for the idea of reflectivity as a core characteristic of teachers' professionalism. Although nowadays one will hardly find anyone in education who denies the importance of reflection, the actual reflective practices in teaching and teacher education are most often dominated by instrumental concerns: finding the appropriate means to achieve the desired ends. Through reflective analysis one strives to acquire knowledge and skills in order to improve the effectiveness of one's teaching or the reflection is driven by a concern for technical problem-solving. This thinking (and the research based on it) remains embedded in what Schön (1983) called a rational, instrumental and technical approach to reflection. A lot of research aimed at the development of 'knowledge for practice' (Cochran-Smith & Lytle 1999) also echoes this idea. Of course, technical issues are neither irrelevant nor illegitimate. Teachers do need a solid knowledge base and the mastery of a broad range of teaching skills (Korthagen 2001). Teachers live and work under the pressure of day-to-day practice. They must maintain the smooth functioning of the classroom and the school. This pressures them to ask for simple, quick-fix solutions, because schooling has to go on (Hopkins 2001).

Yet, my analysis of vulnerability and responsibility indicates that teachers as reflective practitioners (Schön 1983) need to broaden and deepen the content of their reflection, beyond the technical and instrumental concerns that most often dominate. This broad and deep reflection acknowledges and encompasses the moral, political and emotional dimensions in teaching and educational relationships (Hargreaves 1995; Kelchtermans 2009).

Teaching is 'a profoundly moral activity' (Fenstermacher 1990: 132): firstly, because it contributes to the creation and recreation of future generations; and secondly, because teachers constantly make small but *morally* significant judgements in their interactions with children, parents and one another (Hargreaves 1995: 14). What appears to be technical decisions on teaching strategies, on the use of instructional materials or on interventions for classroom management, are moral decisions in their consequences (Nias 1996; Oser, Dick & Patry 1992). The moral dimension in teaching fundamentally refers to the question of what is educationally in the best interest of the students and thus what one should do as a teacher. There is, however, no agreement about what is best for the students and what actions might best achieve that purpose. It follows that responsible teaching implies taking up the moral duty of thoughtfully trying to do justice to the students' needs.

Yet, issues and dilemmas in teaching that appear moral at first sight, often hide questions about power and interests. Who benefits from what I/we as a teacher/teachers do? In whose interests are we working? Who is actually determining the what and why questions in my/our work? These are not only matters of values and norms, but refer to the *political* dimension of teaching and teacher development. *Power* and *interests* are words that still carry a strong taboo for many teachers and teacher educators. Many teachers feel uncomfortable when these issues are raised as integral elements of their work. The political is often still considered as something improper, marginal, just an unfortunate aspect of the particular working conditions or at best a peripheral phenomenon that does not really belong to teaching. This denial makes it more difficult for teachers to see the intrinsically political nature of their work and its fundamental relevance to their effectiveness, job satisfaction and the quality of learning opportunities for their pupils (Kelchtermans 1996).

These political issues go beyond the level of the individual teacher and his/her group of students (class). They also include context issues at the level of the school as an organisation (for instance, relationship with heads of department, management staff) and at more central levels of educational policy. Discussions about values, goals and teaching procedures can, in fact, carry a strong political agenda that is sometimes disguised as technical or moral.

Finally, over the last 15 years, it has become widely accepted that *emotions* play a central part in teaching. As with the political, it is still often hard for teachers to see that emotions are not simply a matter of personality or idiosyncratic teaching style, but constitute a fundamental aspect of the job. Emotions have to be acknowledged as part of educational practices, driven by moral commitment and care for others for whom one feels responsible (see e.g. Schütz & Zembylas 2009). They reflect teachers' experience of their job situation and commitment and as such constitute one dimension of teachers' professionalism (Hargreaves 1995; Kelchtermans & Hamilton 2004; Nias 1996). Acting responsibly implies getting personally involved and thus being 'emotionally non-indifferent', as Filipp (1990) phrased it using a double negation to stress the positive affirmation.

A concept of reflection in responsible teaching does not only need to be broad or wide in its content but also deep enough. By this depth I mean that it should move beyond the level of action to the level of underlying beliefs, ideas, knowledge, value choices and norms. In other words, it implies reflection on what I have called the *personal interpretative framework* (Kelchtermans 1993, 2009), a set of cognitions or mental representations that operates as a lens through which teachers look at their job, give meaning to it and act in it. This framework thus guides their interpretations and actions in particular situations (context), but, at the same time, it is also modified by and results from these meaningful interactions (sense-making) within that context. As such it is both a condition for and a result of the professional interactions, and represents the – always preliminary – 'mental sediment' of teachers' learning and developing over time. Since teaching always involves the investment of oneself as a person (see also the examples of the favourite teachers), the interpretative framework encompasses, on the one hand, one's professional self-understanding: the normative, evaluative and motivational ideas that constitute one's sense of self at a particular point in time. On the other hand, the framework entails the professional know-how or subjective educational theory: one's knowledge and beliefs about how one can make teaching work (Kelchtermans 2009).

Taking up responsibility as a teacher demands that one critically examines time and time again one's deeply held ideas and beliefs about teaching and being a teacher, because these elements in the personal interpretative framework constitute the very basis for professional judgements and decision making. Furthermore, it is only by making this underlying framework the object of reflection that teachers' thinking becomes genuinely *critical*. By examining and unmasking the moral and political agendas in the work context and their impact on one's self-understanding, one's thinking and actions, reflection can open up perspectives for empowerment and for re-establishing the conditions for teaching and learning that allow for pedagogical processes to take place in which people can regain the authorship of their selves (see also Zembylas 2003a, 2003b).

Conclusion

To sum up, I want to repeat that thinking about teaching from the concept of responsibility is a more appropriate way to capture the full picture of education (compared to an accountability approach), yet it does complicate the idea of teachers' work lives and teacher professionalism. Apart from being knowledge-able about one's subject, responsibility implies that teachers commit themselves personally and by doing that become emotionally and morally involved with their students' lives. This commitment implies judging situations, taking a stance, making choices and acting, yet without ever knowing for sure that one's actions will work out as planned or without ever being certain that one has done the right thing. Educational decisions can always be questioned; there is no uncontested ground on which to base one's judgments and actions. This vulnerability that goes with the responsibility in teaching is inherent and even constitutive for the educational relationship. It needs to be endured and embraced. A carefully developed attitude and skill of broad and deep reflection can help teachers to enact responsible teaching but, again, without taking away the inevitable uncertainty, vulnerability and risk that characterise their work. Professional responsibility in teaching demands persistent commitment while living with the perpetual vulnerability. These conditions, however challenging and difficult, are at the same time the ingredients because of which teachers are remembered by their former students as being the 'favourite'.

Note

1 In the rest of the chapter, I shall cite from these articles by mentioning the date on which it appeared in the newspaper. For further information about the newspaper, I refer the reader to the website: www.destandaard.be

References

Achinstein, B. & Ogawa, R. (2006) (In)Fidelity: what the resistance of new teachers reveals about professional principles and prescriptive educational policies. *Harvard Educational Review* 26(1), 30–63.

Ball, S.J. (2003) The teacher's soul and the terrors of performativity. *Journal of Education Policy* 18(2), 215–28.

Blase, J. (1988) The everyday political perspectives of teachers: vulnerability and conservatism. *International Journal of Qualitative Studies in Education* 1, 125–42.

Bullough, R. (2008) The writing of teachers' lives: where personal troubles and social issues meet. *Teacher Education Quarterly* 35(4), 7–26.

Cochran-Smith, M. & Lytle, S.L. (1999) Relationships of knowledge and practice: teacher learning in communities. *Review of Research in Education* 24, 249–305.

Fenstermacher, G. (1990) Some moral considerations on teaching as a profession. In Goodlad, J., Soder, R. and Sirotnik, K. (eds) *The Moral Dimensions of Teaching.* pp. 130–51. San Francisco: Jossey-Bass Publishers Inc.

Filipp, S.H. (1990) *Kritische Lebensereignisse* [Critical incidents]. München: Psychologie Verlags Union.

Hargreaves, A. (1995) Development and desire. A post-modern perspective. In Guskey, T.R. and Huberman, M. (eds) *Professional Development in Education: New Paradigms and Perspectives.* pp. 9–34. New York: Teachers College Press.

Hopkins, D. (2001) School improvement for real. London: Routledge-Falmer.

Kelchtermans, G. (1993) Getting the story, understanding the lives. From career stories to teachers' professional development. *Teaching and Teacher Education* 9, 443–56.

Kelchtermans, G. (1996) Teacher vulnerability. Understanding its moral and political roots. *Cambridge Journal of Education* 26, 307–23.

Kelchtermans, G. (2005) Teachers' emotions in educational reforms: self-understanding, vulnerable commitment and micropolitical literacy. *Teaching and Teacher Education* 21, 995–1006.

Kelchtermans, G. (2007) Teachers' self-understanding in times of performativity. In Deretchin, L.F. and Craig, C.J. (eds) *International Research on the Impact of Accountability Systems. Teacher Education Yearbook XV.* pp. 13–30. Lanham: Rowman and Littlefield Education.

Kelchtermans, G. (2008) Study, stance, and stamina in the research on teachers' lives. A rejoinder to Robert V. Bullough, Jr. *Teacher Education Quarterly* 35(4), 27–36.

Kelchtermans, G. (2009) Who I am in how I teach is the message. Self-understanding, vulnerability and reflection. *Teachers and Teaching: Theory and Practice* 15, 257–72.

Kelchtermans, G. & Hamilton, M.L. (2004) The dialectics of passion and theory: exploring the relation between self-study and emotion. In Loughran, J., Hamilton, M.L., Kubler LaBoskey, V. and Russell, T. (eds) *The International Handbook of Self-Study of Teaching and Teacher Education Practices.* pp. 785–810. Dordrecht: Kluwer Academic Publishers.

Korthagen, F. (2001) *Linking Practice and Theory. The Pedagogy of Realistic Teacher Education.* Mahwah, NJ: Lawrence Erlbaum.

Measor, L. (1985) Critical incidents in the classroom. Identities, choices and careers. In Ball, S. and Goodson, I. (eds) *Teachers' Lives and Careers.* pp. 61–77. London: Falmer Press.

Nias, J. (1996) Thinking about feeling: the emotions in teaching. *Cambridge Journal of Education* **26**(3), 293–306.

Noddings, N. (1984) *Caring. A Feminine Approach to Ethics and Moral Education.* Berkeley, CA: University of California Press.

Oser, F., Dick, A. & Patry, J. (eds) (1992) *Effective and Responsible Teaching.* San Fransisco: Jossey-Bass Publishers Inc.

Schön, D. (1983) *The Reflective Practitioner: How Professionals Think in Action.* London: Temple Smith.

Schutz, P. & Zembylas, M. (eds) (2009) *Advances in Teacher Emotion Research: The Impact on Teachers' Lives.* Dordrecht: Springer.

Zembylas, M. (2003a) Caring for teacher emotion: reflections on teacher self-development. *Studies in Philosophy and Education* **22**(2), 103–25.

Zembylas, M. (2003b) Interrogating 'teacher identity': emotion, resistance, and self-formation. *Educational Theory* **53**(1), 107–27.

9   Leadership

Professionally responsible rule bending and breaking?

Ciaran Sugrue

Introduction

Addressing the question: 'what is enlightenment' in 1874, Kant replied that it is the individual capacity to think for oneself. Its absence, he suggested, stemmed from lack of courage rather than intellectual capacity. The hallmark of enlightenment is 'intellectual autonomy':

> If I have a book to serve as my understanding, a pastor to serve as my conscience, a physician to determine my diet for me, and so on, I need not exert myself at all. I need not think, if only I can pay: others will readily undertake the irksome work for me.
>
> (http://www.english.upenn.edu/~mgamer/Etexts/kant.html)

Kant's thoughts above are more contemporary than may initially appear. Relying on others to do my thinking for me is tantamount to an abnegation of 'responsibility' (Durkheim, 1957/2001). Kant's solution was to recognise that such 'rules and formulas' were 'mechanical aids' that served to shackle and maintain the individual in a permanent state of immaturity. Consequently, codes of conduct are necessary but not sufficient conditions for professionals to behave responsibly (Solbrekke 2007). However, both pre- and post-enlightenment thinkers have invented rules to avoid anarchy by reference to a common good construed in various ways. Thus, there is the Gospel exhortation provided by St Luke: 'Do unto others as you would have them do to you' (Luke 6: 31), Kant's own 'categorical imperative'[1] or Bentham's principle of 'the greatest happiness of the greatest number'(Burns & Hart 1970), a more quantitative approach to determining 'good' or 'appropriate' behaviour or acting responsibly.

This is not the place for a treatise on the attractions or limitations of these competing perspectives. Suffice to say there are inherent tensions between the Enlightenment exhortation to be autonomous while simultaneously advocating adherence to a rule or principle, to exercise professional discretion. Leading citizens, however, have broken the rules in order to bring about improvements for themselves and others. Socrates may be the iconic rule breaker, refusing to behave according to the 'rules' of the Athenian polis and paying the ultimate price. Similarly, Martin Luther King Jr 'had a dream' and from that vantage point he could see beyond legislative segregation and discrimination to a more equal society, and he too paid with his life. Leadership thus, it seems, or at least particular forms of it, implicitly suggest that breaking the rules of convention are a necessary if not sufficient ingredient of leadership, at least in certain circumstances, with overtones also of self-sacrifice rather than self-interest, an ideal type embedded in more classical as well as more recent formulations of what it means to be a professional (Eraut 1994; Fullan 2003; Noddings 1994; Parsons 1968). Is there an onus therefore on professionals to challenge the status quo publicly, to become public intellectuals (Said 1994), or is this an ideal beyond the pale of professionals? (May 1996).

Rapid transition to the twenty-first century does not permit escape from such underlying tensions. For example, a recent report emanating from European Union (EU) identifies 'autonomy' as the dominant and persistent policy pursued in education during the past two decades (Coghlan & Desurmont 2007: 4). Similarly, the Organisation for Economic Co-operation and Development's (OECD's) contribution to international policy- making indicates: 'School leadership is now an education policy priority around the world' (Pont, Nusche & Moorman, 2008: 3). The report continues 'many countries have moved towards decentralisation, making schools more autonomous in their decision-making' and such moves have added to the leadership responsibilities of principals. However, 'holding them more accountable for results' is the other side of the autonomy equation – while readily recognising that accountability and responsibility are far from being synonymous (Biesta 2010; see also Chapter 4).

Leadership (in a variety of contexts) has been seized on and promoted as the means of addressing such complex challenges in increasingly uncertain, insecure and rapidly changing workplace contexts (Bauman 2000/2006; Gardner 2007; Sullivan 1995). Recently, there has been a plethora of high-profile examples of blatant disregard for rules and regulations, and publics have been outraged by the manner in which perpetrators have been 'rewarded' with scandalously large severance sums and pension pots. Against this disconcerting de-regulated contemporary landscape, is it possible for leaders to bend and break rules in a professionally responsible manner?

In response, this chapter is in five parts. First, connections between cultural formation and transformation and the role of rules, norms, so on. within this cultural dynamic are initially outlined. Second, this initial cultural analysis is connected in broad brush strokes with prominent leadership literature and the role of rules within it. Third, the significance of rules, their use and misuse within cultures is taken up in the context of scandals on both sides of the Irish Sea – politician's expenses in UK, sexual abuse of children in Ireland by Catholic priests. Fourth, vignettes from the professional deliberations of school principals are critically analysed to gain insight into how leadership is enacted by them and the prevalence of rule bending and breaking within their practice. Fifth, the concluding part builds on the foregoing analysis while focusing on its impact on conceptions of leadership, leadership preparation and learning and what is entailed in fulfilling inherent obligations in a professionally responsible manner.

Culture: rules were made to be broken?

A vibrant culture appears to necessitate a tension between established rules of the game, and a reforming tendency to seek to have such norms breached and amended by appeal to principles, insights and new understandings, often in light of changed or changing circumstance. Culture, whether of a high or popular variety as well as distinct sub-cultures, *avant-garde* even, that are often in opposition to 'mainstream' culture, have their own distinct rules, customs, conventions and mores. For new, novel and emerging sub-cultures these may be much more fluid and malleable than mainstream norms. A good example in this regard is the manner in which jazz and blues migrated northwards in the US, and gradually moved from 'speak easy' to Carnegie Hall – mainstream and main street!

Part of the postmodern condition is the acceleration of a blurring of more traditional boundaries and, in the process, a mangling of rules that until recently were thought, by some at least, to be immutable (Appiah 2010). Nevertheless, history casts shadows on the present, while a veritable panoply of symbols, artefacts and ideas all contribute to the shaping of the future (Deal & Peterson 2009). Nevertheless: 'every repetition is a form of variation. Every iteration transforms meaning, adds to it, enriches it in ever-so-subtle ways' (Derrida, quoted in Post 2008: 47). For other cultural commentators, the predominance of a neo-liberal agenda has led to a 'hollowed out democracy, aggravated social inequality and ... the normalization of an individualistic consumerist ethos' (Clearly 2007: 96). Taylor asserts 'we seem to be left with a standing problem of how to induce or force the individual into some kind of social order, make him conform and obey the rules' (Taylor 2004/2007: 18). He suggests that we are left to reconcile distinct legacies from the past: 'individualism and mutual benefit are the evident residual ideas that remain after you have sloughed off the older religions and metaphysics' (Taylor 2004/2007: 18). Nevertheless, he asserts, essential to this ongoing tension is a sense of 'moral order'. Consequently, rules are not entirely technical and rational, but rooted within cultures, traditions, values, ideas, etc. It is within this contemporary 'social imaginary' which is 'that common understanding that makes possible common practices and a widely shared sense of legitimacy' (Taylor 2004/2007: 20) that leadership is understood and practised. From an educational perspective, the pervasiveness of a technical rational 'means-end' approach results in 'the normative dimensions of educational decision making' disappearing from consideration, and when this occurs, 'it also limits the opportunities for educational professionals to exert their judgements' (Biesta 2010: 47). Is leadership generally and educational leadership particularly impoverished and hollowed out when professional responsibility is treated in such a reductionist fashion?

Cultures of leadership?

On both sides of the Irish Sea, as well as in dispatches from North America, a persistent recent refrain has been 'lack of leadership', captured in Iaccoca's title *Where Have All The Leaders Gone?* (Iacocca 2008). There may be a hint of nostalgia in his assertion: 'there was a time … when the voices of great leaders lifted us up and made us want to do better' (Iacocca 2008: 5). Nostalgia apart, this iconic figure of successful leadership begins to put flesh on his avatar alter ego when he declares: 'if a leader never steps outside his comfort zone … he grows stale'. Consequently, 'leadership is all about managing change – whether you're leading a company or leading a country … things change, you get creative. You adapt' (Iacocca 2008: 6–7). While such catchy sound bites have the allure of authenticity, in the hands of buccaneer leaders, such assertions quickly become recipes for flagrant breaches of some key rules of the game.[2] Nevertheless, wider cultural norms play a role in this regard also. While key powerful players in American institutions served time for their breaking of financial 'rules', in the Irish context, such clarity is strangely absent:

> When the events that destroyed the economic well-being of the country are examined, those who clearly broke, rather than bent, the laws, or those who took advantage of poorly written laws, may have little to fear, other than a reduction in their wealth.
>
> (Cooper, 2009: 408)

Context matters in how leadership is conceptualised and constructed in practice. Until relatively recently, some suggest that leadership was about following predictable paths – in terms of career advancement – 'organisational man' (Whyte 1956) being the mascot of such a conceptualisation. The implicit contract was: 'follow the rules and obey authority, and things will work well' (Bennis & Thomas 2002: 27). While such an approach to building a career 'implied knowledge … it demonstrated acceptance of the legitimacy of the rules of the game' (Bennis & Thomas 2002: 27). However, in the post-Cold War period, when neo-liberal ideas combined with global forces to become the most pervasive influence, the 'old order changeth' and at an unprecedented pace.

Consistent with this perspective, and reflective of turbulent rather than predictable contexts, more recent research literature on school leadership has sought to provide direction in 'changing times' (Hargreaves 1994; Leithwood, Jantzi & Steinbach 1999). In the absence of consensus, Gronn captures the zeitgeist of this fluid world when he posits various forms of 'hybrid' leadership as the most likely and appropriate in differing contexts (Gronn 2009). Consistent with this general effort to give direction in the absence of empirical evidence, such exhortations create a 'normatively oriented literature' rather than one based on empirical evidence (Leithwood, Mascall & Strauss 2009: 2). There emerges therefore a kind of 'split' between a more empirical approach to leadership – an emphasis on 'what works' that is often critical or negative about a normative leaning literature. 'Adjectivalism' pervades contemporary leadership literature (Gronn 2009) thus contributing to fragmentation in the field rather than coherence; a 'boutique' or 'niche' approach to leadership (Sugrue 2009). However, while those with empirical evidence to support their claims may downplay if not disparage 'normative' aspects of leadership, closer scrutiny of their own evidence provides considerable testament to the importance of vision and values, the power of ideas, the influence of biography, as well as the character and disposition of those in leadership positions (Bennis & Thomas 2002; Hargeaves 2009; Leithwood & Jantzi 2000, 2005).

Throughout the 'roaring nineties' (Stiglitz 2003), the pace and pull of a rapidly advancing future sought to unfetter itself from the straightjacket of tradition; jettisoning the rules, rituals and routines that provided continuity and stability was actively encouraged. When rules are perceived solely as an encumbrance rather than beacons on the horizon that point to possible (moral) hazards, navigation becomes more like a game of Russian roulette – leadership becomes more arbitrary, less predictable and unstable; the 'moral order' becomes more chaotic, risk assessment replaces integrity and professional judgement. This new promised land, it is asserted with no false modestly, is where 'the greatest managers in the world ... first break all the rules of conventional wisdom' (Buckingham & Coffman 2005: 3). Leaders hewn from this (synthetic) fabric are 'revolutionaries' who have 'toppled conventional wisdom' and in the process have minted 'new truths' (Buckingham & Coffman 2005: 3). Such new truths are extolled in titles such as *The Seven Habits of Highly Effective People* (Covey 2007) or *The Six Secrets of Change* (Fullan 2008). These are the new 'sacred' texts that animate new leaders who will bring mere mortals to the promised land. Like Aladdin's lamp, old (rules) may be traded for newer, more glittering replacements. However, as another piece of conventional wisdom suggests, 'all that glitters is not gold'. What emerges here is that, by changing the discourse through the pervasive use of a technical rational language, there is a consequent hollowing out of how leadership is understood and practised.

Politicians and priests: making a mockery of the rules?

Politicians and priests belong to distinct sub-cultures situated within mainstream socio-cultural contexts, and are expected to provide leadership to their respective flocks; the latter in particular were traditionally perceived as providing 'moral leadership' (Coles 2000). A focus on recent events provides a 'measure' of their leadership, of how they have exercised their professional responsibilities.

Politicians

In May 2009 the broadsheet *Daily Telegraph* began to publish individual expenses claims submitted by Members of Parliament in the UK. Details of this 'scandal' have been publicised exhaustively and need not detain us here. Rather, I focus on aspect of the Legg report (Legg 2010), which was established by the politicians to re-assess their claims, while the Kelly report is a more exhaustive analysis of the propriety of the system and how it may be improved (Kelly 2009). Legg's re-calculation required that more than 400 MPs, from a total of 650, repay sums that ranged from £65,000 to as little as £100 (Legg 2010: 7). The public, angered by their political representatives' behaviour, were further outraged when it became clear that expenses were secured for such exotic indulgences as a duck house, cleaning a mote, claims for food, light bulbs, furniture, electronic equipment, gardening and cleaning, pornographic videos, and employment of family members on rather ambiguous contractual terms. However, the most significant sums of money revolved around 'flipping' homes.[3]

One explanation proffered by way of explanation for this 'un-parliamentary' behaviour was the nurturing of grievance regarding salaries. Kelly challenges this directly:

> Some have argued that the situation has been caused by the unwillingness of successive governments to contemplate increases in MPs' pay.... This unwillingness has created a sense of grievance. It has also led to a tendency to regard the expenses system, quite wrongly, as a substitute for higher salaries.
>
> (Kelly 2009: 7)

This inward-looking, self-referential grievance gained further credence in a context where 'the city' was encountering 'regulation light', while paradoxically teachers and schools were being policed by unprecedented levels of surveillance by Ofsted. Legg too, dismissed claims by politicians that they made a 'mistake' or their claims were justified under the rules, merely rudimentary or arbitrary requirements. Rather, 'the rules and standards included fundamental principles which were also laid down and published by the House and its authorities at the time' (paragraphs 51–3, 59–68) (Legg 2010: 6). Since principles are at stake, it is unacceptable on the part of politicians to protest ignorance of the rules, or the fact that payments were made – such pleading is 'misconceived' (paragraphs 72–3) (Legg 2010: 6). With echoes of Kant therefore, ignorance, lack of knowledge, is not a defence. Rather, being professionally responsible implies being appropriately informed.

Principle, 'propriety' and attendant probity, seem very similar to many of the qualities expected of leaders: integrity, character, trust; whatever the terms, they add up a sense of 'moral compass' (Bennis & Thomas 2002: 145ff). However, principles were (conveniently) ignored. A purely procedural, instrumentalist, technical-rational application of rules, cut adrift from their anchoring principles, their underlying values of honesty and public mindedness, facilitates bending and in some instances flagrant breaking of them. Scrutinised more thoroughly and broadly, the needle of the moral compass seems to point towards a black hole of unprincipled pragmatism. It may be suggested also that initial outrage on the part of politicians was about being caught in the public gaze; it was never anticipated by them that this information would be in the public domain. This was a private matter, thus the full rigour of 'public' rules did not apply! Professional and personal responsibility were being accorded differential status. Is such a convenient separation between personal (and private) and professional lives legitimate within the contours of conceptions of professional responsibility? But could similar questions be raised regarding the professional responsibility of clergy?

Priests

In Ireland, there has been widespread abuse of children by Church and state in a variety of institutions, run by the former ostensibly on behalf of the latter (Arnold 2009). However, focus here is on the recently published Murphy report on the sexual abuse perpetrated by priests during the past four decades in the Dublin Catholic archdiocese (Murphy 2009). Despite dealing with a total of 46 cases, the report rather chillingly indicates that the more than 800 pages contains 'a representative sample of allegations and suspicions of child sexual abuse', since the total number of legitimate cases will never be known (Murphy 2009: 1). Another important dimension of rule bending and breaking in this context is the manner in which the rules of 'cannon law' were invoked as being superior to the civil law, thus having a prior claim on loyalty – reinforcing the view that hiding behind any set of rules is an abnegation of responsibility. Since these scandals too have been widely reported nationally and internationally, the Murphy report is selectively quoted to gain insight into how professional responsibility was exercised.

Murphy's remit was 'concerned only with the institutional response to complaints, suspicions and knowledge of child sexual abuse' (Murphy 2009: 2). A prominent member of the Diocesan clergy in a 2007 publication argued that the avalanche of abuse cases had taken all concerned by surprise – a 'sunami ... deep below the surface hidden from view' (quoted in Murphy 2009: 3). Consequently, this popular narrative among senior clergy goes – they were on a 'learning curve'. Murphy emphatically rejects this thesis:

> The Dublin Archdiocese's pre-occupations in dealing with cases of child sexual abuse, ... were the maintenance of secrecy, the avoidance of scandal, the protection of the reputation of the Church, and the preservation of its assets. All other considerations, including the welfare of children and justice for victims, were subordinated to these priorities. The Archdiocese did not implement its own canon law rules and did its best to avoid any application of the law of the State.
>
> (Murphy 2009: 4)

There was blatant disregard for the civil law since 'it was not until late 1995 that officials of the Archdiocese first began to notify the civil authorities of complaints of clerical child sexual abuse' (Murphy 2009: 7). However, fidelity to

perspective, my ability to retain these teachers would be compromised by the receipt of any letters of retirement. I am anxious to secure the long term future of each of these excellent young educators as members of our staff and, therefore, it is neither in my or their interest that I receive any letters of retirement. I have received no letters of retirement to date! Should the procedures with regard to panels remain unaltered, I would continue to hold the same view.

This principal feels justified in his actions ('I would act similarly'). However, if every principal adopted a similar stance, the panel would become inoperable. Though it may be perceived as laudable that a principal would stretch such requirements to these lengths out of loyalty to teaching colleagues, the decision might also be construed as being overly focused on an individual school to the relative detriment of the profession as a whole. However, the panel may be understood also as privileging the interests of the profession more than concern for the quality of teaching and learning. In a more competitive climate, the principal may be understood as acting in the best interest of the school. In such circumstances is professional responsibility understood too narrowly, where the local takes precedence over 'common good'? Is it possible also that this principal is refusing to be merely accountable, to be bound by the 'rule' and takes responsibility for the good of the school community as a whole? Is this evidence of 'the zeal and leadership of people committed to the new orientation' (Lipsky 1980: 209), and if so, who decides?

Breaking rules: professionally responsible leadership?

This illustrative incident of rule breaking contains the additional intent to defy those who have recommended compliance with the rule being breached. The school was permitted to appoint a Home School Community Liaison (HSCL) teacher. The appointee had received initial teacher education abroad and thus did not have the Irish language qualification for 'full' recognition.[6] The principal continues:

> I appointed ... a UK trained probated and experienced staff member to the position because of the clear and obvious qualities that he would bring to the position despite a warning in the relevant DES [Department of Education and Skills] circular that such a teacher must be fully Irish probated. .... An ability to teach and speak Irish is irrelevant to the role of HSCL. In the period since he has become the HSCL he has been excellent in the role and ... has obviously established leadership credibility. However, only last week we were evaluated by a team of DES inspectors ... and while finding many laudable aspects of practice in our school this 'anomaly' featured prominently in our written report. It was made clear to me that the Inspectorate expect me to 'rectify' this anomaly immediately. However, I do not intend to.

In remaining defiant, the principal is seeking to have the rule overturned – a semi-public stance against authority. If the teacher in question is doing good work, and the Irish language requirement a perceived irrelevance, then quality service rather than compliance is the judgement being made. Similarly, the vast majority of informants suggested they would do the same in similar circumstances unless the 'health and safety' of a pupil was at stake or the 'integrity' of the school – that rule breaking is inherent in the leadership role, in the exercise of professional responsibility. The veracity of rules or requirements are questioned by these leaders, they are exercising their autonomy and professional judgement, but are such leadership decisions taken in a professionally responsible manner, and by what criteria or standards are such decisions to be judged responsible or otherwise?

Another respondent provided reflective comments on the relationships between leadership and rule breaking that afford additional insight into the practice of leadership and sheds additional light on professional responsibility.

This principal has been leader of a disadvantaged school for a decade, and adopts a critical stance towards rules and those they are designed to serve, and appears guided by a moral compass in determining a 'right' course of action:

> Breaking a rule: Cui Bono? You must take the rules and the situations they apply to and ask who benefits. I will bend and/or break whatever rules made by the advantaged to the benefit of the advantaged as I see fit, but not just for the sake of it and not without an amount of soul searching balancing evidence with experience etc. However, in a final analysis for society to work we must work broadly within its parameters and by taking the kings shilling as a primary P[rincipal] I've signed up for that and by doing so in a Catholic school I must respect and promote that ethos. However, when rules from whomever are better honoured in the spirit than the letter ... in the best interests of those they should serve then I feel I have a duty to so lead.

This principal views the rules through the lens of the disadvantaged community served by the school, while also being mindful of the bigger picture; mediator between State and individual (Durkheim, 1957/2001). It seems reasonable to suggest that such deliberations regarding rules are guided by a (personal and/or professional) sense of equity and/or social justice, while respect for and promotion of a particular ethos might be inimical to the interests of disadvantaged learners. How are such Gordian dilemmas to be resolved? By way of response, this principal articulates the rules of rule breaking:

> You have to know the rules to bend or break them,
> There are some rules that you do not break.
> With money you have to be creative in a poor school to succeed. But when
>   DES gives grants for specifics like Dormant Accounts[7] or ICT play

it straight. Ancillary services though, I interpreted as for paying the cleaners, with the 'milk money' as a top up.

Be ambitious, never greedy and you're less likely to be caught out.

Lead and make the decision yourself, if caught apologise – you're balancing staff resentment against faceless bureaucratic official irritation.

Be accountable, take responsibility for your actions, it's a novel and not much practiced habit across senior leadership in this country!

The final comment above could indeed be levelled at both politicians and clergy; that being accountable is not merely rule application or compliance – it is about taking responsibility. It indicates clearly that this principal's practice includes rule breaking as integral to the role in the particular circumstances, while reference to not being 'caught' seems redolent of a wider cultural commentary that 'you can do as you like once you say the right thing'! (see Gleeson 2010: 9–56). Illumination of the rules of rule breaking indicates more clearly the extent to which context, disposition and moral commitments are inherently involved and that the process of deliberation necessitates weighing the evidence while being informed by the value stance of the decision maker as professional. In this respect, there is a seamless connection between personal commitments and professional judgements. The moral disposition invoked in this school leader's deliberations is that frequently systemic rules are prejudiced against schools that serve disadvantaged communities. Consequently, in the exercise of professionally responsible leadership, it becomes a necessity to break such rules in the interest of the local community and, in so doing, serve the common good while acting in a manner consistent with values of fairness and social justice (May 1996).

Professionally responsible leadership?

The snapshots of the life worlds of politicians, priests and principals portrayed here reveal pervasive breaching of norms, rules and principles. Consequently, in light of such conduct, how is professionally responsibly leadership to be understood? In the 'real' world, the expectation of conformity to, or slavish adherence to established codes of conduct is naive and possibly also dangerous as well as being inimical to the exercise of professional responsibility. As Macklin suggests: 'being moral in everyday life is messy, complicated, perplexing, fluid, and cannot be made safe or explained by philosophy, clear ethical principles, or reified sociological theories' (Macklin 2009: 86). Additionally, it makes sense to agree that 'practising 'professionally' for any group is norm driven and therefore culturally, temporally and politically framed' (Macklin 2009: 87). It appears therefore that Kant's insight into the importance of challenging authority and conventional wisdom has gained widespread acceptance as one of the Enlightenment's legacies to contemporary society, even if such challenges are not always motivated by desirable values. Yet, leadership practices in particular appear to garner additional discretionary space or autonomy that renders rule breaking a permanent feature of the leadership landscape, but by no means confined to it. Nevertheless, the many politicians who applied the rules governing expenses claims to maximise their 'take', reduced their professional mandate to mere accounting – a managerialist understanding of the term (see Biesta 2010: 50–72). Thus their hollowed out sense of responsibility, devoid of normative content, could be expressed: 'but this was allowed under the rules' or simply 'I made a mistake' – an error of calculation rather than a dereliction of responsibility.

Similarly, the case of clerical abuse indicates that, while it is essential to be up to date – knowledgeable and appropriately informed, this is a necessary but not sufficient condition for professional responsibility. These clergy too assumed that their actions would never enter the public sphere. Here again, therefore, is a key consideration for professional responsibility – the relationship between personal and professional integrity – their seamlessness rather than separation. Are higher standards of professional responsibility expected of professionals in their professional rather than their personal lives? The clerical case gives rise to the additional consideration also of values and their relationship to discretion and judgement. Though it is evident that a normative dimension is inherent, and values play a role, the analysis indicates that which values are prioritised renders such judgements adequate or inadequate. Consequently, even after the normative element of professional judgement is asserted and accepted, which values and how they are chosen and prioritised is critical; the Kantian courage to challenge various elements of tradition were sorely lacking.

It is in the nature of exercising professional responsibility that the outcome is in doubt – deliberation is open, thus it is only after the fact that the veracity of the professional judgement may be determined. Otherwise, professionals would be denied the possibility of exercising discretion; professional responsibility is not reducible to the application of a set of rules or code of conduct (see Chapter 1). Professional responsibility necessitates learning to live with and act within a context of uncertainty and competing considerations. As my principal informant suggests above, it necessitates taking responsibility, and while deliberating 'broadly within … parameters' continuously reserve the right to break the rules in the interest of serving a particular (disadvantaged) community while being mindful also of the common good. Such deliberations 'cannot be programmed' (Lipsky 1980). However, culture and context have a major presence in professionally responsible deliberations. When such deliberations are perceived to be inimical to individuals and/or the common good, more communal notions of service and professionalism strongly suggest that exercising responsibility in such circumstances necessitates becoming a whistleblower (Freidson 2001; May 1996) or is this expecting too much of professionals, tilting towards self-sacrifice to the discomfort of self-interest? Is this, as Brint suggests, 'a movement from *social trustee professionalism* (as found in classical theories) to *expert professionalism*' (quoted in Solbrekke 2007: 35); professionals who (conveniently) compartmentalise expertise from ethics?

An additional consideration flows from the stance of the principals, particularly where an existing rule is being challenged. In such circumstances, is there an additional professional responsibility to 'go public', to air the unfairness of the rules governing the appointment of teachers to particular leadership roles? Is there an additional professional responsibility on the principal who has circumvented the rules regarding panel rights of teachers to challenge such rules in the public domain? Such a public stance would almost inevitably lead to conflict with public positions espoused by teachers' unions regarding protection of members' interests. Burke, Irishman and Enlightenment thinker, would not approve as evidenced by his oft-quoted statement: 'the only thing necessary for the triumph of evil is for good people to do nothing'. In a tradition going back at least as far as Aristotle, it appears that leadership is not merely about bending and breaking rules, but challenging them publicly also when circumstances warrant such dissent. There is an individual and collective responsibility therefore to prepare professionals for such uncertainties, of instilling the necessity for attention to moral compass in the exercise of professional responsibility, including the possibility of taking a public stance, while simultaneously recognising that it is in the nature of professional responsibility that uncertainties are cherished as integral to professional thinking and conduct rather than being reduced to rules and procedures; to mere certification of skills and competencies.

These considerations represent a considerable challenge to professional programmes, professional associations and professionals. In a climate and context where the technical language of new public management and its ideological neo-liberal 'home' have marginalised considerations of the common good, leadership discourses in particular, given the importance of its discretionary role, need to create and renew its horizons of professional responsibility.

Notes

1 The categorical imperative is the centrepiece of Kantian moral philosophy; it is a syllogism that includes the following maxims. The first premise is that a person acts morally if his or her conduct would, without condition, be the 'right' conduct for any person in similar circumstances (the 'First Maxim'). The second premise is that conduct is 'right' if it treats others as ends in themselves and not as means to an end (the 'Second Maxim'). The conclusion is that a person acts morally when he or she acts as if his or her conduct was establishing a universal law governing others in similar circumstances (the 'Third Maxim').
2 In popular culture these 'leaders' have been variously named: 'cowboys', 'chancers' 'goboys', 'sharks' but redeemed by a sanitised (more technical) language that recasts them as 'risk takers', 'entrepreneurs' and 'developers' even!
3 This process enabled MPs from outside the London areas to secure mortgages to buy accommodation in the city. However, they were also allowed to make this their primary residence. Consequently, during the property boom of the past 15 years, they could sell this property as their primary dwelling and avoid paying capital gains tax on the significant profits, and, when it suited, 'flip' back to their country residence as their primary abode. In this manner, the taxpayer subsidised the mortgages on these

properties, and then had to forego capital gains also, thus a double whammy to the exchequer.

4 Both the Irish Primary Principals' Network (IPPN), and the National Association of Principals and Deputies (NAPD) provided practical support while former colleague Catherine Furlong also provided practical assistance with contact details of some informants.

5 It should be noted that in the Irish context, there is an absence of structures between the Ministry and individual schools; there are no local authorities. Consequently, teachers are hired by individual schools, by their Boards of Management, thus in practice, it devolves to the principal to recruit and retain teachers.

6 Under EU regulations, there is common recognition of qualifications. However, in order to teach in Irish primary schools, where it is compulsory for all to learn the Irish language, those without a qualification to teach the language are given a limited time period in which to acquire this qualification. Without it, it is not possible to secure a permanent position within the system.

7 A number of years ago, it was established that there were thousands of bank accounts in branches around the country, particularly in rural areas that had remained untouched for years – thus the designation dormant. The Government decided that the contents of these accounts could be used for worthy causes, and in this regard proposals could be made for access to some of these funds.

References

Appiah, K.A. (2010) *The Honour Code How Moral Revolutions Happen*. New York, London: W.W. Norton & Company.

Arnold, B. (2009) *The Irish Gulag How the State Betrayed its Innocent Children*. Dublin: Gill & Macmillan.

Bauman, Z. (2000/2006) *Liquid Modernity*. Cambridge: Polity Press.

Bennis, W.G. & Thomas, R.J. (2002) *Geeks & Geezers How Era, Values, and Defining Moments Shape Leaders*. Cambridge, MA: Harvard Business School Press.

Biesta, G. (2010) *Good Education in an Age of Measurement Ethics, Politics, Democracy*. Boulder, London: Paradigm Publishers.

Buckingham, M. & Coffman, C. (2005) *First Break All the Rules What the World's Greatest Managers Do Differently*. London: Pocket Books.

Burns, J.H. & Hart, H.L.A. (eds) (1970) *An Introduction to the Principles of Morals and Legislation*. London: The Athlone Press.

Cleary, J. (2007) *Outrageous Fortune Capital and Culture in Modern Ireland*. (2nd ed.). Dublin: Field Day Publications.

Coghlan, M. & Desurmont, A. (2007) *School Autonomy in Europe Policies and Measures*. Brussels: Eurydice.

Coles, R. (2000) *Lives of Moral Leadership Men and Women Who Have Made a Difference*. New York: Random House.

Cooper, M. (2009) *Who Really Runs Ireland? The Story of the Elite Who Led Ireland from Bust to Boom ... and Back Again*. Dublin: Penguin Ireland.

Covey, S. (2007) *The Seven Habits of Highly Effective People*. London, Sydney: Simon & Schuster.

Deal, T.E. & Peterson, K.D. (2009) *Shaping School Culture Pitfalls, Paradoxes, & Promises*, 2nd edn. San Francisco: Jossey-Bass Publishers Inc.

Durkheim, E. (1957/2001) *Professional Ethics and Civic Morals*. London: Routledge.

Eraut, M. (1994) *Developing Professional Knowledge and Competence*. London: Falmer Press.

Freidson, E. (2001) *Professionalism: the Third Logic*. Cambridge: Polity Press.

Fullan, M. (2003) *The Moral Imperative of School Leadership*. Thousand Oaks: Corwin Press.

Fullan, M. (2008) *The Six Secrets of Change: What the Best Leaders do to Help Their Organisations Survive and Thrive*. San Francisco: Jossey-Bass Publishers Inc.

Gadamer, H.G. (1975/1989) *Truth and Method* (trans. J. Weinsheimer, J. and Marshall, G.), 2nd edn. London: Sheed & Ward.

Gardner, H., Csikszentmihalyi, M. & Damon, W. (2001) *Good Work When Excellence and Ethics Meet*. New Yor: Basic Books.

Gardner, H. (2007) *Responsibility at Work How Leading Professionals Act (or Don't Act) Responsibly*. San Francisco: John Wiley & Sons, Inc.

Gardner, H. (2008) *5 Minds for the Future*. Boston: Harvard Business Press.

Gleeson, J. (2010) *Curriculum in Context Partnership, Power and Praxis in Ireland*. Bern: Peter Lang Ltd.

Gronn, P. (2009) Hybrid leadership. In Leithwood, K., Mascall, B. and Strauss, T. (eds) *Distributed Leadership According to the Evidence*. pp. 17–40. London, New York: Routledge.

Hargreaves, A. (1994) *Changing Teachers, Changing Times*. London: Cassell.

Hargeaves, A. & Shirley, D. (2009) *The Fourth Way The Inspiring Future for Educational Change*. Thousand Oaks: Sage.

Iacocca, L. (with Whitney, C.) (2008) *Where Have All The Leaders Gone?* New York, London: Scribner.

Kelly, C. (2009) *MP's Expenses, Supporting Parliament, Safeguarding the Taxpayer*. London: Her Majesty's Stationery Office.

Legg, T. (2010) *House of Commons Members Estimate Committee Review of Past ACA payments First Report of Session 2009–10*. London: House of Commons.

Leithwood, K., Jantzi, D. & Steinbach, R. (1999) *Changing Leadership for Changing Times*. Buckingham: Open University Press.

Leithwood, K., & Jantzi, D. (2000) The effects of transformational leadership on organisational conditions and student engagement. *Journal of Educational Administration* **38**(2), 112–129.

Leithwood, K., & Jantzi, D. (2005) *A Review of Transformational School Leadership Research*. Paper presented at the AERA.

Leithwood, K., Mascall, B. & Strauss, T. (eds) (2009) *Distributed Leadership According to the Evidence*. London, New York: Routledge.

Lipsky, M. (1980) *Street-Level Bureaucracy Dilemmas of the Individual in Public Service*. New York: Russell Sage Foundation.

Macklin, R. (2009) Moral judgement and practical reasoning in professional practice. In Green, B. (ed.) *Understanding and Researching Professional Practice*. Rotterdam, Sense Publishers.

May, L. (1996) *The Socially Responsive Self. Social Theory and Professional Ethics*. Chicago: Chicago University Press.

Murphy, Y. (2009) *Commission of Investigation Report into the Catholic Archdiocese of Dublin*. Dublin: Department of Justice, Equality and Law Reform.

Noddings, N. (1994) Foreword. In Brophy, C.M. and Wallace, J. (eds) *Ethical and Social Issues in Professional Education*. Albany: State University of New York Press.

Parsons, T. (ed.) (1968) *International Encyclopedia of the Social Sciences* (Vols 12). New York: The Free Press and Macmillan.

Pink, D.H. (2008) *A Whole New Mind why righ-brainers will rule the future.* London: Marshall Cavendish Business.

Pont, B., Nusche, D. & Moorman, H. (2008) *Improving School Leadership:* Volume 1. *Policy and Practice.* Paris: OECD.

Post, R. (ed.) (2008) *Another Cosmopolitanism Selya Benhabib with Jeremy Waldron, Bonnie Honig, and Wuikk Jympicka, The Berleley Tanner Lectures.* Oxford: Oxford University Press.

Said, E.W. (1994) *Representations of the Intellectual. The 1993 Reith Lectures.* New York: Pantheon Books.

Solbrekke, T.D. (2007) *Understanding Conceptions of Professional Responsibility.* Oslo: University of Oslo.

Stiglitz, J. (2003) *The Roaring Nineties Seeds of Destruction.* London: Allen Lane.

Sugrue, C. (2009) From heroes and heroines to hermaphrodites: emancipation or emasculation of school leaders and leadership? *School Leadership and Management* 29(4), 361–72.

Sullivan, W.M. (1995) *Work and Integrity. The Crisis and Promise of Professionalism in America.* New York: HarperCollins.

Taylor, C. (2004/2007) *Modern Social Imaginaries*, 4th edn. Durham, London: Duke University Press.

Whyte W. (1956) *Organizational Man*, New York: Simon & Schuster.

Zimbardo, P. (2007) *The Lucifer Effect How Good People Turn Evil.* New York: Random House.

10 Evidence-based practice, risk and reconstructions of responsibility in nursing

Sally Wellard and Kristin Heggen

Introduction

What it means to be professional has changed profoundly in the course of the last decades. In contemporary society, professionals are expected to produce new knowledge, in addition to creating new relationships of commitment and trust in a changing society (Nerland & Jensen 2007). Professionals work within contours of a 'web of commitments' (May 1996) and multifaceted responsibilities of professional work, and these are accompanied by dilemmas embedded in professional responsibility. A significant pressure on professionals is related to the current 'public control regimes' that have evolved in the last 20–30 years. New methods of steering in the public field, introduced by the ideas of neo-liberalism are often described as New Public Management and are accompanied by demands for greater 'oversight', 'transparency' and 'accountability' (Svensson & Karlsson 2008). States (politicians and bureaucrats) in their regulation and audit of the delivery of public goods, such as public health care, have developed restrictive demands through greater externally prescribed accountability systems to ensure professionals are loyal to predefined political and economic goals. Making professionals' work more transparent has become an important management strategy to facilitate control and reduce the cost of health care.

Minimising risks and replacing uncertainty with rationality and predictability are within the new public management discourses considered to be promising management strategies. Evidence-based practice (EBP) and its potential for reducing risks has become a major theme in health care. In principle, EBP requires decision making to be based on verifiable evidence and knowledge obtained via particular forms of clinical studies. EBP as a new framework for clinical practice, and its potential for reducing risks, has become a dominant component of professional accountability in Western health care systems, despite significant debate about what constitutes evidence. The plurality of discourses surrounding EBP and risk management are linked to an expectation that risk is reduced if clinical practice is based on scientific evidence. The focus of this chapter is the impact of risk management and EBP on the contemporary constructions of professional responsibility in nursing. We begin by outlining our understanding of the notion of professional responsibility in nursing, followed by a brief exploration of Michel Foucault's concept of governmentality. Our analysis of the influences of risk and EBP on professional responsibility draws on Foucault's use of governmentality to describe the variety of ways different levels of governance are linked, including the ways groups and individuals conduct everyday life. The presentation of a case from a nursing home where residents were denied access to the outdoors due to concerns based on the evidence about risk of fracture provides a context for the subsequent discussion of risk, risk management and the various controversies associated with the dominance of EBP in contemporary nursing practice. The final part offers a challenge to re-consider professional responsibility in nursing as engaging in a contest and balancing the dominance of discourses of risk and EBP with discourses of care and consumer engagement.

Professional responsibility in nursing

Professional work entails a specific body of knowledge, skills and deliberative processes that are exclusive to that profession. Additionally, professionals have a shared set of values and rules of conduct that guide their practice. The privileges of professional status accompany the requirement to provide a role in society and, as Solbrekke (2005) identified, professional responsibility in this context includes: placing service before profit; being prepared to deal with conflicts between societal and individual interest; speaking out in the interests of the broader society, and using one's expertise in the interests of social equality. Professional responsibility involves not only taking responsibility for one's local practices but also enacting a role within a larger civic and social responsibility (Solbrekke 2008; Solbrekke & Heggen 2009; Sullivan 2005).

Nursing arguably claimed professional status in the late twentieth century, and has defined the knowledge, skills and values required for entry and maintenance of the role of professional nurse. Conventional views of nurses' responsibility are associated with the ideas of selfless service, nurturing care for patients and duty to the organisation, all indications of a heritage from religious and military organisations. This might mean that in nursing responsibility and accountability were derived within hierarchical models, where obedience to institutional values was fundamental. Within this tradition, nurses have worked within a culture marked by collective shared responsibility for patient care. This culture has been described as a 'we'-oriented culture where sharing responsibility for all the patients on a ward was a characteristic. It was 'our' patients and 'our' responsibility to offer necessary care to patients (Elstad & Hamran 1995).

Responsibility is often viewed as a twin partner to freedom, or autonomy, where you cannot have freedom without taking responsibility for preserving the systems that give you that freedom (Dworkin 1988). The preservation of autonomy relies on taking responsibility for actions within the scope of the autonomy. Nursing in shaping a place as a profession within the health care system has attained a degree of autonomy, which varies according to the scope and specialisation of the various roles held.

Responsibility involves both the taking of actions, and being able to explain how and why those actions were taken. Eby (2000) described four components of responsibility that influence individual responsibility in the practice of health care professionals: social, ethical, legal and professional. These provide a useful framework to examine influences on responsibility in nursing, and while presented separately here, it is important to view them as overlapping. The social component of responsibility involves acting as a responsible citizen, meeting societal expectations of being a professional through following social norms, showing respect for others and promoting good health for all. Gottlieb and Robinson (2006) argued that civic responsibility means active participation in the public life of a community with a focus on the common good. This participation should be informed, committed and constructive.

Professional nurses argue that practice is developed in ethical ways and nurses must demonstrate values and principles including having a duty to respect and value the patient as central in health service delivery, a duty to be honest and trustworthy; a duty to do no harm and to promote wellbeing (Johnstone 2008). Clancy and Svensson (2007) in an examination of ethical duties in public health nursing in Norway argues that these duties may not have been of our choosing but we have an obligation to accept them nonetheless.

Nurses are required to demonstrate responsibility within a legislative framework that governs both their nursing practice specifically and the conduct of health care within the jurisdiction where they practise. Compliance requirements with laws relating to privacy, consent, mandatory reporting and restraint are among the broad array of parameters for the conduct of nurses. Regulatory authorities interpret the legislative constraints on practice through registration and monitor nurses' compliance with the terms of their registration.

Nurses have a range of professionally directed influences on their responsibilities in practice. The International Nursing Council specifies both ethical and professional codes for the conduct of nurses in practice, which member nations agree to and these codes become the foundation for national codes of conduct for nurses. Both Norway and Australia have articulated standards and competencies that nurses must demonstrate to gain and maintain their registration to practise. As members of the nursing profession, individual practitioners are required to accept the rights and responsibilities that accompany that status. The public entrust professional regulators and organisations to develop and monitor the standards and competencies required, as well as ensuring that the professional practices within that scope.

Governmentality

Responsibility within nursing practice we argue is 'governed' by a number of competing and coexisting discourses, and of particular interest in this analysis are discourses of risk and evidence-based practice. We have taken considerable inspiration from the French philosopher Michel Foucault, and his repeated reminders that seemingly uninteresting everyday practices often play a little recognised but vital role in social life. He used the term *governmentality* to describe the ways governance occurs in modern societies (Foucault 2001), not only the formal political governance, but to link different levels of governing life, including the way groups and individuals conduct everyday life (Danaher, Schirato & Webb 2000). Foucault referred to governmentality as the 'conduct of conduct' (Lemke 2001), and this is often invisible to us because it governs our thoughts within institutions, and language that we hardly notice, nor question. In representing the ideas about governmentality, Foucault drew attention to 'how' we are governed and self-govern. Others have built from his work and developed analysis of the discursive fields that frame governance and the practices and techniques that govern individuals and groups (McKee 2009). Amongst the critics of EBP, Traynor (2002) used Foucault's governmentality to analyse how clinicians need to turn problems and uncertainties in clinical encounters into answerable questions, and therefore at risk of overlooking important information from the perspective of the patient. He further argued that whether practitioners accept or express hesitation regarding the new knowledge regimes, EBP discourses have re-shaped the identity of nursing in subtle ways.

Nikolas Rose and colleagues (2006) argue that an analysis of governmentality seeks to identify different streams of thought and the conditions for formation of principles and knowledge. In the next part we describe a clinical case with the aim of identifying how nurses and nursing home residents are governed by discourses of risk management and the knowledge policy where research-based evidence is given priority in decision making about the wellbeing of residents. Following Rose, O'Malley and Valverde (2006) our aim is to identify the operation of governmentality in the way staff restrict the movement of residents. The following questions focus our analysis of the case: Who governs what? With what logic and techniques? And for what ends?

Risk and evidence – an illustrative case

This story is drawn from a residential care setting in Australia (Wellard 2010) but could be from many countries that use a residential model for aged care. During data gathering for a research project in residential settings, the researchers observed that residents with dementia had very limited opportunities to go outside and make use of relatively new and secure dementia gardens. A dementia garden is constructed to give residents the option to be outdoors in a reasonably safe environment with locked gateways to the external community. The gardens are organised with a variety of plants, walkways, benches and water features, all aimed to facilitate memories and sensations for residents with reduced cognitive abilities at the same time as they get fresh air and exercise. Recent studies provide evidence for the positive effects on residents of such facilities (Detweiler et al. 2008, 2009; Hernandez 2007).

The dementia-specific residential settings, in common with most nursing homes, were very busy and the workload of nurses was high, and they frequently complained about all the 'new' paperwork they were expected to do: reporting on the wellbeing, daily activities and care of residents. Nurses in a Norwegian nursing home have labelled similar obligation to document practice as 'paper-care'. In the three study sites, nurses not only complained about too much time required for reporting, but they also commented on the value of the written documentation and the transparency of everyday activities in a nursing home. In addition, there was a request for reporting unexpected events and accidents. Staff identified falls and the potential for fractures to lower limbs and hips as among the major risks residents faced. Research literature has given evidence for high incidence of falls and fracture among residents in nursing homes and the subsequent variety of complications related to surgery and recovery. Guidelines based on research findings are available and are intended to prevent falls (Australian Commission on Safety and Quality in Healthcare 2009; Registered Nurses Association of Ontario 2002). Reports on the number of falls are used as one indicator of quality in nursing homes (Castle & Ferguson 2010).

One of the researchers asked at the three different sites why residents could not be outside. There was a uniform response. A first reason offered related to insufficient time of staff to accompany residents outside, and this was clearly evident in observing the work required by the staff members that were available. When asked if the residents could access the gardens without staff, patient safety and risk of harm to residents were cited as reasons for not allowing such 'open' access. Staff expressed concern that residents might fall if they were unaccompanied and this could potentially result in a fracture. Staff described that the risk of fracture was best managed by removing the risk factors, thus denying residents free access to outdoors. This clearly does not support the standards of liberty, or the benefits from being outdoors in improving gait and behaviour.

The case illustrates how new guidelines for risk assessment have been developed and adopted from research-based evidence. At the same time it is evident that garden walks have a positive effect on the wellbeing of residents, but these reports play a less significant role when it comes to prioritising activities of nurses and residents. The strongest evidence is the one related to risk assessment and documentation. Here it is evident that nurses were practising defensively (Annandale 1996) as a result of the risk assessments. It also shows that viewing risk management as a simple process of measuring and minimising risk does not account for the complexity of clinical situations (Alaszewski 2005).

Risk and responsibility

Dean (2010) starts his discussion of risk by stating two propositions: firstly that 'there is no such thing as risk in reality'; and secondly, that 'the significance of risk lies not with risk *itself* but with what risk gets attached to' (Dean 2010: 206).

Prior to industrialisation risk was not considered. Rather, work and life were viewed as subject to hazards, which were mostly random events of nature. However, the 'Enlightenment narrative of progress' transformed this view and a desire to control and manipulate the environment to support growth emerged (Dean 2010: 209). He argues that the technologies of risk calculation are a product of wealth production, and emerged to reduce the hazards of that production (Dean 2010: 209). Dean (2010) is arguing that the current 'risk' culture is one form of governmentality.

According to Giddens (1990) one of the major consequences of modernisation has been a tremendous intensification of real and perceived, or socially mediated, risk. Indeed, Lupton (1999) and theorists such as Ulrich Beck (1992, 1999) have described modern society as a *risk society*. Both Giddens and Beck posit that *risk society* means risk has become a strategic organising principle guiding both individual and institutional thinking and action in contemporary society (Hall 2002).

In contemporary health care there are two predominant forms of risk analysis. First, clinical risks from an epidemiological perspective provide analysis of population surveillance and screening data to predict risks of particular pathologies within a population and therefore direct treatments and preventative programmes (Dean 2010). Tobacco use is a clear example of this, where predictions of the types of harm caused by tobacco use have led to a range of strategies to reduce the use of tobacco ranging from controls on purchase price and reducing public spaces where smoking is acceptable. The second form of risk analysis is related to the delivery of health services. Over the past decade there has been increasing sophistication in the systems developed in many countries around clinical risk management.

Our interest is more with the influence of these systems of clinical risk management in the ways nurses construct their professional responsibilities. There has been increasing concern with patient safety since the mid-1990s that has resulted in an explosion in the forms of regulation to manage the clinical risks in health care services (Waring 2009). While patient safety is important to safeguard, the interest in clinical risk is also influenced by a need to control costs of health in an industry where costs are constantly escalating and a desire to control professionals who are driving the types of services available (Alaszewski 2005).

In Australia, for example, a national commission on safety and quality in health care was established in 2006 and subsequently the commission established created a number of standardised approaches towards the delivery of health care services (http://www.safetyandquality.gov.au). These include clinical handover, open disclosure, medication safety, health care-related infections, patient identification and managing clinical deterioration. Arguably these standardised approaches in part 'regulate' how professional practice will be enacted, where previously professionals had more autonomy in how they practised in these domains.

'Responsibilise' is a term Löwenheim (2007) uses to describe the transformation of individuals in becoming responsible for risk management in the context of travel, but could equally be adopted to understand the ways individual nurses adopt risk management practices as a responsibility within their practice. Löwenheim (2007) describes responsibilisation as

> the process whereby the state encourages or even impels people and communities to acknowledge – and to – assume – a responsibility to govern their own risks ... this self-management of risk does not mean the state loses interest in how individuals will act to safeguard from risk. Responsibilisation is not the equivalent of anarchy or 'self-help' ... Quite the opposite: the state works to establish the rules and boundaries for such self-management.
>
> (Löwenheim 2007: 204; emphasis in the original)

Changing health care systems have seen the devolving of responsibility to the point of direct service delivery, the point of patient contact (Annandale 1996: 416). This is occurring in the context of societal changes where there is an increased consumer focus. Consumers have different expectations than in the past: they are more informed and prepared to voice their expectations. This trend supports increased public accountability systems and the visibility of risks that were previously obscured, resulting in new systems of vigilance of practices. This is a reflection of the risk society (Hall 2002) where a culture has developed with increased surveillance and scrutiny of practices – by individuals of themselves, peers and organisational surveillance. This arguably does produce benefits, but also can lead to defensive practices, which may or may not benefit clients. As illustrated in our case, the residents with dementia are denied the freedom to move outdoors by themselves because of the fear that this may produce an adverse outcome. This illustrates what Annandale (1996) suggested as consumers being viewed as risk generators, where the awareness of a consumer focus creates a 'cloud' hanging over practice. Nurses perceive an increased personal responsibility and accountability for their practice (Godin 2006). This is a dramatic shift from the previous collective responsibility and potentially results in consumers and professionals being in opposition rather than partnership.

The 'audit society' as described by Power (2000) became increasingly dominant in the UK since the 1980s, and also evident in many other countries. Audit is a by-product of a drive for performance measurement of most aspects of life: we have standards against which our performance is measured, and the audit has become a primary tool for assessing performance. However, there are two issues associated with its rise to dominance: firstly, not everything lends itself to auditing; and secondly, a response to audit is 'creative compliance'. Annandale (1996) describes health staff responses to risk and audit predominance in practice as creating a culture where practitioners constrain themselves. She notes that:

> ...practice decisions made *today* only become problems in the *future*, risks can never be really forestalled. The dilemma is that even though staff may

come to appreciate this, they *still* feel compelled to do all that they can to colonise the future in order to protect themselves.

(Annandale 1996: 417)

Our case illustrates how nurses, on behalf of the institution and preserving its reputation, perceive they are held accountable if patients are injured, and therefore adopt risk-adverse behaviours. Fractures are visible and measurable outcomes, but patients' perceptions of their life quality are less measurable and therefore invisible in the performance measurement systems of health care. These systems transform how nurses take responsibility for the residents and also affect what type of knowledge is considered as valid and relevant in age care.

New knowledge regimes

Within the context of increased awareness of risk, previous views of health care practice as based primarily on tradition, assumptions and precedent have been disrupted. This approach is no longer adequate and the requirements for greater efficiency and quality in health care increasingly demand that practitioners underpin their practice with research evidence.

Evidence-based practice has gained significant authority in nursing over the last couple of decades following the evidence-based medicine (EBM) movement. There are various reasons for the rise of EBP: a response to risk and uncertainty; useful for protection of professional status; and supporting increased economic stringency in the west (Traynor 2002). Arguably the nursing profession, since joining the academy in the late twentieth century, appears to be more aligned with the medical model. If correct, this analysis pinpoints that the nursing profession itself has participated in creating greater tension between 'care' within the traditional models of nursing and the EBP movement. Whether this analysis is valid is not the focus of our discussion, but illustrates the complexity of discourses embedded in EBP and professional identity.

Evidence based is now considered globally as a premise for health care delivery, which reflects that clinical practice should be based on scientific inquiry. When an action is performed in the clinic there should be evidence that the action will produce the desired outcomes believed to benefit patients. EBP/EBM emphasises the evaluation of all relevant research related to a specific clinical question using a systematic review. Practice guidelines are then created from the evidence that has been judged to be best according to strict scientific criteria. Systematic reviews identify which interventions are most effective and incorporate critical evaluation of the associated economics. Soon after EBM was introduced, nursing and other health sciences adopted the same knowledge regime promoted by organisations such as the Cochrane Collaboration and similar centres (e.g. the Joanna Briggs Institute) responsible for systematic reviews, meta-analyses, and development of guidelines for evidence-based clinical practice. Similarly, new EBP journals and research funding schemes have proliferated to encourage development, inquiry and discussions about practical, epistemological and ideological issues.

The most frequently cited definition of EBM remains that of Sackett et al.

> ... the conscientious, explicit and judicious use of current best evidence in making decisions about the care of individuals. The practice of evidence-based medicine means integrating individual clinical expertise with the best available external clinical evidence from systematic research.
>
> (Sackett et al. 1996: 71)

This definition signalled the acceptance of a broad view of what might constitute evidence, including clinical and practitioner's expertise. However, in reality a hierarchy of evidence exists which privileges some types of research above other forms of evidence. The randomised controlled trial (RCT) continues to be regarded as the golden standard, and is ranked above other methodologies (Derkatch 2008; Kristiansen & Mooney 2006). Sackett & Oxman (1994) have been criticised for using their definition as rhetoric, while their handbook of EBM focuses on methods for dealing with scientific evidence and provides little by way of guidance for the development of individual clinical expertise (Kristiansen & Mooney 2004). Broom, Adams and Tovey (2009) clearly express Australian concerns with EBP in a study of evidence-based health care in oncology practice. A major concern among clinical practitioners was the threat and neglect of the art of patient care.

What counts as knowledge is a question central to the construction of nursing responsibility (as well as other disciplines). Holmes et al. (2006) argue that EBP has become a dominant discourse in nursing and is a dangerously normative, privileging scientific knowledge over other forms of knowledge. This, therefore, has created new regimes of truth where, the RCT is considered sovereign in a hierarchy of methodologies that produce evidence. These regimes of truth form part of the *governing* of practices of nurses and have supplanted the previous understandings about knowledge for clinical work which included the value of practical, tacit and experiential forms of knowing (e.g. Benner 1984, Eraut 1994; Schön 1987). The nursing profession then, in some respects has become complicit in the privileging of scientific knowledge over more traditional notions of care. Therefore the regimes of truth that influence their practices create tensions between traditions of care that privileged a particular 'knowing-in-action' that are in conflict with externally imposed but also professionally appropriated forms of EBP.

The recent work of Norwegian philosopher Grimen (2010) supports this shift when he argues that a new epistemological division of labour is a possible consequence of the growth of EBP. The establishment of a new type of organisation (e.g. Clearinghouses and Cochrane Collaboration) mandated to assess the quality of research and generate reports and guidelines to support professional practice signals a change in knowledge generation. These new knowledge houses do not undertake research but undertake systematic reviews. Therefore, their role becomes that of interpreter and disseminator of knowledge produced at universities and research centres. Power over knowledge production has moved from universities to new expert groups at the EBP centres, and professionals in the field are reduced to accepting and managing evidence that is defined outside their own workplace. Professionals like nurses and doctors rarely have the skills and resources necessary for assessing the quality of reviews and therefore rely on the output of the new knowledge houses. The premises for decision making have changed and being responsible can now be interpreted as following the latest update from the new knowledge centres and the locus of control for professional responsibility is increasingly located outside the community of practice rather than within.

Governance of professional responsibility

Rose, O'Malley and Valverde (2006), as discussed earlier, suggested understanding governmentality by identifying the sphere of governance and the operational techniques of that governmentality. We have argued that professional responsibility in nursing forms the sphere of governance and that EBP together with the culture of risk surveillance are the operational techniques of that governmentality.

The operational can be understood as functioning across two distinct axes. First, the political axis where new knowledge regimes, audit systems and economic discourses influence the operation of health care institutions. Second, a personal axis of the governance of self through the cultivation of attitudes and qualifications needed to be compliant with EBP and risk policy.

Systematic structuring of nursing work through evidence-based guidelines is a new way of making nursing visible and demystifying practice. This is a new form of visibility based on guidelines that give detailed information about best and often the most cost-effective practices. The guidelines provide information that becomes operationally governing of the work of nurses. A problematic aspect of EBP is that there is rarely universal agreement about what is the best and valid evidence for a certain practice. Guidelines do not include procedures for their own use. It takes discretion to translate and transform evidence to suit the needs of individual patients in distinct situations (Grimen 2010; Heggen & Engebretsen 2009).

Returning to our case of residential care and the use of gardens, the practice of nurses is illustrative of the governance of self through risk avoidance. Clearly it is important to understand the risks of fracture in elderly residents and how to implement health promotion across a variety of sites. The information/evidence about risk factors may be used to instruct nurses about their work. Being responsible is understood as being compliant with general guidelines made outside the workplace in the new EBP centres. The guidelines represent a regime of knowledge and truth which presuppose trust in the integrity of those developing the guidelines by those nurses responsible for their implementation. As illustrated in our case, there is evidence of privileging certain practices for reducing the risk of falls and fractures, but at the same time research-based evidence exists about the positive impact of letting residents use dementia gardens.

Being responsible is in this context being compliant; and the level of compliance is controlled through the audit practices or what nurses in our case define as 'paper care'. Audit is one of the techniques of governance where performance is measured against standards and often against individual perform-ance. This is another drive for changing how responsibility is constructed in nursing. There has been a shift from collective shared responsibility for patient care in nursing to greater individual responsibility. A critical aspect of the risk and audit culture is, as exemplified in the case, a practice marked by caution and 'watching your back' or defensive strategies. In this case, being responsible was making sure residents did not have free access to using the dementia garden because of a perceived risk of injury. Nursing practices are perceived as constantly under surveillance and therefore are revised in response to perceived risks and mitigation strategies.

In addition to new forms of visibility and new ways of practising as a respon-sible nurse, the evidence-based movement has introduced new dominant codes for knowledge production and giving science what Foucault has called a disciplining and normalising form of social control. Making science the dominant way of knowing has been the subject of considerable critique. Such criticisms do not necessarily argue against the value of science per se, but rather are directed against the hegemonic positioning of abstract knowledge at the expense of creativity, embodied and intuitive tacit knowledge (Benner 1984). Ignoring what Sennett (2008) calls the craftsmanship of professional work and others have labelled the art of patient care is at the core of the EBP critiques.

For Foucault the self is a cultural and historical phenomenon created through discourses that include practices. To fulfil the personal axis related to governance EBP requires individual nurses to adopt certain practices, such as implementa-tion of guidelines to improve health care, monitor their own practice, promote risks and perform risk management. The strategies are often built on the need for individuals to govern themselves and behave independently and responsibly in daily practice. One of the appealing aspects in EBP is its ability to tap into the highest form of accepted contemporary authority, namely science (Winch, Creedy & Chaboyer 2002: 159). Taking responsibility for being a high status knowledge worker with the potential of reducing risks and documenting effects of your own practice might be interpreted as a tempting invitation and rather easy to recruit 'volunteers'.

Conclusion

In this chapter we have argued that what professional responsibility means for nurses has changed profoundly in the course of the last decades. We have focused on two driving forces. One relates to the development of the risk society and how risk operates in the context of health care services where patient safety is the focus of attention. Diminishing patient risk is done in a variety of ways, including protecting patients from possible injuries and harm. The second driving force is the emergence of EBP where evidence for best or safe practice is offered. Risk and evidence are closely connected, like a hand in a glove and also within the wider economic interests of gaining more health care for less money.

We have argued that shifts in the political governance (including knowledge policy) of nursing have changed how nurses perceive responsibility. Nurses previously perceived their responsibility as providing selfless service, giving priority to what might serve as the best care for patients, having a duty to the organisation and loyalty to the fellowship of nurses. Now there is a focus on individual responsibility for practice, demonstrating accountability through written documentation of practice (audit) and compliance with guidelines produced by experts outside the ward. These shifts signal the construction of responsibility in nursing as a form of governmentality, where discourses of risk and evidence shape the way nurses work.

Although discourses of risk and EBP are dominant, there is no single 'right' way, and nurses need to develop their capability to navigate their way in this new form of governance. Frequently *'evidence is against evidence'* and responsibility in nursing requires interpretation of what evidence will best support the care and treatment of each individual patient in different situations. There is clearly value in a focus on risk and building care on research based evidence but these need to be understood within context; nurses must reflect about what evidence to use and how to use it to reduce risks to patients. Responsibility in nursing should include balancing the risks to patient safety with the risks to patient wellbeing.

It is necessary for the collective culture of nurses to be re-built and therefore strengthen the profession (not only fighting for increase of salary). We are not romantic about the past, but argue that the new contours in the web of commitments require a renewal of the collective aspects of nursing. Building practice on a platform of both individual and collective responsibility will strengthen the awareness and critical reflections about the impact of these new discourses on practice. This could facilitate a practice environment which diminishes the defensive practices that arise in the accountability systems that focus on individuals. Increasing the transparency of patient care and professional work and analysing the effects of risk management and EBP on patient care and nursing as a profession is urgently needed. If such a re-constitution of the field of nursing is to be possible, then the current dominance of particular regimes of risk management and EBP will need to be challenged and resisted, while recognising that escalating costs of health care will continue to colonise more traditional collective commitments to care.

References

Alaszewski, A. (2005) Risk, safety and organisational change in health care? *Health, Risk & Society* 7, 315–18.

Annandale, E. (1996) Working on the front-line: risk culture and nursing in the new NHS. *The Sociological Review* **44**, 416–51.

Australian Commission on Safety and Quality in Health Care (2009) *Preventing Falls and Harm from Falls in Older People: Best Practice Guidelines for Australian Residential Aged Care Facilities.* Canberra: Commonwealth of Australia. Available online at: http://www.health.gov.au/internet/safety/publishing.nsf/content/FallsGuidelines-AustRACF (accessed 30 October 2010).

Beck, U. (1992) *The Risk Society: Towards a new Modernity.* London: Sage.

Beck, U. (1999) *World at Risk.* Cambridge: Polity Press.

Benner, P. (1984) *From Novice to Expert. Excellence and Power in Clinical Nursing Practice.* Menlo Park: Addison-Wesley.

Broom, A., Adams, J. & Tovey, P. (2009) Evidence-based healthcare in practice: a study of clinician resistance, professional de-skilling and inter-specialty differentiation in oncology, *Social Science and Medicine* **68**, 192–200.

Castle, N.G. & Ferguson, J.C. (2010) What is nursing home quality and how is it measured? *The Gerontologist* **50**(4), 426–42.

Clancy, A. & Svensson, T. (2007) 'Faced' with responsibility: Levinasian ethics and challenges of responsibility in Norwegian public health nursing, *Nursing Philosophy* **8**(3), 158–66.

Danaher, G., Schirato, T. & Webb, J. (2000) *Understanding Foucault.* Sydney: Allen & Unwin.

Dean, M. (2010) *Governmentality: Power and Rule in Modern Society,* 2nd edn. London: Sage.

Derkatch, C. (2008) Method as argument: boundary work in evidence-based medicine. *Social Epistemology* **22**(4), 371–88.

Detweiler, M.B., Murphy, P.F., Myers, L.C. & Kim, K.Y. (2008) Does a wander garden influence inappropriate behaviors in dementia residents? *American Journal of Alzheimer's Disease and Other Dementias* **23**(1), 31–45.

Detweiler, M.B., Murphy, P.F., Kim, K.Y., Myers, L.C. & Ashai, A. (2009) Scheduled medications and falls in dementia patients utilizing a wander garden, *American Journal of Alzheimer's Disease and Other Dementias* **24**(4), 322–32.

Dworkin, G. (1988) *The Theory and Practice of Autonomy.* Cambridge: Cambridge University Press.

Eby, M. (2000) The challenges of being accountable. In Brechin, A., Brown, H. and Eby, M. (eds) *Critical Practice in Health and Social Care.* pp. 187–208. London: Sage.

Elstad, I. & Hamran, T. (1995) *Et kvinnefag i moderniseringen. Sykehuspleien mellom fagtradisjon og målstyring* [Modernization of a female profession]. Oslo: Ad Notam Gyldendal AS.

Eraut, M. (1994) *Developing Professional Knowledge and Competence.* Washington, DC: Falmer Press.

Foucault, M. (2001) Governmentality. In Faubion, J.D. (ed.) *Essential Works of Foucault 1954–1984: Vol. 3. Power.* pp. 201–22. London: Penguin Books.

Giddens, A. (1990) *The Consequences of Modernity.* Cambridge: Polity Press.

Godin, P. (2006) *Risk and Nursing Practice.* Hampshire: Palgrave MacMillan.

Gottlieb, K. & Robinson, G. (2006) *A Practical Guide for Integrating Civic Responsibility Into the Curriculum.* Washington, DC: American Association of Community Colleges.

Grimen, H. (2010) Debatten om evidensbasering – noen utfordringer [The debate about EBP – a few challenges]. In Grimen, H. and Terum L.I. (eds) *Evidensbasert profesjonsutøvelse.* Oslo: Abstrakt. 191–222.

Hall, D.R. (2002) Risk society and the second demographic transition. *Canadian Studies in Population* 29(2), 173–93.

Heggen, K. & Engebretsen, E. (2009) En dekonstruktiv nærlesning av arbeidsbok for sykepleiere [A deconstructive analysis of a Norwegian textbook in nursing]. *Sykepleien Forskning* 4(1), 28–33.

Hernandez, R.O. (2007) Effects of therapeutic gardens in special care units for people with dementia: two case studies. *Journal of Housing for Elderly* 21, 117–52.

Holmes, D., Murray, S.J., Perron, A. & Rail, G. (2006) Deconstructing the evidence-based discourse in health sciences: truth, power and fascism. *International Journal of Evidence Based Healthcare* 4, 180–6.

Johnstone, M.J. (2008) *Bioethics: A Nursing Perspective,* 5th edn. Chatswood, Australia: Elsevier.

Kristiansen, I.S. & Mooney, G. (eds) (2006) *Evidence-based Medicine in its Place.* London: Routledge.

Lemke, T. (2001) 'The birth of bio-politics' – Michel Foucault's lecture at the Collège de France on neo-liberal governmentality. *Economy and Society* 30(2), 190–207.

Lupton, D. (1999) *Risk.* London: Routledge.

Löwenheim, O. (2007) The responsibility to responsibilize: foreign offices and the issuing of travel warnings. *International Political Sociology* 1, 203–21.

May, L. (1996) *The Socially Responsive Self, Social Theory and Professional Ethics.* Chicago: The University of Chicago Press.

McKee, K. (2009) Post-foucauldian governmentality: what does it offer critical social policy analysis? *Critical Social Policy* 29(3), 465–86.

Nerland, M. & Jensen, K. (2006) The construction of a new professional self: an analysis of the curricula for nurses and computer engineers in Norway. In Brown, A., Kirpal, S. and Rauner, F. (eds) *Identities at Work.* Dordrecht: Kluwer Academic.

Power, M. (2000) The audit society – second thoughts, *International Journal of Auditing* 4, 111–19.

Registered Nurses Association of Ontario (2002) *Prevention of Falls and Fall Injuries in the Older Adult.* Toronto: Registered Nurses Association of Ontario.

Rose, N., O'Malley P. & Valverde, M. (2006) Governmentality. *Annual Review of Law and Social Science* 2, 83–104.

Sackett, D.L. & Oxman, A.D. (1994) *The Cochrane Collaboration Handbook.* Oxford: Cochrane Collaboration.

Sackett, D.L., Rosenburg, W.M.C., Muir Gray, J.A., Haynes, R.B. & Richardson, W.S. (1996) Evidence-based medicine: what it is and what it isn't. *British Medical Journal* 312, 71–2.

Schön, D. (1987) *Educating the Reflective Practitioner.* San Francisco: Jossey-Bass Publishers Inc.

Sennett, R. (2008) *The Craftman.* London: Yale University Press.

Solbrekke, T.D. (2005) *Understanding Conceptions of Professional Responsibility.* Ph.D. dissertation. Series of dissertations submitted to Det utdanningsvitenskapelige fakultet, Universitetet i Oslo, No. 88.

Solbrekke, T.D. (2008) Professional responsibility as legitimate compromises – from communities of education to communities of work. *Studies in Higher Education* 33 (4), 485–500.

Solbrekke, T.D. & Heggen, K. (2009) Sykepleieansvar – fra profesjonelt moralsk ansvar til teknisk regnskapsplikt? [Professional responsibility in nursing – focusing the tensions between moral values and audit]. *Tidsskrift for Arbejdsliv* 11(3), 49–61.

Sønbø Kristiansen, I. & Mooney, G. (2004) *Evidenced Based Medicine: in its Place.* London: Routledge.

Sullivan, W. (2005) *Work and Integrity: The Crises and Promise of Professionalism in America,* 2nd edn. San Francisco: Jossey-Bass Publishers Inc.

Svensson, L.G. & Karlsson, A. (2008) Profesjoner, kontroll og ansvar [The professions, control and responsibility]. In Molander, A. and Terum, L.I. (eds) *Profesjonsstudier.* Oslo: Universitetsforlaget.

Traynor, M. (2002) The oil crisis, risk and evidence based practice. *Nursing Inquiry* 9(3), 162–9.

Waring, J.J. (2009) Constructing and reconstructing narratives of patient safety. *Social Science and Medicine* 69, 1722–31.

Wellard, S.J. (2010) Challenges in designing a resident centred dementia garden in a risk adverse culture. Presentation to the *Australian Association of Gerontology Conference,* November 24th, Tasmania.

Winch, S., Creedy, D. & Chaboyer, W. (2002) Governing nursing conduct: the rise of evidence-based practice. *Nursing Inquiry* 9(3), 156–61.

11 Teacher education for professional responsibility

What should it look like?

Berit Karseth

Introduction

Teacher education as a professional programme consists of different school subjects, educational sciences as well as practical training. As a professional programme, teacher education is concerned with conceptual and technical competence. These competencies indicate that students have learned the knowledge base and the technical skills needed to practise (Stark & Lattuca 1997). Furthermore, the development of professional identity, ethics and moral competence have always been seen as important aspects of teacher education. Additionally, connection to the practical fields is essential and the ability to meld concepts and skills in practical training is emphasised. Consequently, an integrated approach to theory and practice is a hallmark of the narrative of teacher education.

Although people engaged in teacher education generally would agree that all the aspects mentioned are crucial in the education of prospective teachers, there are various opinions about the significance and weight to be attached to the different elements. Teacher education as a 'tribe' is based on a divergent rather than a convergent approach (see Becher & Trowler 2001). The meaning of 'good work' is disputed by the profession itself. Moreover, the nature of teacher professionalism and the meaning of professional responsibility are contested not only at the level of the profession and practice, but also at the level of policy. The teacher profession as well as teacher education in many countries is highly regulated through national curricula. That does not however change the fact that teacher education, like other professional education, is an important institution to look into as it reflects what is at stake for the profession concerning knowledge base, standards, skills and professional ethics.

In this chapter I elaborate on professional responsibility by addressing different approaches to what teacher education is or should be about. The arguments put forward are theoretically grounded rather than empirical. However, in order to illustrate my points, I refer to the recent reform in teacher education for primary and lower secondary education in Norway. Even though this is restricted to one national context and one profession, I believe the discussion is relevant beyond the limits of teacher education and national boarders.

With reference to my reading of the curriculum and research literature on teacher education, I discuss three approaches. By doing so, my intention is to retain the complexity of the profession and the issue of an education fostering professional responsibility without being caught in polarities. There is, I will argue, no consensus or hegemonic discourse on the purposes of teacher education, therefore a dynamic approach which captures the interplay between different stakeholders is needed.

The first approach argues that teacher education should be based to a significant extent on research and academic work. The second underscores teacher education as a moral activity. The third places teacher education in a global context where it is seen as embedded in the national as well the global landscape of higher education where scientisation and competitiveness are fundamental characteristics. How these three approaches capture and define professional responsibility is at the core of the discussion. My analysis borrows some concepts from Paula Ensor (2004) and Hugh Sockett (2008) that I find useful and relevant. In advance of this analysis, some words about the recent curriculum reform in teacher education in Norway are necessary.

The curriculum reform of teacher education for primary and secondary education in Norway

In 2006 teacher education for primary and lower secondary education in Norway was evaluated by the Norwegian Agency for Quality Assurance in Education (NOKUT 2006). The evaluation executive (nine experts) concluded that there is a great variety between the institutions offering teacher education with regard to the quality of the educational programmes. One reason for this according to the evaluation is the differences in conditions when it comes to the size, structure and organisation of the programme, leadership, level of competence, students and the nature of the cooperation with schools. The evaluation also emphasises other aspects that are more controlled by the particular institution itself, such as students' participation and engagement, subject teachers' commitment to subject didactics and their engagement in research. The main concerns expressed are the lack of coherence between the different elements of the programme (school subject, subject didactics, pedagogy and practical training) and between theory and practice.

Three years after the evaluation executive delivered its report, the Ministry of Education proposed a new teacher education programme for primary and lower secondary education and published a White Paper on Teacher Education entitled 'The teacher – the role and the education' (St.meld.nr. 11 2008–2009). An important suggestion was to strengthen the emphasis on subject knowledge and teaching skills, the quality of the programme and research orientation. One of the principal elements proposed is a dual-level teacher education meaning two programmes geared to the different levels of schooling (years 1–7 and years 5–10). Furthermore, and in order to create better integration, a new expanded educational science subject 'Pedagogy and pupil-related skills'

(PPS) is suggested. Additionally, improved quality of practical training is emphasised.

The White Paper sets out seven fundamental areas of competence essential for all teachers where one concerns ethical awareness in line with the school's value base and educational theory and subject didactics, that is, insight into how children and young people learn, and the ability to plan, deliver and assess instruction to promote pupil learning (Rundskriv F-05-10: 5; Fact Sheet 2009).

The Parliament decided that a new national curriculum regulation as well as national curriculum guidelines should be developed and the Government appointed a committee in the spring of 2009. The committee delivered its report at the beginning of 2010 and the new curriculum was put into action in autumn 2010. The committee mandate stated that the curriculum should build on the fundamental areas of competence mentioned in the White Paper. Furthermore, the curriculum should be based on descriptions of learning outcomes in line with the national qualifications framework for higher education.

The new curriculum for primary and lower secondary teacher education programmes for years 1–7 and years 5–10 (KD 2010) consists of the national curriculum regulation that represents the legal binding text of the curriculum and national curriculum guidelines describing the main principles and the curriculum for each of the school subjects (including educational science and practice) for the two programmes (years 1–7 and years 5–10).

In the curriculum regulation it is stated under the heading 'Scope and objective' that:

> The objective of the Regulations is to ensure that teacher education institutions provide integrated, professionally oriented and research-based primary and lower secondary teacher education programmes of high academic quality. These study programmes must comply with the Education Act and the prevailing curriculum for primary and lower secondary education and training. The institutions are to facilitate integrated primary and lower secondary teacher education programmes showing coherence and cohesion between theoretical and practical studies, between subjects and subject didactics and between subjects. The primary and lower secondary teacher education programmes are to provide the candidates with sound academic and didactic knowledge and to qualify them for research-based professional performance and continuous professional development. The education programmes are to demonstrate close interaction with the professional field as well as the society of which schools are part. The education programmes are to place the teaching profession in a historical and social context and contribute to critical reflection and professional understanding.
>
> (KD 2010: 1)

This text illustrates the complexity of teacher education and its academic and professional orientation, but it also demonstrates the absence of a language of ethical and moral issues in defining the scope and objective. In the following discussion, I draw on the quotation in addition to examples of learning outcome descriptions.

Teacher education as a research-based enterprise

There is a strong argument among politicians, teacher educators as well as educational bureaucrats that the purpose of teacher education is to offer an education where scientific knowledge makes up one of the most significant frames of reference. Teacher education should be anchored in scientific knowledge and relevant research.

The new curriculum regulation referred to above reflects such an orientation by emphasising the importance of research-based teaching and to qualify the prospective teachers for research-based performance. Furthermore, the curriculum reflects the increased emphasis on securing knowledgeable professionals that are able to work in a systematic and knowledge-based way. The new differentiated structure of teacher education (grade 1–7 teacher and grade 5–10 teacher) creates an image of the teacher as an expert in particular school subjects as well as having an in-depth knowledge about students as learners. The inclusion of a 15 ECTS[1] credit (half a semester of study) bachelor thesis including an introduction to scientific theory and methods, further underlines the need for a scientific basis of teacher's work.

A statement by the Minister of Education and Research also illustrates this point. Teachers in compulsory education, she argues, should have a research-oriented approach to their teaching practice, have access to research and be competent to apply research results in their teaching. Thus during teacher education, students should come in contact with research and gain experience with research (Aasland 2008).

The emphasis on research-based teacher education can, however, be analysed from two different points of departure.

First, research-based teacher education can be viewed as an academic education where the curriculum emphasises acquisition of scientific content knowledge in particular academic disciplines and a general problem-solving capacity (Musset 2010: 5). This is consistent with what Ensor labels the disciplinary discourse of higher education, which emphasises the mastery of concepts and modes of analysis or as an 'apprenticeship of a student into those largely self-referential knowledge domains that we call disciplines' (Ensor 2004: 343). According to Sockett (2008), such teacher education represents a *scholar-professional model* characterised primarily by interest in an intellectual endeavour where the curriculum approach is tightly located in a discipline. The epistemic purpose is to develop teachers who are subject specialists and who see themselves as historians, scientists, linguists, etc. The epistemological nature of the discipline provides intellectual virtue, which, Sockett maintains, defines the moral virtue (Sockett 2008: 49–52). Mastery of the disciplinary knowledge is the main objective in educating towards professional responsibility.

The idea of the unity of teaching and research in higher education is often traced back to Humboldt and the beginning of the nineteenth century. However, when examining the history of teacher education for basic education in Norway, teachers were ambivalent in their attitudes towards an academic orientation (Hagemann 1992).

An interesting case in this regard arose from a dispute regarding teacher education in Norway in 1929 where questions were raised as to whether or not the education of teachers should build on 'examen artium' [the examination for the General Certificate of Education (Advanced Level)]. In the discussion, references were made to the reforms of teacher education in Germany and the abolition of the distinction between academia and the seminary. However, the opponents representing seminaries and local schools argued in favour of teacher education based on local and rural culture and advocated that, if 'artium' is the foundation, the schools will get teachers that are theoreticians and thereby not appropriately trained for teaching (Hagemann 1992).

Secondly, research-based teacher education can be understood as the acquisition of comprehensive research-based knowledge on teaching. Teachers are educated as expert in their precise field as *teachers* (Musset 2010). Sockett (2008) identifies this as a *clinician–professional* model. Within this model the knowledge base is seen as research-driven and 'it celebrates the development of teaching as a profession, with medicine being seen as the benchmarking for its development' (Sockett 2008: 54). Consequently, he argues: 'a model built from this perspective on the profession and its knowledge-base is appropriately described as the (medical-driven) notion of the clinician' (Sockett 2008: 54). The epistemological purpose is rooted in research-based scholarly knowledge and there is an emphasis on social morality where moral purpose is intended to contribute to the development and maintenance of a democratic society.

The comparison with medical education is made explicit by Darling-Hammond (2010) and she argues that the arguments against professionalisation of teacher education today are similar to those used by commentators who were sceptical towards the professionalisation of medicine previously. They used arguments in line with a traditional apprenticeship model and 'felt that medicine could best be learned by following another doctor around in a buggy' (Darling-Hammond 2010: 39). According to Darling-Hammond the central issue teacher education must confront is 'how to foster learning about and from practice *in* practice'. Factors as coherence in standards, clarity about curriculum, and commitment to act based on knowledge about what appears to be effective are pointed to as particularly important in order to improve teacher education (Darling-Hammond et al. 2005: 479). Furthermore, accreditation is seen as essential in order to set a 'clear goal of leveraging improvements based on the practices of successful models and of ending the practice of poor preparation by so-called traditional and alternative programs alike' (Darling-Hammond 2010: 39). With a clear reference to other professions such as medicine and the emphasis of transferring of successful models, the call for a research-based teacher education can be associated with the evidence-based teaching argument towards a knowledge-based teaching practice. To educate towards professional responsibility from this perspective entails emphasis on abilities with regard to work in line with professional standards and to ensure education for all through a systematic evidence based approach to teaching.

Taken together, while a teacher education that is based on a scholar–professional model emphasising an academic orientation puts the different school subjects and their disciplinary anchors to the fore, teacher education based on a clinician–professional model, highlighting expert knowledge, is more concerned about securing necessary teaching skills in line with professional standards. In both cases scientific knowledge and research is essential.

A scholar–professional orientation is visible in the new Curriculum Regulation as stated in the following learning outcome for years 5–10, which states that the candidate 'has sound academic and subject didactic knowledge in the subjects making up the education programme and knowledge of the subjects as school subjects and research subjects' (KD 2010: 2). The clinician–professional orientation is noticeable in the learning outcomes descriptions for both programmes which state that the candidate

> is able to assess and use relevant research results and carry out systematic development work … is able to evaluate and document the pupils' learning and development in relation to the objectives of the education, give feedback that promotes learning and contribute so that the pupils can evaluate their own learning.
>
> (KD 2010: 3)

With regard to professional responsibility, both models, it may be argued, define the teacher as either a knowledgeable expert or a scholar, while moral issues are described in a scientific manner. But while knowing the content is essential in the scholar–professional model, the clinician–professional model emphasises usable knowledge where teachers are committed to seek research-based knowledge throughout their careers in order to make professional judgements based on evidence about what works. These two models indicate also that the question of professional autonomy is addressed differently. Within the scholar–professional model, autonomy means individual freedom and is an important fundament and an institutionalised value widespread in higher education. In contrast, professional autonomy within a clinician–professional model is limited by the development of guiding standards based on evidence. Consequently, professional responsibility in the latter sense is tightly linked to the ability to live up to standards defined scientifically and formal rules of conduct. Although these authorised norms, according to Solbrekke (2008: 498), are important for preventing unlawful or unethical conduct, there is a risk, however.

> that 'externally' defined regulations become detailed and begin to function as a 'rule-book', thus diminishing the need for a professional to make

reflective judgments. ..., it is tempting to question whether an apparent over-emphasis on formal knowledge and predefined norms is sufficient to encourage reflexive conceptions of moral and societal responsibility that are robust enough to endure throughout a work career.

(Solbrekke 2008: 497)

Teacher education as a moral activity

The judgments teachers make are not simply of a technical or instrumental nature; they are not simply about finding the most effective means to achieve certain ends. Rather, they always also involve an *evaluation* of the means and hence require *value-judgment* about the desirability of the ways in which particular aims and ends might be achieved.

(Biesta 2009: 185–6)

The above quotation emphasises the moral aspect of teaching and the importance of judgement about what is educationally desirable and worthwhile. The question of 'doing good' according to ethical, cultural and pedagogical criteria has been central in teaching as well as teacher education and there is a strong narrative in the scholarly literature of seeing teaching as a moral enterprise (see Bullough 2010). The moral purpose of education was placed to the fore in Norwegian teacher education from the beginning and Christianity was the main subject. Baune (2001) argues that the teacher in the 1850s still was a

a pious minded man who in life and living was a true Christian example for his students. In fact all activities and all that took place at the teacher training seminaries [colleges] were prepared and arranged to fulfil this purpose. According to regulations a strict selection procedure for accepting students was demanded from the seminaries and material should be handled in a way consistent with their religious and moral aims. The teacher training seminaries consequently were more like religious institutions more so than educational institutions. The students should be educated – not only to become pious and moral Christians – but also to become good and obedient members of the common people's class of society.

(Baune 2001: 86, author's translation)

The teacher training seminaries were often located in rural areas and the students had to stay in dormitories/boarding schools. This made it possible for the teacher educators to control and follow the students closely, and according to the rules, see to it that the students used their spare time in a useful way (Baune 2001). Teachers at that time were perceived as dedicated to humanity, as well as showing a personal engagement and willingness to take the role as enlighteners of the people in the service of the nation. Michelsen (2002) argues that institutional autonomy, Christian values and national state formation were key elements in the seminary tradition. The need to be independent of the

'Bildung' tradition of the university and its value neutrality (Michelsen 2002: 37) was also important in the narrative of teacher education for primary school. Hench, the Norwegian seminary tradition rests upon a rural orientation rather than an urban one. This also means a resistance to development of elites in society: 'The elite is seen as alien, effete or exploitive. The good sense and rights of ordinary people are stressed. They are the carriers of national identity' (Lauglo 1990: 72).

This historic image of the purpose of teacher education still makes sense and underscores the moral aspect of education. Within Sockett's *moral agent professional model* teaching is defined as moral activity. Consequently, there is no aspect of teaching or teachers' engagement to which the moral is irrelevant. Sockett (2008: 59) argues that: 'to have a moral purpose *is* thus to have an epistemic purpose'. Furthermore, 'proponents of the model, derived from Aristotle, would urge a radical re-thinking of teacher education, rooted in an institutional ethos, intellectual rigor and the articulation and discussion of the profound character of moral issues confronting the teacher' (Sockett 2008: 62). Within this model moral considerations are placed at the heart of the enterprise of teaching. Education is concerned with human betterment and is therefore a moral business.

With this perspective in mind, it is appropriate to ask if the new national curriculum regulation for teacher education for primary and lower secondary school, with its emphasis on learning outcomes, represents a new curriculum genre where the moral aspect is approached differently? By way of response, I compare two texts, the first is from the new regulation and the second is from the former regulation.

The new curriculum regulation specifies learning outcomes with regard to expectations of the candidates' general competence as follows:

> is able to contribute to a professional teaching community with regard to the further development of good practice and a professionally ethical platform ... is able to stimulate an understanding of democracy, democratic participation and the ability for critical reflection adapted to the year in question ... is able to contribute to the strengthening of international and multicultural dimensions of the work done in the school and contribute to an understanding of the Sami people's status as an indigenous people, ... is able to identify his/her own needs for learning and competence with regard to the teaching profession ... has adaptive and developmental competence as a basis for his/her encounter with the school of the future.
>
> (KD 2010: 3)

It is also stated that the candidate is expected to have the following skill: 'is able to reflect critically about his/her own and the school's practice in their work for the further development of the role of the teacher and issues of a professionally ethical nature' (KD 2010: 3).

For purposes of comparison, the former curriculum states:

> The teacher needs to apply *professional ethics competence* in all activities. This involves the capacity to see the relations between general morals and ethics and the special requirements of the profession. Relations with children and adults may involve both the duty to disclose information and the duty of confidentiality. The teacher often encounters children in conflict and crisis, and this may result in ethical dilemmas. The teacher role confers power, and the teacher must administer this power in accordance with legislation, acknowledged basic values and children's right to equal treatment. The profession requires the exercise of discrimination and ethical considerations in the selection of learning materials and working methods. Ethical competence provides a basis for the teacher's professional development, and is necessary if the role is to be conducted with honesty, responsibility and humility.
>
> (UFD 2003: 3).

The former curriculum text uses words that connote specific values such as honesty and humility, while also issues of power and general morals, and duty of confidentiality to describe the moral aspects of teaching. This leaves us with the impression that education is a moral enterprise and teachers are expected to act in accordance to specific values. However, there are no defined learning outcomes articulated to be 'measured' in order to determine the extent to which students and teachers are actually practising in accordance with these values.

The text of the new regulation introduces a new rhetoric which is concerned with the candidates *abilities/skill* such as to contribute to an ethical platform and to educate towards democracy. Without mentioning what values that should underlie teachers' practice, the new vocabulary connotes expectations of action. Teachers should be able to 'build' an ethical platform (however that may be understood) and to 'educate' for democracy (whatever is meant by that concept). Additionally, learning outcomes represents a new way of formulating what education is about. In other words, the new curriculum is embedded in a discourse where *outcome* is the privileged word. Although we may argue that teacher education to some extend has always been geared towards social ends (social legitimation) rather than towards knowledge for its own sake (epistemological legitimation), the new language of learning outcome defined as 'statements of what a learner is expected to know, understand and/or be able to do at the end of a period of learning' (Bologna Working Group on Qualifications Framework 2005: 29) has moved teacher education towards a more measurable enterprise and in line with predefined standards.

Historically, as already mentioned, Norwegian teacher education was rooted in a discourse where morality was linked to Christianity. Teacher education today, however, is embedded in another discourse and attendant institutional norms. One such norm is that students and schools should value *the differences* of opinion. According to McEneaney and Meyer (2000: 201), there is 'growing empirical evidence of a historical shift toward "omnivorousness" among high-status individuals'. This tolerance or cultural openness is highly visible in educational discussions where we find arguments about the importance of opening up the school for all types of cultural activities. This openness, however, must be analysed through the lens of a changing global order as well as an increased emphasis on competitiveness and scientisation. These aspects will be elaborated on below.

Teacher education in a global context

Before the 1990s, as pointed out by Hudson and Zgaga (2008), teacher education in Europe was mainly a closed 'national affair'. However, there has been increasing attempts in the last 20 years to develop and strengthen a European teacher education policy. These efforts point to the emergence and activities of different organisations such as the *Association for Teacher Education in Europe* (ATEE) and the *European Trades Union Committee for Education* (ETUCE). However, teacher education is not only affected by what goes on in the teacher education sector, but also the ongoing restructuring of the higher education system in Europe and the intense effort to develop a coherent system that facilitates mobility, transparency and recognition of qualification from one educational setting to another. The main drive for these attempts in Europe is the Bologna Process and its attempt to organise higher education within a more coherent and compatible European framework. Parallel activities are also pursued by the European Union. In 2000 the European Council in Lisbon stated that by 2010 the Union should become 'the most competitive and dynamic knowledge-based economy in the world, capable of sustainable economic growth, with more and better jobs and greater social cohesion' (Lisbon Strategy 2000). This indicates that debates and policy-making processes with regard to higher education have emerged on a European level that call for research that takes this activity into account.

We may argue that the Bologna process has been revolutionary for cooperation in European Higher Education and represents a concerted attempt to strengthen the linkage between higher education and society. The locus for changes is not just the individual nation state, but European society. The process has mobilised numerous ministers of higher education and high-ranking bureaucrats as well as leaders, staff and students in higher education institutions in Europe towards the development of a European Higher Education Area (Bologna Beyond 2010, 2009). The ambition from the beginning was to consolidate and enrich the European citizenship, develop and strengthen stable, peaceful and democratic societies, social and human growth by enhancing the employability and mobility of citizens and to increase the international competitiveness of European higher education (Bologna Declaration 1999: 1). In order to do that the development of compatible and easily readable degrees and programmes became essential objectives (Bologna Declaration 1999). Standardisation of higher education can be seen as an attempt to manage uncertainty and to create a predictable system. Standardisation is important in order to manage a European higher education system that emphasises universal participation as well as employability, mobility and competitiveness. The Bologna process not only represents an avenue for reforming higher education in Europe, it is also faced with increasing attention from other parts of the world. This global interest is well illustrated by the American researcher Clifford Adelman's argument that the Bologna Process 'has sufficient momentum to become the dominant global model of higher education within two decades' (Adelman 2008: 2).

According to Jon Meyer, the promotion of global models is most dramatic through national educational systems which 'expand isomorphically around the world and which tie individuals into globalised models of modernity' (Meyer 2000: 242). Drori & Meyer (2006) point to the scientisation of modern society and emphasise the extraordinary authority of modern scientific rationalisation to the point where 'the science speaks with highly legitimate authority on the widest range of questions' (Drori & Meyer 2006: 40). This means that national policies as well as institutional practices are highly dependent and constructed within rapidly expanding myths of rationality (Meyer 2008). Consequently, Meyer questions the role of states in creating a global heterogeneousness through national reform. Formal curriculum documents refer to multiple contexts, from the global to the local. Moreover, a current trend is that individuals are seen as promoters of their own learning capacities. To empower the individual person by emphasising the rights and capacities of the individuals, can therefore be seen as a worldwide curricular trend, describing a global language for the curriculum.

Analysed from this perspective, the meaning of educating towards professional responsibility follows a global script where scientisation 'disciplines and rationalises the chaotic uncertainties of social environments, facilitating the creation of articulate rule systems, so that social actors can organise to deal with them' (Drori & Meyer 2006: 31). Consequently, the penetration of scientisation indicates that how professional responsibility is institutionalised follows a science-like logic that works as a paradigmatic umbrella (Drori & Meyer 2006: 46). Within this paradigm the rules of professional responsibility are linked to what is measurable as well as global scripts of transparency and accountability. When taken to extreme, the logic of this argument is that science defines what moral is about.

Apparently, there are signs in the new curriculum of emergent standardisation and scientisation. The use of learning outcomes, the emphasis on the individual learner and an idea of universal skills and qualifications are examples. A curriculum based on descriptions of learning outcomes becomes the national and European currency that enables students and graduates to circulate in a predictable system. Ensor (2004) labels this curriculum as the 'credit exchange discourse' or 'credit accumulation and transfer discourse'. It has a projective orientation towards the global world, and it underlines the importance of students' choices.

It is in the nature of curriculum that it also works as a preserver of institutional practices. Consequently, as long as a national state such as Norway continues to produce national curricula characterised by certain procedures and substantial patterns, the curriculum represents a continuation. Likewise, the purpose of teacher education can be interpreted and translated in different ways and thereby opened up for contesting discourses. Nevertheless, the global knowledge economy and the increased emphasis on competition threaten the power of the national curriculum and its role as a national voice.

According to the discourse of credit exchange and competition, professional responsibility is linked to *delivery*; the teacher needs to be accountable in the sense of producing competences in line with what is specified. This represents a perspective of teaching as an instrumental activity that is far removed from Sockett's model of the teacher as a moral agent–professional. Although my analysis does not give any evidence that the curriculum reform in Norwegian teacher education for primary and lower secondary school moves the role of the teacher as Hopmann (2003) puts it, towards the role of 'stand-up-and-deliver' pedagogy, the emphasis on new assessment strategies and external control of outcomes of schooling as well as the political imperative of the need to improve the students' scores on international tests support arguments based on the logic of science as well as the logic of bureaucracy. These arguments challenge the narrative of teaching that has been advocated by the *Union of Education*, the largest trade union for teaching personnel in Norway, who call attention to professional knowledge as personal and contextual. The Union also emphasises professional diversity and the importance of the freedom of the individual teacher in carrying out his or her pedagogical practice in a personal way (Karseth & Nerland 2007).

Conclusions

In this chapter I have discussed the meaning of professional responsibility in light of three different approaches to the construction of teacher education. To some degree, the approaches are reflective of different historical periods. Viewing the teacher as primarily a moral agent and role model was central in earlier times. Similarly, the emphasis on the scientific base of being a professional teacher has been foregrounded for all teachers, regardless of level. The global context as a frame of reference for education is rather new, although there has been some attempt to stimulate cooperation (for instance, through the EU-funded Erasmus Mundus programme). Within these three approaches, different meanings and aspects of professional responsibility are brought to the fore, and others are left aside.

Although it seems reasonable to see teacher education as increasingly embedded in global scripts of education, it continues to be the case that the translation of these scripts into national and institutional meanings differs (Karseth & Solbrekke 2010).

An alternative approach to the accountability discourse highlighted in various ways in this book, with its instrumental turn on the meaning of professional responsibility, is to investigate how teaching is understood within the tradition of *Bildung*[2] (Karseth & Sivesind 2010). My analysis above suggests that it is timely and appropriate to propose, by way of alternative, a perspective which demands didactical reflection among teachers concerning Bildung and the balance between the inner and outer world. As Hopmann suggests:

> In the perspective of Bildung and Didaktik there are no facts or objects of teaching as factum brutum .... Any given matter (Inhalt) can represent many different meanings (Gehalt), any given meaning (Gehalt) can be opened up *by many different matters (Inhalt). However, there is no matter without* meaning, and no meaning without matter.
>
> (Hopmann 2007: 116)

According to the quotation we may argue that a curriculum based on expected learning outcome overlooks the relationship between meaning and matter. From a Bildung approach, the question to ask is not to ascertain what students should be able to do, instead higher education institutions as teacher education should ask what is the character-forming significance of the knowledge and skills that a culture has at its disposal (Künzli 2000: 46). Moreover, the idea of becoming educated (*gebildet*) embodies a lifelong course, where citizens continuously generate knowledge and virtue through their experiences with the world. In schooling, this means creating an educational process, not in terms of individualistic modes of learning, but by participating in a 'reciprocal exchange of information, consideration and argumentation' (Klafki 2000: 93). Teacher education as all education is about the responsibility of providing opportunities for the learner to develop towards a state of independence and responsibility for their own actions ('Mündigkeit') (Klafki 1998: 308).

Professional responsibility allied to Bildung is a possible way forward in order to (re)claim the importance of seeing teacher education as a place for critical reflection and self-reflexivity. Teacher education can never (and should not) prescribe who the students are to become, but it needs to take seriously the role of providing opportunities epistemologically, socially as well as morally.

Notes

1 ECTS, European Credit Transfer System, is the credit system for higher education used in the European Higher Education Area, involving all countries engaged in the Bologna Process. 60 ECTS credits are attached to the workload of a full-time year of formal learning (academic year) and the associated learning outcomes.

2 Bildung is derived from *bilden*, to form or, in some instances, to cultivate. It is conventionally translated as 'education', although this does not cover the connotations the word has in German. Therefore, I leave the term in German. However, Gert Biesta's way to approach the concept seems fruitful to remind us of the complexity and situateness of the concept: 'The concept of *Bildung* brings together the aspirations of all

those who acknowledge – or hope – that education is more than the simple acquisition of knowledge and skills, that it is more than simply getting things "right," but that it also has to do with nurturing the human person, that it has to do with individuality, subjectivity, in short, with "becoming and being somebody." *Bildung* is a rich, but also a complex concept – a concept, moreover, with a long history' (Biesta 2002: 343).

References

Aasland, T. (2008) Lærerutdanning for framtida. *Utdanning* 17, 34.

Adelman, C. (2008) *The Bologna Club: What U.S. Higher Education Can Learn from a Decade of European Reconstruction.* Washington, DC: Institute for Higher Education Policy.

Baune, T. (2001) Mellom profesjon og academia: Norsk allmennlærerutdanning I historisk perspektiv. In Kvernbekk, T. (ed.) *Pedagogikk og lærerprofesjonalitet.* pp. 83–110. Oslo: Gyldendal Akademisk.

Becher, T. & Trowler, P. (2001) *Academic Tribes and Territories: Intellectual Enquiry and the Culture of Disciplines,* 2nd edn. Buckingham: Open University Press.

Biesta, G. (2009) Values and ideals in teachers' professional judgment. In Gewortz, S., Mahony, P., Hextall, I. and Gribb, A. (eds) *Changing Teacher Professionalism.* pp. 184–93. London: Routledge.

Biesta, G. (2002) Bildung and modernity: the future of bildung in a world of difference. *Studies in Philosophy and Education* 21(4–5), 343–51.

Bologna Beyond 2010 (2009) *Report on the development of the European Higher Education Area Background paper for the Bologna Follow-up Group prepared by the Benelux Bologna Secretariat.* Leuven/Louvain-la-Neuve Ministerial Conference 28–29 April 2009.

Bologna Declaration (1999) *Joint Declaration of the European Minister of Education.* Bologna 19 June 1999.

Bologna Working Group on Qualifications Frameworks (2005) A framework for Qualifications of the European Higher Education Area. Copenhagen: Ministry of Science Technology and Innovation. http://www.bologna-bergen2005.no/Docs/00-Main_doc/050520_Bergen_Communique.pdf.

Bullough, R.V. Jr. (2010) Ethical and moral matters in teaching and teacher education. *Teaching and Teacher Education* doi:10.1016/j.tate.2010.09.007.

Darling-Hammond, L. (2010) Teacher education and the American future. *Journal of Teacher Education* 61(1–2), 35–47.

Darling-Hammond, L., Pacheco, A., Michelli, N. LePage, P., Hammerness, K. & Youngs, P. (2005) Implementing curriculum renewal in teacher education: managing organizational and policy change. In Darling-Hammond, L. and Bransford, J. (eds) *Preparing Teachers for a Changing World.* pp. 442–79. San Francisco: Jossey-Bass Publishers Inc.

Drori, G.S. & Meyer, J.W. (2006) Scientization: making a world safe for organizing. In Djelic, M-L. and Sahlin-Andersson, K. (eds) *Transnational Governance: Institutional Dynamics of Regulation.* Cambridge: Cambridge University Press.

Ensor, P. (2004) Contesting discourses in higher education curriculum restructuring in South Africa. *Higher Education* 48, 339–59.

Lisbon Strategy (2000) Lisbon European Council 23 and 24 March 2000. Presidency conclusions. http://www.europarl.europa.eu/summits/lis1_en.htm

Fact Sheet (2009) *White Paper on Teacher Education 'The teacher – the role and education'.* Report to the Storting No. 11 (2008–2009 Principal elements). handbooks/2009/factsheet-white-paper-on-teacher-educati.html?id=545075 (accessed 21 July 2010).

Hagemann, G. (1992) *Skolefolk*. Oslo: AdNotam Gyldendal.

Hopmann, S. (2003) On the evaluation of curriculum reforms. In Haug, P. and Schwandt, T.A. (eds) *Evaluating Educational Reform*. Connecticut: IAP.

Hopmann, S. (2007) Restrained teaching: the common core of didaktik. *European Educational Research Journal* 6, 109–24.

Hudson, B. & Zgaga, P. (2008) Introduction. In Hudson, B. and Zgaga, P. (eds) *Teacher Education Policy in Europe: A Voice of Higher Education Institutions*. Umeå: University of Umeå, Faculty of Teacher Education.

Karseth, B. & Nerland, M. (2007) Building professionalism in a knowledge society: examining discourses of knowledge in four professional associations. *Journal of Education and Work* 20(4), 335–55.

Karseth, B. & Solbrekke, T.D. (2010) Qualifications frameworks: the avenue towards convergence of european higher education? *European Journal of Education* 45(4), 563–576.

Karseth, B. & Sivesind, K. (2010) Conceptualizing curriculum knowledge within and beyond the national context. *European Journal of Education* 45(1), 103–20.

KD (2010) Forskrift om rammeplan for grunnskolelærerutdanningene for 1-7.trinn og 5.-10.trinn [Regulations concerning a national curriculum for primary and lower secondary teacher education programmes for years 1–7 and years 5–10, English draft version]. Oslo: Kunnskapsdepartmentet [Ministry of Education and Research].

Klafki, W. (1998) Characteristics of Critical-Constructive Didaktik. In Gundem, Bjørg B. and Hopmann, Stefan (eds): Didaktik and /or Curriculum - an International Dialogue. New York: Peter Lang Publishing, 307–330.

Klafki, W. (2000) The Significance of classical theories of Bildung for a contemporary concept of Allgemeinbildung. In Westbury, I., Hopmann, S. and Riquarts, K. (eds) *Teaching as a Reflective Practice. The German Didaktik Tradition*. London: Lawrence Erlbaum Associates.

Künzli, R. (2000) German Didaktik: models of re-presentation, of intercourse and of experience. In Westbury, I., Hopmann, S. and Riquarts, K. (eds) *Teaching as a Reflective Practice. The German Didaktik Tradition*. London: Lawrence Erlbaum Associates.

Künzli, R. (1998) Characteristics of critical-constructive Didaktik. In Gundem, B.B. and Hopmann, S. (eds) *Didaktik and/or Curriculum – an International Dialogue*. pp. 307–30. New York: Peter Lang Publishing.

Lauglo, J. (1990) A comparative perspective with special reference to Norway. In Granheim, M., Kogan, M. and Lundgren, U.P. (eds) *Evaluation as Policymaking*. pp. 66–88. London: Jessica Knigsley Publishers.

McEneaney, E.H. & Meyer, J.W. (2000) The content of the curriculum: an intuitionalist perspective. In Hallinan, M.T. (ed.) *Handbook of the Sociology of Education*. pp. 189–211. London: Kluwer.

Meyer, J.W. (2000) Globalization: sources and effects on national states and societies. *International Sociology* 15, 233–248.

Meyer, J.W. (2008) Reflections on institutional theories of organizations. In Greenwood, R., Oliver, C., Suddaby, R. and Sahlin-Andersson, K. (eds) *The SAGE Handbook of Organizational Institutionalism*. Los Angeles: Sage.

Michelsen, S. (2002) Når styringsambisjoner møter en profesjonsutdanning. In Michelsen, S. and Halvorsen, T. (eds) *Faglige forbindelser. Profesjonsutdanning og kunnskapspolitikk etter høgskolereformen*. pp. 17–52. Bergen: Fagbokforlaget.

Musset, P. (2010) Initial teacher education and continuing training policies in a comparative perspective: current practices in OECD countries and a literature review on potential effects. *OECD Education Working Paper*, no 48. France: OECD Publishing. Doi:10.1787/5kmbphh7s47h-en.

NOKUT (2006) *Evaluering av allmennlærerutdanningen i Norge 2006*. Del 1: Hovedrapport. Rapport fra ekstern komité. Oslo: NOKUT.

Rundskriv F-05-10 (2010) *Forskrift om rammeplan for grunnskolelærerutdanningene for 1.–7. trinn og 5.–10. trinn og forskrift om rammeplan for de samiske grunnskolelærerutdanningene for 1.–7. trinn og 5.–10. trinn*. Skriv til høyere utdanningsinstitusjoner som tilbyr lærerutdanning, datert 21.03.10. Kunnskapsdepartementet.

Sockett, H. (2008) The moral and epistemic purposes of teacher education. In Cochran-Smith, M., Feiman-Nemser, S. and McIntyre, D.J. (eds) *Handbook of Research on Teacher Education*. pp. 45–65. New York: Routledge.

Solbrekke, T.D. (2007) *Understanding Conceptions of Professional Responsibility*. Ph.D. dissertation. University of Oslo: Faculty of Education.

Solbrekke, T.D. (2008) Professional responsibility as legitimate compromises – from communities of education to communities of work. *Studies in Higher Education* 33(4), 485–500.

Stark, J. & Lattuca, L.R. (1997) *Shaping the College Curriculum. Academic Plans in Action*. Boston: Allyn and Bacon.

St.meld.nr- 11 (2008–2009) *Læreren, rollen og utdanningen*. Oslo: Kunnskapsdepartementet.

UFD (2003) *Rammeplan for Allmennlærerutdanningen med Endringer av 10.nov. 2009*. [*Curriculum Regulations and Guidelines for Teacher Education* 2003, Chapter 1, English version] Oslo: Utdannings- og forskningsdepartmentet [Ministry of Education and Research].

Part 3

Professional responsibility

Possible Futures?

12 Professional responsibility

New horizons of praxis

Ciaran Sugrue and
Tone Dyrdal Solbrekke

Introduction

When Martin Luther King Jr electrified a massive crowd from the steps of the Lincoln Memorial on 28 August 1963, when he departed from his prepared script and began 'I have a dream today', this was not mere idle talk nor simply daydreaming. Rather, in a Wittgensteinian sense he was going 'back to the rough ground' (Dunne 1993), to a messy and far from satisfactory reality, to play a particular 'language game', that of re-configuring elements of previous speeches and preaching, to forge new horizons. His words gave verbal reality to the world he envisaged, thus paving the way for others to step their way towards an alternative future with some confidence, a sense of purpose and direction. The future he envisaged had to be brought into being by the actions of others, individually and collectively. In similar vein, though much less dramatically so, and without the benefit of a live audience, we too find ourselves faced with the challenge of addressing the future of professionals – how they understand their respective roles, and deliberate on their actions, while recognising that there are different audiences, different constituencies within the diverse professional field:

1   those who are already established members of professional groups or associations;
2   those who are being prepared for entry into a profession whatever that might be; and
3   those whose responsibility it is to prepare new entrants, or existing members, for the life of a professional.

Less directly, it is evident from the foregoing chapters that the various publics and civil societies from whom professionals garner legitimacy in return for quality professional service are legitimate participants in the conceptualisation of professional responsibility, theoretically and practically. However, this is not a static world. Rather, there is the additional and onerous necessity to ensure that those already part of a plethora of professional communities that continues to expand and mutate, are kept up to date in knowledge and skills. Updating knowledge and expertise, however, is scarcely adequate either. It is necessary also to connect these knowledge bases with wider social concerns through creating and nurturing a sense of professional responsibility as it continues to be buffeted by the inevitable tensions created between governments, citizens and professional groups, and increasingly also by international change forces.

Neither is this enough, however. We understand our task as something akin to a 'fusion of horizons' in the Gadamerian sense and, in the process, to create new horizons, new possibilities for professional responsibility, while recognising as King suggested 'business as usual' is an inadequate response. Consequently, at this juncture, it is necessary to re-visit perspectives articulated in Chapter 1 in light of the contributions in each subsequent chapter, to forge new horizons of praxis. It is necessary to summon the courage to get off the academic fence, to grasp the nettle of professional responsibility and to transform the various perspectives espoused in the foregoing chapters into a different weave, to thread the distinct voices into a fabric that, while of our making, remains sensitive to context, culture and particular circumstance. We take up the challenge of meaning making, to engage in inter-subjective sense making while being mindful and respectful of our differences – language, culture, gender, professional lives and work.

We have determined that a shift in writing genre is appropriate, to speak to professionals whatever their milieu, while seeking to avoid artificial boundaries between thought and action, theory and practice. Such considerations provide justification also for persisting with the word 'praxis' in the title of this chapter, since the term 'practice' in English tends to focus more exclusively on the doing, the action to the exclusion of thought and intention. We have a strong preference therefore for the Greek conceptualisation of praxis and its close relative 'phronesis' as something more than mere enactment of a professional role. Elaboration *of* praxis *and praxis* artistry by Higgs, McAllister & Whiteford's (2009) are particularly useful in this regard as they combine critical and ethical reflection with other essential ingredients, such as expertise, humanity, morality and finesse, all of which are embodied in high-quality professional practice.[1]

While committing to these points of departure, our intention is to construct a deliberative conversation.[2] The genre is conversational in style, while academic connections are more often confined to endnotes, though they are sometimes included as they might be in a more typical conversation on this topic. As reader, we invite you to become an active if absent presence in this conversation, thus making your own contribution to the meaning-making process. In this manner, your voice, along with ours and the others that populate the various chapters, becomes active in the deliberative conversation of constructing new horizons of and for professional responsibility. As an active participant you are already in the process of rehearsing (new) conversations, constructing new horizons of praxis in your context with your colleagues, weaving new tapestries of professional responsibility in ways that cannot be anticipated here. Two additional considerations are intended to facilitate this process. First, it is inevitable in a conversation that there is some repetition due to the back and forth nature of meaning making, though we have sought to keep this to a minimum. However, such interwovenness is also indicative of the seamlessness of professional responsibility, thus indicating simultaneously its complexity as well as the necessity for holding its diverse elements in productive tension. Second, while not wishing to constrain unduly the spontaneity of the conversation, we provide some sub-headings as a means of enabling the reader to remain a connected participant as our deliberations progress. Echoing King, this concluding chapter is a beginning rather than an end.

As we began to grapple with the import of the individual chapters for this conversation, an immediate pressing concern raised its head.

Professional responsibility: prescriptive or authoritative?

Tone: It strikes me Ciaran that the contributions in this book are, in many respects, quite normative? And while I am comfortable with this, I also feel a little uncomfortable about being so prescriptive. So why are academics in general so reluctant to be prescriptive?

Ciaran: You believe in beginning with 'easy' questions obviously! Apart from left leaning liberalism, in this instance there is a tendency to hide behind the increasing complexity argument, but this is most likely merely ducking the question. Consequently, I would like to distinguish between being prescriptive and being authoritative. Perhaps another way of thinking about and connecting with this issue is consideration of courage and vulnerability, both issues that have been raised in various chapters. So, I might venture – it is a considerable challenge to be courageous while recognising one's vulnerability, *and* to be authoritative about values, standards, service to public and profession. What the various voices are insistent upon, without being prescriptive, is that the normative dimension of professional responsibility has been impoverished, hollowed out, due to the dominance of a technical rational discourse.

Tone: I would like to go one step further though, to argue that, such a stance may also entail being 'prescriptive' – that there are elements of professional responsibility that are non-negotiable. Is it too idealistic, for example, to re-iterate a phrase that has been around for a long time – 'above and beyond the call of duty' and that this is the requirement or standard that is expected by professionals of themselves? This is both prescriptive and authoritative?

Ciaran: OK, as long as prescriptive here means insisting on an ethical dimension as inescapable, and that complexity cannot be used as an excuse for not grasping the ethical element, thus deliberations may be authoritative without being prescriptive in the sense of the outcomes of deliberations being predictable or pre-determined. Consequently, I think we should simply acknowledge that complexity is inherent in

professional responsibility in the same way that we assert the inescapable presence of moral obligations.

Professional responsibility: expert and normative?

Tone: I agree, but I'm rather uncertain that responsibility ends with either
accepting complexity or a normative dimension. Wouldn't it be necessary also to challenge the prevailing culture and how it has been influenced by dominant approaches to accountability – that create, as
indicated by the nurse participants in Chapter 10, 'paper care' rather
than proper care?

Ciaran: Well, would you like to have a go at answering your own question?

Tone: Thank you! We should keep in mind here, Chapters 3 and 10 in
particular. What they indicate and illustrate is that care may be marginalised when a premium is put on efficiency, leading to defensive practices whereby professional care is denied in the interests of safety – a
'cult of efficiency'.[3] Chapter 3 advocates care as integral to professional responsibility while Chapter 10 signals clearly that external
accountability puts a premium on 'paper care', actually trumps quality
care, and restricts the sphere on which professionals are willing to
exercise judgement. It serves then as a good example of how accountability or a more technical–rational approach reduces professional
responsibility in comparison with what one might wish for a loved one
in a nursing home.

Ciaran: OK, so in such circumstances, are you suggesting that professional
responsibility obliges them to have the courage to resist such pressures, to recognise their vulnerability, and accompany the patients to
the garden?

Tone: Yes, I do! I think courage needs to be taken seriously ... and brought
into the discussion on professional responsibility. However, even
though I see it as an important 'virtue',[4] it is necessary to move
beyond an individualistic perspective on courage to one connected to
a communitarian approach consistent with May's perspectives (see
Chapter 1). Individual professionals need support from their respective professions in order to be responsible, and to be encouraged to
act with integrity.

Ciaran: It sounds to me that you are supporting the call (in Chapter 2) for an
ecological professionalism, a recognition that everything is connected
with everything else. When an ethical dimension is silenced or marginalised by the dominance of a language of efficiency, professionals begin
to be reductionist in the exercise of their responsibilities – compliance
trumps comprehensive service to the client.

Tone: Perhaps you have forgotten, but in Chapter 1 we indicated that at
different time periods across the twentieth century, various aspects of
professional responsibility – ideals, expertise, moral mandates, etc.

have been foregrounded. That account has resonances with Gert Biesta's (2010) elaboration on what he describes as the three periods in the history of professionalism: *client-emancipation*, which enhanced responsibility; *the new public management* that shifted the main focus from client to targets and an erosion of responsibility; which more recently has shifted further to a preoccupation with *evidence-based practice* and a consequent erosion of discretion and client emancipation. In such circumstances, it is necessary and worthwhile to consider why professions came into being. For some, Durkheim's ideas may be anachronistic, but a more ecological consideration suggests that old ideas may breathe new life into contemporary discourses on professional responsibility.

Professional responsibility: more than accountability

Ciaran: But I think there is an added urgency to recapitulate understandings of professional responsibility since 'accountability' looms so large in the English language and in contemporary discourses on professionalism (Cunningham 2008; Gewirtz, Mahony, Hextall & Cribb 2009; Green 2009).

Tone: Fine, but Chapter 4 is primarily devoted to arguing that responsibility is more than being merely accountable. In fact your own chapter (Chapter 9) makes this point too when it says that politicians and clergy followed various rules but neither behaved responsibly. In many respects, therefore, current preoccupations with accountability are impoverishing professional responsibility by reducing it to the application of rules, checklists and codes of conduct. For example, if evidence-based practice is the sole means of determining or measuring the nature of service, conformity and compliance dominate to the detriment of professional judgement and the exercise of professional responsibility.

Ciaran: I couldn't agree more, but is that all there is to professional responsibility then, to say that it is more than being accountable?

Tone: I would say that it is understandable and necessary in various workplace contexts to follow checklists and rules as a means of managing complexity. However, I would like to add the following – in a paradoxical manner such behaviour is recognition of complexity, a way of dealing with it, of reducing it to manageable proportions, yet not sufficient as a professional response to it.

Ciaran: May I stop you there until I make sure I am getting the gist of your argument. Is the argument then that just applying the rules, or just to answer to prescribed routines is never an adequate fulfilment of professional responsibility or that it is only in some circumstances that this might be the case?

Tone: Complexity is here to stay, and, at one level, professionals need to recognise that it goes with the territory. Part of being a professional means living with complexity, dealing with it through the deliberative process of exercising professional judgement, and living with the uncertainties and insecurities that attach to such situatedness – the 'messiness' as indicated in Chapter 1. And it is this messiness that cannot be captured by predetermined performance indicators that have become pervasive as part of new accountability systems such as the logic inherent in new public management.

Ciaran: From a theoretical or conceptual perspective, I can go along with what you say, but I'm thinking also of the harried, hard-pressed professional who is quite likely to say in response: 'in a low-trust, high-risk environment such as my workplace, you are asking me to walk a tightrope without a safety net', is it reasonable in such 'high stakes' circumstances to put additional pressure on already over-stretched professionals to go that extra mile, to be professionally responsible rather than play by the rules?

Tone: I think that this is a critically important question, and one we have to grapple with if this conversation is to 'cut it', to have credibility in diverse professional fields, because in low-trust, high-risk environments (as Chapter 6 illustrates), professionals are more likely to be cautious and conservative in their deliberations when such courses of action may not always be in the best interest of the client. Of course, it is not possible to address this concern without situating it within a number of other considerations – the general policy environment membership of professional bodies, the professional preparation of professionals for a life of professional responsibility, as well as the relationship of professionals to the public – both as members of the public as well as providing a service to that public in a public or private capacity.

Ciaran: Wow! Just when I thought things were coming together – this is definitely complexity at work, but we will have to wade through these issues, not all at once, as that would be impossible, but nevertheless, deal with them while also indicating how they form part of the tapestry of professional responsibility – a 'web of responsibilities', as you might say, inspired by Larry May (1996).

Professional responsibility: 'capital commitments'

Tone: Before we deal with these inter-related issues, I want to say something about the notion of a web of commitments …

Ciaran: Feel free …

Tone: Once we accept that professionals do not work in a vacuum, then they are hooked into a whole plethora of commitments, but it is possible to understand a web in a number of ways. You could understand a web, from the spider's perspective – as an elaborate network that is intended to ensnare – to capture unsuspecting or naive members of the insect community. Such 'ties that bind' have a particular kind of self-serving 'capital'.[5] However, it is also possible to understand a web as an intricate work of art, carefully and systematically created over time, that despite its apparent fragility, is extremely robust, flexible and fit for purpose. Though each strand may be thin and fragile, collectively, they reinforce one another, thus it is the web as a collective, as a system that is important. This more composite view of web enables the spider to survive and thrive, as part of a more elaborate, integrated ecology. These are robust but 'loose ties' that create a more ecological sense of capital. By extending the metaphor in this manner, I like to think that the web of commitments that connect professionals to their fields of responsibility and influence, as well to their professional communities, make them robust in the sense that the web provides a firm basis for excellence in service provision, but when its fragility is exposed, too much effort may be spent on defending the citadel rather than using it as a basis for serving the client and wider community. Understood in this manner, it is these internal and external ties that provide professionals with the bridging capital to behave with integrity as members of professional communities, while simultaneously drawing on this web as a resource to (re-)build trust with client and public.

Ciaran: Again, if I am understanding this appropriately, professionals are bound together by webs of professional association, but these are the same agencies and associations that create and influence codes of conduct, and professional ethics. This suggests that there is a need to encourage professionals to adopt such codes. However, it is not simply a matter of adopting, but deliberating on them in ways that do not result in behaviour that works on 'automatic pilot' – that being a responsible professional carries the additional responsibility of being alert to the strengths and limitations of any set of rules or procedures as they are brought to bear in particular contexts as part of the deliberative process. And, I think there is a subtle but important distinction between a web of commitments and a web of responsibilities. The latter is more open to questioning and deliberation than the former. To extend the point you made just now – professionals must strive to occupy a space that is always bridging, connected to fellow professionals through the ties of association and shared commitments, while retaining the autonomy conferred by loose ties to be able to act independently of, and possibly in defiance of, that same web of commitments in the interest of client and community; no pun intended, but this bridging positioning might be said to be their 'over-arching' professional responsibility!

Tone: I concur since your comments imply the additional responsibility of continuously questioning the appropriateness of rules in the workplace, in the processes of arriving at professional judgements, uncomfortable and time consuming though that may be. However, it is one thing to have the courage to challenge dominant forms of accountability, but doing so responsibly requires suggesting possible alternatives, does it not?

Ciaran: While I can subscribe to this view in an ideal world – professionals' sense of 'belonging', their professional identity straddles or bridges the professional–public interface, and in a somewhat different manner than expressed in Chapter 8, there is a 'perpetual vulnerability' inherent in professional responsibility given this borderland positioning. But, contemporary policy environments are far from ideal, heavily laden with various technologies of accountability, as Chapter 6 indicates, aren't professionals more likely to be risk averse, to play safe rather than pushing the boat out regarding standards?

Tone: It may be more appropriate to suggest that, while standards are important, an integral element of maintaining high standards is recognising the necessity for 'legitimate compromise'. Where there is low trust (and here I subscribe to the view that trust in professionals has declined), there is an additional responsibility to (re-)assert the highest standards and to go that extra mile to try to ensure that these standards are maintained, upheld and promoted despite current demands and difficulties. But, and this is an important caveat, we need to deliberate on what we mean by 'highest standards' because you cannot live up to all ideals all the time. Instead, professional discretion relies on the ability to negotiate the most appropriate solution in a particular situation, having considered all possibilities and arrived at a legitimate compromise. This is demanding, I agree. However, I think the most important principle or standard that may guide you as a professional is the one that you can never escape the responsibility of putting the interest of the client and society before your own interest. ...

Ciaran: In that sense, drawing on comments a little earlier, the bridging undertaken by professionals is an ongoing negotiated compromise between competing interests, while you are arguing that in these deliberations the interest of clients and public must be accorded priority over self-interest. I have two observations in relation to this. First, and with respect, this may be a particularly Norwegian, Scandinavian or even northern European perspective, that may be much more superficially shared, if at all, in the Anglo-Saxon or US context. Second, and with respect to the logic of what 'legitimate compromise' entails, a legitimate rapprochement between self, client and public interest seems both necessary and desirable. However, in the current policy climate, where often trust is notable by its absence between professional and public, what counts as legitimate or illegitimate becomes more contested.

Tone: Quite right, unless professionals not only aspire to the highest standards, but also seek to vindicate these standards in their professional work, then low trust and perhaps even more draconian accountability measures will be imposed from without, rather than professionals and their representative bodies insisting on the most exacting professional standards. And, I hasten to add, if professional associations have been complicit in a decline of trust by being perceived as putting self-interest ahead of service, this too calls on those associations to re-engage in public discourses beyond sound bites and spin, to re-connect meaningfully with the publics they serve. In order to do this, and it will undoubtedly take time, there needs to be a subtle mixture of vigilance in promoting the highest standards, defending those who seek to vindicate them, while being prepared to both question and defend those standards publicly, and where necessary point a finger when such standards are seriously compromised. To avoid compromising standards, the art of legitimate negotiated and acceptable professional judgements requires continuous vigilance and attention.

Ciaran: Phew! At this point, I need a coffee and a pit stop, and may be even the reader does too! Perhaps we should take a break, digest what we have discussed so far, and when we return, take up some of the issues raised above.

Tone: OK, let's do that, but we did also indicate earlier in the conversation that it would not be possible in this conversation to exhaust all possibilities. Rather, we are initiating a conversation while inviting readers to be partners, with the additional expectation that these conversations will be extended through their own professional ties, networks, communities of practice ....

Ciaran: Let's drink our coffee while continuing the conversation?

Tone: Sure, of course.

Ciaran: One of the elephants in the room in an age of expert professionalism is a separation of ethics or moral responsibility by privileging expert knowledge. So from a complexity or ecological perspective, and within the postmodern condition, how do you address the issue of the normative element of professional responsibility?

Personal and professional responsibility: what values, who decides?

Tone: Well, we have already agreed that moral dimensions of professional responsibility are inescapable – that much is clear. Expert knowledge per se does not commit you to a particular course of action – rather it is how that is used in the deliberative process of professional judgement that counts, and in that process values matter. I think that Chapter 7 illustrates this rather well in the case of the professional preparation of nurses in the US, while Chapter 5 indicates that virtues too play a critical role.

Ciaran: Yes, agreed, but in a cultural climate of relativism, there is a sort of retreat from the public sphere, whereby values belong in the personal or private domain rather than informing and shaping professional thinking, deliberation and practice?

Tone: I think there is truth in what you say, and another aspect of understanding professional responsibility is connecting the personal and the professional....

Ciaran: OK, but what values are to be included or considered, and, importantly also, who gets to decide?

Tone: Let's begin with what values, for me that question is easier than who has the power to decide. First, in choosing to become a member of a particular professional community, you are not signing up to a blank canvas. Rather, there already exists – rules of the game, codes of conduct that are intended to spell out the standards of service demanded of you. But more fundamentally, you are signing up to provide a service – to individuals, families, communities, and the public and this is inherent in the social contract – between the state and the profession – a mandate.[6] You are obliged, therefore, to provide the highest possible quality service – you are obliged to have expert knowledge, to commit to updating that knowledge continuously or regularly and in this way the value of service and all that entails is part of the relationship, implicitly and explicitly. And, even though we asserted this in Chapter 1, such deliberations often remain rather abstract. In order to come to grips with what it means, reflective conversations with colleagues and peers are a necessity – rather like the conversation we are having right now. It is necessary to ask: what are the values that should guide our professional work – and how do we understand them in practice – and how are they embedded both in our deliberations and our actions? We know that there is a lack of such discussion in both higher education and professional work (Fishman et al. 2004; Gardner, Csikszentmihalyi & Damon 2001; Solbrekke 2008) . I think, if we want to take responsibility for vindicating those values embedded in the notion of social trustee articulated in Chapter 1, we need to become more self-conscious about what is guiding our own choices in everyday practices. It is as easy and as difficult as that ... particularly in a pluralistic and super-complex world.

Ciaran: But don't we need to go a step beyond saying this is difficult and challenging? And, I think here is where the work of Charles Taylor (1989) (*Sources of the Self*) is particularly useful, although his work is not directly linked to professions.[7]

Tone: Please say more ...

Ciaran: His thesis is that the frameworks in which we make sense of our lives, and how identities are constituted occurs through the taking of moral stances, and, in my view, the processes of becoming and being a professional are identical. Both Taylor and May (1996) are 'on the same page' when I say that a professional with integrity, is an individual who has successfully integrated the principles of his or her profession with the principles of personal life, including the society and family (May 1996). But I am less confident in my own mind regarding the seamlessness or indivisibility between the personal and professional.

Tone: In so far as we are ever confident about anything, and perhaps professional humility is an underused virtue also, my understanding of Taylor is that without commitment to some moral order, the individual is lost.[8] There is a mutual shaping between individuals and their respective communities such that both identity and morality develop through engagement and exchange with others in the communities in which they participate. Becoming a professional, and, taking on as well as shaping its responsibilities, is an ongoing conversation that encourages articulation of the moral content, values if you like, embedded in theories and actions (Solbrekke & Jensen 2006).

Ciaran: So, I assume also that it is for this reason that ongoing reflective conversation is vital if professional responsibility is to remain vibrant. I would like to add though that this is where important echoes of Durkheim's work continues to have relevance – there needs to be a kind of realignment between the individual and the collective, between individuals and their professional communities, and, as May suggests, between the professional, the professions and their publics.

Professional and personal responsibility?

Tone: I couldn't have put it better myself!

Ciaran: Oh thank you! So, active participation in a vibrant professional community carries the additional responsibility of challenging our colleagues – as the chapters in this book tend to do – by raising questions regarding: power in our professional–client relationship, trust, risk, vulnerability, dilemmas, professional judgement, and deliberations about what counts as responsible behaviour in 'real' situations so that we are better equipped to act in a professionally responsible manner and to continue to be both critically reflective on, and articulate about, our professional deliberations and actions. While I can live with these realities, I have two additional concerns – is the relationship between the personal and professional entirely seamless, and does such intimate alignment have implications for the notion of the 'boundless' professional?

Tone: What do you mean – boundless professional?

Ciaran: What I mean is – borrowing from the commercial or economic notion that 'the market never sleeps' and in a world where you can be online 24/7, trading futures somewhere in the world, is the professional similarly always on duty, is there no respite? Is there a kind of panopticon professional responsibility? Am I never off duty?

Tone: There are two issues here as I see it. The first is the personal and professional life. Here is how I understand the relationship. As an individual in my private life, I operate to a personalised moral code, I set my own standards, espouse a set of values that are shaped by family background, education, friendships and professional life also, so in that sense they are not exclusively my personal code – they are shaped by the influences just mentioned. However, in the professional sphere, I opt to become a member of a particular profession, a professional community, where there is already a history of standards, of values and expectations that I may influence, but I am expected also to internalise. Consequently, by becoming a member, I take on responsibility for upholding, developing and promoting that inheritance or legacy and, in turn, seek to pass it on to subsequent new members of the profession. And, there is the additional responsibility, to question critically those values, particularly in contexts where legitimate compromises need to be negotiated.

Ciaran: So, is there a definite break, a clear distinction then, between how I lead my personal and my professional life? As a professional, I am not answerable to a personal code of conduct; rather I have an obligation to uphold the standards and integrity of the profession to which I belong. If for whatever reason I fail to do this, I not only let myself down, I also leave the profession down, both in the eyes of the professional community as well as in the eyes of the public.

Tone: Yes, I agree if you are saying that it is not possible to separate one's personal and professional lives. May (1996) makes this point that some continuity and transfer is to be expected between how an individual behaves in private and while acting in a professional role.

Professional responsibility: perpetual duty?

Ciaran: While I am inclined to agree, I'm mindful also of professionals who work in the private sector in particular, and the words of the song that come to mind are: 'I owe my soul to the company store',[9] or we say the 'company owns you body and soul' meaning that you can be expected to work ridiculously long hours, because your 'boss' demands it of you? So, are you expected to be a professional 24/7, in which case you have no personal life, or the professional colonises (entirely) the personal sphere?

Tone: If I am a novice professional, then I am more susceptible to the overtures of a demanding employer to be in the office or workplace early and late, but in my view beyond a certain point, admittedly difficult to determine precisely, such demands are excessive, unreasonable and, I would suggest, unprofessional – I am entitled to a family life too.

While such demands might very well meet accountability criteria, in the longer term they are likely to undermine or erode professional responsibility, resulting in compliance rather than the exercise of professional discretion and judgement – your behaviour becomes (entirely) predictable – anathema to professional responsibility.

Ciaran: So, let's assume that I am that novice professional and you are my overly demanding boss, and I say 'Sorry, I cannot remain at work, I have other responsibilities', and I do that on a number of occasions, and on one of those your response is: 'Well in those circumstances, I think you would be better to seek alternative employment'. Now, it may be that in Norway such a response would not be permitted, and I am aware that in other jurisdictions there is legislation that protects against unfair dismissal, but I am aware also that in the private sector, such protections are frequently circumvented.

Tone: Let me respond directly while I want to bring in a related issue also. If this employer were putting pressure on me to deal with more clients in order to maximise company profits or in the interest of greater 'efficiency' to the point where I felt very genuinely that I could no longer stand over the quality of the work I was doing, how would I deal with that? In my view, in both instances there are issues about professional standards at stake. In the first instance, it is unfair, and unacceptable to make excessive work demands on a professional employee. In the second, I feel my work is compromised, I can no longer uphold the standards of professional responsibility, due care and diligence that I signed up to, as I am expected to work at a pace that does not allow due diligence.

Ciaran: Well, in both instances, on the assumption that my protests fall on deaf ears, and that my employer is not prepared to negotiate either on time at work (the length of my working day) or on the amount of work I am expected to complete, then it seems to me that my options are limited: I can complain to my professional association, I can do the best I can in the circumstances – and this might mean compromising on professional standards and values, or I could seek alternative employment.

Tone: For now, let us rule out the 'nuclear' option and assume you stay. In exercising the first option, I can initiate a grievance procedure, but I need to be very convinced of the 'rightness' of my perceptions, and recognise that in pursuing such a process, I may be jeopardising my career prospects longer term – a very serious decision. I become something of a whistleblower on my employer, and presumably the profession in general would not be enamoured by such a course of action since it is like 'washing one's dirty linen in public', and my professional association might caution against such a course of action. If I remain, and chose to do the best I can, is this a 'legitimate compromise' as Larry May suggests?

Ciaran: My concern is that seeking to vindicate my sense of professional responsibility in such circumstances may require a superhuman effort on my part, or when does 'legitimate compromise' become illegitimate?

Tone: But I would never argue for professionals to be superhumans. On the contrary, we have to argue for a middle ground, a *via media* – it is not by accident that Romans coined the phrase – *virtus in medio stat* (virtue stands in the middle). Take, for example, the prevalence of 'paper care' in Chapter 10, where access to the therapeutic garden is denied to elderly patients. I would be rather insistent in those circumstances that the nurses need to take a stand by drawing attention to the impact of policy on practice. In such circumstances, they are obliged, in my view, even at some risk to their own employment security, to raise the matter through whatever channels are available to them – management, professional bodies, and in the event of not having the matter resolved in a professionally responsible manner, as a last resort to air the matter in public.

Ciaran: For some reason or other, more perverse perhaps rather than linguistic and cultural, I am more comfortable with *via media* than 'legitimate compromise' and accept that it is not possible in all circumstances to attain the ideal. But, as suggested earlier, if professionals are to connect with the public and re-build trust, apart from a professional commitment to provide the best possible service, then perhaps recognising that such selflessness (if not self-sacrifice) may be necessary, but should not be required routinely. Such demands are what Appiah (2010: 193) refers to as 'supererogatory – acts that are morally desirable but which ask too much of us to be morally required'.[10] However, even if such demands are expecting too much of some, they nevertheless draw attention to moral dimensions of professionals' work that are inextricably entwined with respect, dignity and integrity, and if these were more to the fore, then perhaps contemporary preoccupations with accountability and attendant technologies of surveillance and 'paper care' could be relegated to an appropriate subservient rather than superordinate role.

Tone: In response, I might invoke the question with which we began this conversation – a reluctance to be prescriptive, and suggest that, for professional responsibility to be treated with the utmost seriousness, with the care and attention it deserves, demands even, when any one individual falls short of these demanding responsibilities, all members of that professional group or association, in fact you might say all professionals, but perhaps less so, have their reputations tarnished. So, while I recognise the point made with reference to Appiah, there are times when it is necessary for individuals to insist publicly on those standards being upheld, even if such supererogatory stan ces are exceptional. However, it is not just the individual who is obliged to 'stand up and be counted' in the name of professional responsibility but the profession – collective solidarity that is more than self-interest.

Ciaran: So where does that leave the issue of always being on duty?

Tone: There isn't a simple answer to the question other than to assert – professionals are entitled to a private life, to assert otherwise is potentially detrimental to professional responsibility.

Ciaran: OK, so even if it isn't possible to indicate what is 'reasonable' in the abstract, let me try the following by way of 'legitimate compromise' while building on an earlier part of the conversation. This is where I think the idea of bridging capital is useful. It is to be expected and desirable that there will be some overspill between the personal and professional life, it is vitally important also, on occasion, at the end of the working day or week and so on, to be able to pull up the drawbridge and to retreat into one's private, personal or family life, to leave the professional behind, temporarily. This may not be a satisfactory response for some, but it may have to suffice in current flexible and fluid circumstance. Maybe it's time to turn some attention to educating for professional responsibility?

Tone: I agree …

Professional responsibility: initiation into a way of life

Ciaran: It seems sensible to separate this task into initiation into a professional community and to follow with some discussion of sustaining professionals' sense of professional responsibility across the lifespan?

Tone: So, let's begin with professional schools?

Ciaran: Alright, in a generic sense then, are there key ingredients of professional preparation?

Tone: I would say that, in the first instance, it is important to recognise that, in many instances, contemporary preoccupation with expertise and expert knowledge has tended to marginalise other important elements of professional formation. Dealing with professional responsibility in an integrated, coherent and complete manner within programmes has been largely neglected. I think that the three apprenticeships (expert knowledge, skills and competencies, and ethics) indicated in Chapter 7 have much to recommend then.

Ciaran: I agree with the attractiveness of the three apprenticeships approach, but does this approach run the risk of fragmentation in a number of senses? And I have some difficulties with the term 'apprenticeship'.

Tone: But don't you think that the arguments in Chapter 7 promote integration rather than fragmentation – even though they use the concept of apprenticeship? Are they not primarily used for analytical purposes?

Ciaran: While I agree that these are useful analytical tools, my experience of teacher education over many years is that with disciplinary boundaries, status hierarchies, planning and delivery of programmes, shared responsibility and collective ownership are intractable challenges.

Tone: But even if these challenges are intractable as you suggest, the dictates of professional responsibility suggest that it is necessary, as Tennyson put it: 'to strive, to seek, to find, and not to yield,'[11] so whether or not there is a division of labour approach or a more integrated holistic view of professional preparation, either view has potential to lead to superficial or inadequate treatment of professional responsibility. As an addition to or development of the three apprenticeships therefore, I want to argue that professional responsibility needs to be the anchoring for the other two.

Ciaran: But what about my concern regarding apprenticeship and its training connotations?

Tone: If you hadn't interrupted me, I would have continued, Chapter 5 makes reference to a 'golden mean' and here is where planning across the three apprenticeships is critical, while I take your training/apprenticeship connotations seriously – but here too there are cultural and linguistic considerations at play. My view is that preparation for professional responsibility needs to be undertaken within as well as between all three apprenticeships, and this necessitates all contributors having a comprehensive overview of the entire programme and how they are expected to contribute to it. This may also mean altering existing pedagogical approaches so that there is real engagement with learners, beyond the kind of compliance approach evident in the case of nurse preparation (in Chapter 7), and teacher education (see Chapter 11).

Ciaran: Apart from pedagogical innovation – which I recognise as being a necessary part of more comprehensive provision, this also raises questions about time allocation, and how much may be achieved realistically in initial professional preparation programmes, but we will come to that in a minute. Meantime, I want to add: isn't there also a golden mean to be developed in an open-ended, ongoing manner between claims to expertise, robust procedures and practices, while recognising an essential fragility, and indeterminacy at the heart of professional responsibility?

Tone: If I may, I would like to add to that – developing a professional identity, within any professional community necessitates getting to grips with its traditions, its expert knowledge and related skills, while the vulnerability and professional humility derives from saturating these elements of what it means to be a professional in its various moral commitments and values – you might even say, these values lend unity to professional preparation. Consequently, professional preparation is also about creating a professional identity, as well as creating a professional disposition, a way of being in the world that respects tradition, but also challenges it when it conflicts with professional judgements. Issues about time, duration of programmes, etc., I don't think we can deal with in any meaningful sense other than to indicate their importance.

Professional responsibility: (re-)new(-ed) learning

Ciaran: I agree, so what about ongoing professional learning or renewal?

Tone: I'm not sure that we can add much to what we have said just now other than to indicate in professional workplaces, where the pace of change and new challenges are a regular feature of daily practice, there is greater need than ever before for more imaginative ways of what I might call 'doing professional renewal' with combinations of the three apprenticeships in mind, and Chapter 5 captures the necessity for the inclusion of all elements rather well.

Ciaran: It will require considerable advocacy on the part of professional leaders and their respective associations to persuade employers, either in the public or private sector, that more time and space will be necessary if professionals are not to be 'running on empty' rather than being renewed and revitalised.[12] It is unlikely to happen, I would suggest, unless, as professionals, we develop collective courage and capability to articulate, deliberate and dare to confront questions raised here, and to challenge our colleagues, to raise legitimate questions regarding professional judgements. This is difficult, I'll admit, requiring a professional culture that is more open to scrutiny, particularly if a sceptical public is to be convinced, and to trust that professionals are taking their responsibilities seriously rather than being self-serving.

Tone: All I will say in response is that this too needs to be part of an ongoing conversation around professional responsibility and, in this regard, those in professional schools, professionals in workplace settings and their representatives need to take up these issues individually and collectively, and create the public spaces and opportunities whereby what is at stake is part of a wider deliberative conversation about professions, professionalism and what professional responsibility entails.

Ciaran: I sense that this conversation may be coming to an end?

Tone: I thought you were going to say – grinding to a halt! Though I agree, I think we should conclude by addressing the reader directly regarding new horizons of professional responsibility as colleague and fellow professional.

Ciaran: I am more than happy to assent to that!

Professional responsibility: new horizons of praxis

We have had our say. It behoves us to be brief. This conversation is inexhaustible, and that is why finding your own voice in this deliberative process is a necessary next step. We began this chapter with the stirring voice of King, and towards the end invoked the more sombre tones of Tennyson, while a multiplicity of voices populate the pages of this text. It is from this profusion of perspectives that new fusions of praxis will be propounded, and you and your colleagues are henceforth the primary actors in this unfolding drama – building 'bridges' to the future. It is our fervent hope that the polyphony evident here provides important ingredients for your ongoing deliberations that will enable a multiplicity of horizons to be forged, and that the deliberative process in this concluding chapter, provides you with a head start in the challenging but vitally necessary process of breathing new life into professional responsibility. We hereby pass the baton and depend on you to (re-)enkindle the flame of professional responsibility in all your deliberations, reflections and actions.

Notes

1 For further elaboration on the significance of praxis and phronesis for understanding and shaping the life worlds of professionals, see particularly, Green (2009) and Dunne (1993).
2 We make a crucial distinction here between deliberative communication as envisaged by Habermas in contrast to a Socratic dialogue, the latter being understood more as a master–apprentice relationship – question and answer, but with a particular end in view. In the present context, the deliberative conversation is communication among equals, and though bringing different contributions to the discussion, we seek to create inter-subjective, shared meanings. And, in many respects, we consider that such conversations are a necessity to the promotion and longer term health of professions by taking professional responsibility more seriously as integral to and an unavoidable element of professional judgement and not a luxury to be indulged in when time, space and convenience allow.
3 In this regard, see the work of Gross Stein (2001) in the field of medical care, and that of Hargreaves (2003), who identifies 'performance training sects' in education where preoccupation with improvement of test scores trumps every other educational consideration as a consequence of policy climate. Similarly, Chapter 5 indicates and illustrates how a lack of a more holistic, coherent and comprehensive approach to academic life hollows out what it means to be an academic by separating teaching, service and research.
4 It is worth noting in this regard that the Greek word *areté* means both 'courage' and 'virtue'.
5 The notion of 'capital' as it is used here has resonance with the work of Bourdieu (Bourdieu 1977; Bourdieu & Wacquant 1992) and that of Putnam (Putnam 2000; Putnam & Feldstein with Cohen 2004). However, the most significant point being made is that capital, whether economic, cultural or social, may be deployed primarily for self-interest or in the service of others and for the good of society.
6 In this regard, it is worth noting that other possible words for mandate include permission, authorisation, consent and go-ahead – all of which imply notions of trust, obligation and responsibility.
7 For further elaboration on the relevance of Taylor's work in the context of professional responsibility, see Solbrekke & Jensen (2006).

8 In support of this claim, and in acknowledgement of Taylor's influence on this element of the conversation, the following quotation is apposite: 'To know who you are is to be orientated in moral space, a space in which questions arise about what is good and what is bad, what is worth doing and what is not, what has meaning and importance to you and what is trivial and secondary' (Taylor 1989: 28).

9 This line is borrowed from the song 'Sixteen Tons', first recorded in the US in the late 1940s, and became controversial during the cold war anti-communist, McCarthyism period. The line refers to the practice of coal companies selling basic foodstuffs to miners, often at extortionist prices, while retaining wages to pay the bills – a form of indentured labour.

10 For a more extensive account of supererogatory responsibilities, see Appiah (2010: 175–204).

11 This line is from Tennyson's poem *Ulysses*, first published in 1842.

12 In the Fourth Way (Hargreaves & Shirley 2009), the authors identify 'catalysts of coherence', and we consider that 'professional responsibility' has potential to serve this function (see pp. 71–111).

References

Appiah, K.A. (2010) *The Honour Code How Moral Revolutions Happen*. New York, London: W.W. Norton & Company.

Biesta, G. (2010) *Good Education in an Age of Measurement Ethics, Politics, Democracy*. Boulder, London: Paradigm Publishers.

Bourdieu, P. (1977) *Outline of a Theory of Practice* (trans. Nice, R.). Cambridge: Cambridge University Press.

Bourdieu, P. & Wacquant, L.J.D. (1992) *An Invitation to Reflexive Sociology*. Chicago: University of Chicago Press.

Cunningham, B. (ed.) (2008) *Exploring Professionalism*. London: Institute of Education.

Dunne, J. (1993) *Back to the Rough Ground 'Phronesis' and 'Techne' in Modern Philosophy and in Aristotle*. Notre Dame: University of Notre Dame Press.

Fishman, W., Solomon, B., Greenspan, D. & Gardner, H. (2004) *Making Good: How Young People Cope with Moral Dilemmas at Work*. Cambridge, MA: Harvard University Press.

Gardner, H., Csikszentmihalyi, M. & Damon, W. (2001) *Good Work When Excellence and Ethics Meet*. New York: Basic Books.

Gewirtz, S., Mahony, P., Hextall, I. & Cribb, A. (eds) (2009) *Changing Teacher Professionalism International Trends, Challenges and Ways Forward*. New York, London: Routledge.

Green, B. (2009) The primacy of practice and the problem of representation. In Green, B. (ed.) *Understanding and Researching Professional Practice*. pp. 39–54. Rotterdam: Sense Publishers.

Gross Stein, J. (2001) *The Cult of Efficiency*. Toronto: Anansi Press.

Hargreaves, A. (2003) *Teaching in the Knowledge Society*. Buckingham: Open University Press.

Hargreaves, A. & Shirley, D. (2009) *The Fourth Way The Inspiring Future for Educational Change*. Thousand Oaks: Corwin.

Higgs, J., McAllister, L. & Whiteford, G. (2009) The practice and praxis of professional decision-making. In Green, B. (ed.) *Understanding and Researching Professional Practice*. pp. 101–20. Rotterdam: Sense Publishers.

May, L. (1996) *The Socially Responsive Self. Social Theory and Professional Ethics*. Chicago: University of Chicago Press.

Putnam, R. (2000) *Bowling Alone: The Collapse and Revival of American Community*. New York, London: Simon & Schuster.

Putnam, R. & Feldstein, L.M., with Cohen, D. (2004) *Better Together Restoring the American Community*. New York, London: Simon and Schuster Paperbacks.

Solbrekke, T.D. & Jensen, K (2006) Learning the moral order of professions; the contrasting approaches of nursing and clinical psychology, i. *Learning in Health and Social Care* 5(4), 181–93.

Solbrekke, T.D. (2008) Professional responsibility as legitimate compromises – from communities of education to communities of work. *Studies in Higher Education 3*, no. 4: 485–500.

Taylor, C. (1989) *Sources of the Self the Making of Modern Identity*. Cambridge: Cambridge University Press.

Index